About the author

Brian J Smith was one of a large family, born into poverty and what would now be called, a slum dwelling.

He did his part - passed the 11 plus, but poverty denied him a grammar school education. It seemed he was destined to be amongst the 'also- rans'. As if in confirmation, he left secondary school at 15 years of age without a solitary citation and spent a few years meandering between jobs.

Then came the change – Brian returned to school, college to be precise. His achievements there earned him a position with a major High Street banks. He passed his professional examinations and was admitted into the Chartered Institute of Bankers. He went on to qualify to lecture at colleges and universities and to earn a BSc (Hons) in psychology.

He is now a member of the British Psychological Society, registered as a debt psychologist.

D1799410

The Life of Brian –
the Other One

Brian J. Smith

 New Generation Publishing

'Because I could not stop for death
He kindly stopped for me'

Emily Dickinson – (1830 – 1886)

In memory of brother Barry
17 February 1938 – 11 December 2018

Thank you for the invaluable contributions you made in
helping to get this project off the ground.

PROLOGUE

Paleoanthropologists and geneticists generally agree that modern humans emerged out of Africa some 200,000 years ago, that's a long way to track back the family tree and if such a task were ever completed we would have a tome that would make the Encyclopaedia Britannica read like a pocket diary. Besides which, there aren't enough 'greats' to describe relatives from so long ago. So, I've decided to limit backward glances of my life to two generations, my parents and grandparents, coincidentally these are also the only ones I have known, well most of them anyway.

In my beginning, then. were my grandparents.

PATERNAL

Hezekiah Smith circa 1880 -??

Jane Smith (nee Worrall) circa 1881 - ??

MATERNAL

Walter Joshua Francis Pittaway 20 June 1879 - 19 February 1967.

Emma Pittaway (nee Parker) 20 June 1885 - 23 February 1960

They respectively begat my parents.

Reginald Percy Smith   - 7 June1911 - 18 November 2001

Millicent Emma Pittaway - 28 May 1914 - 29 April 1981

They married 23 December 1933 and became Mr & Mrs Smith.

Eventually they begat:

Brian James Smith (Me) and 14 others, but you don't want to know about them.

Sadly, two brothers are no longer with us. One died before my time, of diphtheria, another was murdered by the IRA

I am now 2, 436, 262, 399 seconds old.

Sad to say I have no recollection of grandparents on my father's side. I know that dad had four brothers and two sisters. Three of the brothers were to become familiar, the fourth died when I was relatively young and there was little or no contact with the sisters – in fact, it was only following research for this book that I learned there were two sisters, I had lived my life thus far believing there to be only one.

Grandfather Smith worked at a company of lock-makers, Tonks' which later became a part of Yale Ltd. He was an amateur herbalist but there's no evidence of his prowess. I suspect that he was one of thousands who acquired a copy of Nicholas Culpeper's book - Complete Herbal, published in 1653 and reprinted many times over. Culpeper was an apothecary at a time when they, not surgeons or doctors, ran hospitals and ruled medicine. Herbal medicines reigned supreme. Interesting too, Culpeper was a Puritan, Granddad Smith's reported strict disciplinary ways suggests he had similar authoritarian traits and, I suspect by force of his personality convinced many that he was an authority to be reckoned with. I have the impression also, that few would dare to risk an argument with him.

It is said that he was a heavy drinker and had frequent

attacks of what they called then the 'blue devils', nowadays we are better informed and would say that he hallucinated. Drink also triggered a propensity to aggression and violence; woe betide anyone who got in his way at such times.

An intriguing tale promoted by my father concerns an alleged family involvement with the White Star Shipping Line – owners of the ill-fated Titanic. Dad was not very specific, and these stories never got much traction but it's a fascinating thought. He spoke of a lost family fortune and the mysterious disappearance of an important (to the story) 'somebody'. Some dodgy share dealings are suggested. Dad did mention that he, his brothers and grandad had some sort of venture going that involved a truck and potatoes, but I never made much sense out of that. Maybe it would be worthwhile investigating the 'Smith' ancestry.

Even less is known about Grandma Smith. Records confirm that she was in domestic service, likely until she married. The only other comment worthy of note (in a mischievous sort of way) is that it is said that she looked like a witch. Sadly, it is also reported that she was wheelchair bound following ill - treatment inflicted by her husband, my Grandfather. Obviously, she was not a very good witch – where was the spell that turned Grandfather into a harmless frog?

As kids, we saw Mom's parents, Granddad and Grandma Pittaway, regularly. Mom had three sisters and one brother, all of whom we got to know well. Grandma Pittaway was always frail whilst I knew her but ever a kindly soul.

Granddad Pittaway also worked at Yale, but he didn't make locks. He was a lock-breaker (or 'lock-boster' as the local vernacular had it). He offers a most intriguing tale. His father was a Channel Islander, Jersey to be exact. The story goes that Great Granddad Pittaway (GGP) may have been in the military (unconfirmed) and that he absconded because his father would not give permission for him to marry. GGP changed his name, forged a letter of consent from his father (to whom he also gave the false name) and married the love of his life. The fascinating fact is that the false name he chose was Smyth. I understand that's how the French spell Smith and don't forget, the Channel Islands had a heavy French influence. This is evidenced by the fact that his dear beloved was a lady of distinct French origin by the name of Le Bouttillier. How prophetic - GGP chose as his pseudonym, the surname of his yet-to-be-born grandson's daughter's husband. Or is it simply that GGP lacked imagination in choice of an alias? Brian James Le Bouttillier - now that has a ring about it.

Legally, of course, the marriage was void both at law and in the eyes of the church. This misdemeanour came to life many, many years later when a sister and a cousin were tracing the family tree on Mom's side. They found a note in the file pointing out the false name, presumably an attempt to put matters right. This little farce appears to have eluded the authorities and when it was brought to their attention, the registrar on the island asserted that, as the note was unsigned, it had no legal force. However, it was acknowledged that 'an error' appeared to have been made. As it stands GGP and 'wife' were never legally man and wife.

When Granddad Pittaway was born, it seems that he was neither welcomed nor wanted because he was handed over to GGP's sister who brought him to mainland UK and raised him in Worcester.

INTRODUCTION

I pondered long on how to tell this story. I could have gone for a gritty dour approach grounded in hardship and deprivation, a lot shared by many, but especially endured by us – the Smiths. I could have told of the stress and strain, the distress and pain but that would be a maudlin account of a life that had it's good and lighter moments. Besides, I'm no lover of the 'poor me' school of reflection. In the end, I settled for what is essentially my way of remembering and recalling which is heavily laced with humour and irreverence. Behind this lies a belief that we should not take this life too seriously for if we do it will surely kill us - one way of another. We should also take life as it is – not as we would have it be. I am here reminded of the tale about a man, in the centre of Birmingham, asking for the best way to get to London. He was told – "Not to start from here".

It must be noted too that what follows are my recollections and perceptions. Others may recall and reflect events differently - that is their right. Their perspective is no less valid. Memory is not infallible indeed, it often misleads us, it being a reconstruct and not a sort of video playback. There is too, the need to acknowledge our ability to distort recall, sometimes wilfully. Proof certain that we each see, and record, events differently. I suggest that there are three versions of any story – yours - mine and the truth – and they all present as honest and accurate reflections. Tis prudent to harken to the wise words of Edgar Allan Poe in his tale – 'The System of Doctor Tarr and Professor Tether' - "Believe nothing you hear and only one half of what you see."

Some may point out certain omissions. This is unlikely to be a wilful act of avoidance or evasion. It is impractical to include all that has happened, even if it could be recalled. I have then, exercised the discretion of selection, choosing what to include or exclude.

The use of names in this book is subject to the following guidelines. Where comments and observations are favourable, real names have been used so that those good people can not only identify themselves, but also know that they were appreciated. Where the situations are especially sensitive, names have been changed to protect the feelings of the persons concerned. Finally, where the reflections are not favourable, names have been dropped so as not to cause disquiet.

As I meander through my early life, I stop frequently to take a closer look at an object; a place name or a person. We spend so little time in paying attention to the detail of life that surrounds us. We use objects without a thought as to how they came into being and the inventors, many of whom dedicated their lives in the pursuit of what we now take for granted. When we switch on a light for example, how many of us think, where did the incandescent light bulb come from? We visit places without a thought for how they got the name they bear. My point is that everything has a story, to know that story is to enrich our lives. The world is all around us, yet we 'see' so little of it. So, on my travels in recall, putting this book together, I halt frequently to indulge and enlighten myself and, hopefully, you too dear reader. It may also be a sound camouflage for the lack of excitement

This little poem by W H Davies sums up what I'm driving at in a most genteel style.

WHAT is this life if, full of care,
We have no time to stand and stare? —

No time to stand beneath the boughs,
And stare as long as sheep and cows:

No time to see, when woods we pass,
Where squirrels hide their nuts in grass:

No time to see, in broad daylight,
Streams full of stars, like skies at night:

No time to turn at Beauty's glance,
And watch her feet, how they can dance:

No time to wait till her mouth can
Enrich that smile her eyes began?

A poor life this if, full of care,
We have no time to stand and stare.

(W H DAVIES – LEISURE)

Try it – the name of the city, town, village, the street where you live – what do you know about it? How did it get the name? Your own name – do you know its origin and what it means? Take any object you like – who invented it – when where and how? There has never been a better time to get to know 'things'.

Chapter 1

ARRIVAL – COME OUT NUMBER FOUR, YOUR TIME IS UP

It is Tuesday the 4th June 1940. I arrived just in time for Winston Chur6chill's great speech (I think he might have waited for me).

Even though large tracts of Europe and many old and famous states have fallen or may fall into the grip of the Gestapo and all the odious apparatus of Nazi rule, we shall not flag or fail. We shall go on to the end. We shall fight in France, we shall fight on the seas and oceans, we shall fight with growing confidence and growing strength in the air, we shall defend our island, whatever the cost may be. We shall fight on the beaches, we shall fight on the landing grounds, we shall fight in the fields and on the streets, we shall fight in the hills, we shall never surrender. And, if, which I do not for a moment believe, this island or a large part of it were subjugated and starving, then our Empire beyond the seas, armed and guarded by the British Fleet, would carry on the struggle, until, in God's good time, the New World, with all its power and might, steps forth to the rescue and the liberation of the old" - (Winston Spencer Churchill 4th June 1940)

An extract from what many consider to be Churchill's finest piece of oratory. It was magnificent and reduced several MP's, from both sides of the house, to tears. The speech is defined as a 'peroration' - describing how a speaker concludes by recapitulating and emphasising the important parts of the speech usually with added pathos - and Churchill certainly did all of that. See how often he used the phrase "We shall..." - brilliant, awe inspiring. Be warned dear reader - this volume may be educational at times. But there's more: Churchill is reported as saying to a colleague in an off-the-record aside after his stirring speech.

" And we'll fight them with butt ends of broken beer bottles because that's bloody well all we've got"

Unlike modern politicians, Churchill had first-hand experience of soldiering and war. As a young subaltern, he served in the Sudan in 1898. Later he operated as a war correspondent during the second Boer War (1899-1902). Likely he inherited his fighting spirit from the founder of the Churchill dynasty - John Churchill who fought on the Royalist side during the English civil war. John Churchill won many battles against the French (ruled by Louis XIV) during the late 17th - early 18th century and became a favourite of Queen Anne. She made him Duke of Marlborough - he built Blenheim Palace, named after a famous battle around a small village on the banks of the Danube in 1704. Our Winston Churchill loved Blenheim Palace, despite moving to Chartwell in 1922 and he loved England. I do believe that he would have laid down his life for any of the three. Could I ever have chosen a better day to be born?

*****

Right - that's enough deference to the great man, this is my story. And so, it begins. I was born on the 4th June - I know 'cos I was there (still think I should have taken that corny line out). I had two parents - one of each, that was the norm then. Nowadays you're just as likely to have one only and, increasingly two of a kind. It gets worse, certain sections of the thought police would negate gender altogether – so as not to offend the sensitivities of minority groups apparently, oh and to appease gender equality. That's what happens when people with too much learning and too little common sense are set loose. Anyway, I was born when there were males and females and that little fact went unchallenged. I would eventually become one of fifteen - Mum had ten sons and five daughters. It wasn't that my parents were Catholic, nor did they plan a rugby team. In fact, planning of any kind and the arrival of us kids did not belong in the same thought stream. We were the accidents waiting to happen. More likely we were the consequence of boundless passion and no television.

What timing! Five months after rationing was introduced (8 January 1940) I was 'persuaded' to make my entry. Tuesday the 4th June 1940 - Tuesday derives from Tiw's-day - Tiw was the Norse god of war, how apt. It was a leap year and a momentous day for team UK. Not only the day Churchill made his inspirational speech, but also the ninth and final day of the heroic evacuation from Dunkirk and - last of all – 'tis the day I be born. What a trilogy – Dunkirk, Churchill and Me! Am I the only one that's excited? C'mon, it's my birthday – we should have a party - my first time here (although I did hear in later life that some old sage, looking at me knowingly when I was very small, clucked "he's been here before"). That would make reincarnation the original re-cycling. Anyhow, I reckon that, had Churchill not got so emotional he would have mentioned my arrival - he just forgot in the passion of the moment, or maybe he thought the British people had had enough excitement for one day.

Anyhow, before you scoff at my reverence for the 4th June, consider this: war was declared on Germany 3rd September 1939 – nine months later I arrived to find a desperate world. More than a coincidence does one not think? You might also argue that it was dreadful timing on my part. Noteworthy too that I have little competition – in 1394 Philippa of England was born on the 4th of June and in 1829 Jinmaku Kyugord, a sumo wrestler was born in Japan. No – I've never heard of either of them before, I chose them because the first like me, is British and I'm fiercely proud of that and including Mr Kyugord is surely evidence that I'm no xenophobe. Here's another little gem. A less known, and taught, event that happened on the 4th June 1487 could have changed the course of English history. A young boy - Edmund, earl of Warwick and royal prince of York, had earlier been crowned King of England - in Dublin. Confusing is it not? Seems that King Henry V11 was fearful that this young pretender might have a legitimate claim to the crown of England. So, when the boy 'king' led an army from Ireland to conquer England on the 4th June 1487, Henry Tudor was waiting with a vastly superior army and the rebellion was quashed. The Irish army was slaughtered but Edmund was spared and later put to work in the royal kitchens.

1942, my birthday was marked by the battle of Midway – see, even the Americans wanted to get in on the act as they celebrated by routing the Japanese. Unfortunately, the Allied High Command were wary of sharing momentous events, they moved the Normandy landings (D-day) from the 4th to the 6th June 1944. History books will claim it was because of the weather but you make up your own mind. We're talking about soldiers, highly trained fighting fit men who in recent history had slugged it out on the Somme in the most appalling conditions, they didn't call a halt because it was too muddy (very seriously – it should have been called off for the senseless slaughter that it was; 20,000 British soldiers died on the first day - 1st July 1916) and in the then current conflict I don't recall any talk of calling off the Second Battle of El Alamein (18th November 1942) because it was too hot. Anyhow, that year I got to share the 4th June 1944 with the allies liberating Rome so clearly someone was on the ball. I notice that the Queen's coronation in 1953 was set for the 2nd of June – presumably to avoid clashing with the day I became a teenager. All is forgiven - Her Majesty gladly celebrated 60 years as monarch at a service in Westminster Abbey on the 4th June 2013. I didn't receive an invitation - I assume it got lost in the post - Royal Mail of course (now that's a clever pun). The point of this meandering preamble? That the 4th June, over time, has seen some interesting and significant, events and I am forever a part of that.

*****

Back to the big day – imagine the scene, I'm fully gestated - all snuggled and warm where I am with all my needs catered for. Outside all hell has broken loose so I hesitate to join the melee. Had I not done so I could have arrived 3rd June – bang on nine months, but hey what's the hurry? Truth is I didn't allow for it being a leap year. So, I spent a day weighing up the options – staying where I was or venturing forth to see what the hell was going on. Turned out there was only one option 'cos staying put was a no no. They had ways of persuading babies to evacuate so go go go it was.

Starring in my birth was my mother of course (leading lady) and me obviously (leading man). Forget dad, he was nowhere to be seen, men were not welcome at the big event then - they could start the race, but they were banned from the finishing line. It's common now for a partner to attend the birth at 'her' insistence. Many find themselves in the horizontal position, those that don't pass out may be treated to a torrent of abuse from their nearest and dearest for putting them in this state - 'you did this you *****'. At least one other was present, the mid-wife I suspect (only supposed to be a supporting role) – I believe her attendance was compulsory. I also believe that it was she who gave me a sharp slap on the arse by way of a welcome. Why? So, that I would cry out and prove that I was alive – apparently. Right – now let's get this straight, you've already won the marathon of marathons in being the 'chosen one'. You were the single solitary sperm out of circa 250 million, released at the same time, that made it - you fertilised the egg that became you. That was some race and the competition! - had to put up detour signs to get rid of some of the little spermites. Little wonder that it takes so long to get sorted.

You start out - a little seed that gets steadily bigger until you reach a stage of more-or- less wholeness. It takes about thirty-six weeks give or take, so there's plenty of time to develop nice and easy. You're very relaxed about this and are quite content to lie quietly and patiently until it's time to go. You expect your departure to be equally tranquil. Think again – you can hear the yelling and the screaming – it sounds like bedlam and you pause and think – do I want to go out there, they sound awful mad? The tympanic membranes are perfectly formed and functional in the about-to-be-born so easy on the noise ladies. Not so the visual cortex so no bright lights if you please. Regardless, suddenly you're squeezed out into the light – a blinding light and a cacophony of noise. My point is – you are in no position to do anything, much less make a sound – it's a state of shock. Making a noise, any sort of noise, would surely be pointless because no one would hear you above the racket they were making. So – I ask again – why the slap on the arse? Try that now nurse-whatever-your-name-was and I'd have social services on your case, assault, child-cruelty maybe even a bit of S & M - why the compensation could have set me up for life. The only deliveries you'll be doing in future, assuming you want to keep a uniform, will be post for Royal Mail. (Now there's an interesting role reversal – mid-wives pull 'em out and postmen push 'em in). There you go – there's never a do-gooder around when you need one and solicitors were far too full of their own importance to soil their hands with such a vulgarity as no-win-no-fee work. The 1940's version went something like this – can't afford - can't have. I was so mad with this rough handling that I refused to talk to my parents for at least the first eighteen months of my life, and as for walking - when I could be chauffeur driven? I had my own environmentally friendly carriage, powered by Mum-power.

I was told an entertaining anecdote by a solicitor about the term 'a backhander' and lawyers. The tale goes that lawyers appearing at court were not disposed to openly take money from clients, this was considered as rather vulgar - that's what tradesmen did. The dilemma was neatly navigated by payment being deposited in the folds of the silk gowns worn by lawyers and gathered at the back - hence the term 'backhander' - handed over at the back. No idea if it's true but things have changed - solicitors are no longer shy of quoting and collecting fees.

Many are the times I've heard parents (mine and others) say,

"I'll show you the back of my hand if you don't ......"

There would then be a reference to some perceived unacceptable behaviour or misdemeanour, (likely exaggerated, even untrue). That's the backhander with which I, and very many other kids, were so familiar.

Anyway, when you're out you're out – there's no going back. New-borns have virtually no idea what they are; where they are; who they are and why they are here. Metaphysically many go through their lives permanently perplexed by these questions, especially the 'why' part, the answers to which eludes them to the end. Others take a strong dose of pragmatism and acknowledge that they'll never be smart enough to work it out, so they set about making the best of it. The answers they get, and settle for, are that eventually someone will tell you who you are, and you'll work the geography out. What you are is clear from the start – you're an 'it' a 'thing' a baby, something to be poked and prodded by a seeming endless army of gurning adults. As for 'why' – there are two ways to deal with this, one is to take up religion and bemoan your inferiority to a god (but you do get very accomplished at genuflecting) or there's booze - excess booze to be precise because it is after a gut-filling overdose that the finest philosophers and orators in the land hold forth on the meaning of life and everything and there's not a political, economic, military or social problem to which they don't have the answer (not forgetting the ability to manage a football club better than that *******) pubs at closing time abound with these shamans. On religion, I am ambivalent. I defer to the beliefs of others (their right) but I don't share them. I have issues with a book (the bible) said to have been compiled 200 years after the events it records; some said to be written in ancient Hebrew and some in ancient Greek – translation into English would have been a challenge. Allow me to put it this way – it is now 2017 – imagine scribes writing about 2017 in 2217. I think I finally parted company with religion in 1964 and the disaster at Aberfan. Surely a merciful god would have intervened to saves the lives of those poor children. My last word on the matter – the word 'cretin' is said to be a dialectal French word for Christian – makes one think.

*****

Not sure when exactly I found out who I was but apparently, I was a (and remain) a 'Smith'. There are numerous clones who have 'borrowed' my name, one notable Brian Smith, a Canadian ice hockey player, was born in 1940 - the audacity of the man! He didn't last the distance, seems he died in 1995. I once had a neighbour by the name of Brian Smith – tragically he committed suicide. I came home one day to find numerous police officers in attendance. They asked if I would provide a witness statement and when I told them my name there was much confusion. The name Smith carries one unfortunate cross - the captain of the Titanic was called Edward John Smith, born a landlubber in Hanley, Stoke-on-Trent. Legend has it that his last words to his crew were

"Be British" and in true sailor tradition, he went down with his ship. Magnificent.

According to the scriptures of the new religion, the world-wide - web, there are about 4.5m Smiths in the world. A certain Brendan Cooper suggests that - 'There are so many

Smiths about because they were very good at picking chastity belts' Yes - my thoughts exactly. Anyway, non-believers can do their own head count. It's an impressive number – could be the population of a small country like Scotland – ah no, they'd put Mc in front of it and McSmith just doesn't work. What about Ireland you say? - Similar problem – too reminiscent of a call from my schooldays. Just when I thought I'd got away with a minor misdemeanour I'd hear a teacher shout out.

"O Smith…"

This Irish connection reminds me that circa 941 - 1041 BC there was a certain King of Ireland - King Brian Bore. He founded the O'Brien clan. Just so you know; King Brian died at the battle of Clontarf (1041). Some would suggest that this was a defining moment in Irish history. King Brian was said to be a uniting force, his death marked a retreat into disunity that has prevailed ever since. Methinks he's the one and only King Brian ever. King Brian - just doesn't resonate. Rather like Monty Python's - Life of Brian - why didn't they pick a good biblical name? I wanted to call this book The Life of Brian - still could but I can't afford the lawsuit.

Close to home that only leaves Wales, only got one thing to say to that idea – Jones – Smith and Jones under one flag, never work. Imagine calling the school register, only two names would need to be called. Make that four names if you count those fellows Evans and Davies. The response would be a choral version of

"Here sir/miss"

and they'd do it in harmony. Did you know that one in six Welshmen is named Jones? Population is said to be circa three million so that's five hundred thousand Jones'. It's also a fact then, that there are more Smiths in the world than

Welshmen in Wales. So further afield it is – er, how about New Zealand? Going to share a little secret here – I have an elder brother out there already – he's the advance guard. Give it a century or two and there'll be a name change – New Smithland. And oh joy – we won't have to join the EU.

It is said that there are seven origins of the surnames of the indigenous population of the UK. First is the surname of occupation like Smith and Archer; then there's a personal characteristic such as Short or Black; next comes English place names giving names like Bedford and Hamilton; in fourth place are names from estates - Windsor is the prime example (chosen by King George V). At number five we have patronymic - Johnson (son of John), Jackson (son of Jack); matronymic - Madison from Maude, Emmett from Emma and ancestral - the Scottish clan names. Now, when you get bored you can venture forth and find out where your surname comes from. My favourite category is personal characteristics, explains why we give (and get) nicknames - and some very uncomplimentary ones.

I suspect that we all have those mad moments when we give our minds over to some obscure and pointless thoughts. Here's one to ponder, how far 4.5m Smiths would reach if they were placed in a straight line, end to end. I had to complicate it by deciding whether they would be standing up or lying down head to toe but then I remembered my wife's pearl of wisdom – why stand when you can sit and why sit when you can lie down? So, lying down it is (the preferred position of some on account of their appetite for the local brew), they'd go further too and assuming the average length (they're lying down remember – the only way to travel - and none of your metric nonsense), is six feet (I'm allowed to exaggerate), we would have a line extending over 5,000 miles – New Zealand is 11,682 miles away (London to Wellington). I assume that that is as the proverbial crow flies, in a more- or- less straight line, so we'll get there sooner in the lateral position. Hold on brother, we're coming, nearly half-way there, we only need to double the Smith population plus a few.

My parents did their bit – they produced fifteen Smiths - more a tribe than a family some might think. Five were girls - their status proved temporary as they all got married to men with different surnames. They are now technically defectors – not Smiths. Of the remaining ten boys two are sadly no longer with us; one died in infancy from diphtheria, the other murdered by the IRA. Tis said that I almost made an early exit courtesy of a bout of double-pneumonia (that must be the sickness version of bogof – have one attack of pneumonia and get a second one free). I'm more inclined to the notion that it could have been alcoholic poisoning. The story goes that when I was teething Mum would pour a drop of neat whisky onto the bothersome gum and apparently, it worked. It is reported that I became known as 'whisky boy'. But lest you get the wrong idea, I hate the stuff - might consider it as an anti-freeze for the car but for drinking - never in this or any other lifetime. We, the remaining eight have gone on to add another twelve males to the Smith population. Pathetic really – my old man generated more than the rest of us put together. Credit where it's due – hail the potent one. Bring him back to life and we'll take New Zealand by the turn of the century. For a long time, I believed that my father had no idea where babies came from. Seemed like he'd go out to work in the morning and when he came back in the evening there was a new arrival wailing in the background. I reckoned that he paused long enough to ask – 'where did that come from?' There were a lot of jokes about milkmen doing the rounds (pun intended) then; men left early for work – milkmen arrived early for delivery. There was never much truth in the tales – milkmen started work before dawn and could just about make out the difference between pasteurised and sterilised. Anything more complicated at that hour is mere urban myth and there is this too, many a housewife rejoiced in getting the bed to themselves at last, bed sharing would not be high on their list of things to do.

*****

At birth, I was fourth in the line of succession to our thread of the Smith dynasty – that's allowing big sister equal rights which she would have now – but not then so move over sister, I'm in third place. The Smith clan reflects the social structure of society. At the bottom, there are the common Smiths – that's me and my lot. A few hundred years ago, there was at least one of us in every village – the blacksmith. We were amongst the original metal bashers - appropriate since the name 'Smith' is an old English surname meaning to smite, to hit. Blacksmiths were known as the 'Smithy'; in Scotland, the word was 'Skiddy', now, if they had voted for independence they would have become foreigners and if they moved to England they'd be immigrants - would that mean that they'd have to learn English before being allowed to stay?

Here's a bit of nonsense information; in researching the name Smith I came across a reference to a Greek mythological character called Procrustes. He was a metal basher - a blacksmith, only the term hadn't been coined then. The story goes that Procrustes had 'guests' who were adjusted to fit the iron beds he had made. Those that were too tall had their legs cut off whilst those that were too short were stretched to size. I reckon this was the first example of one size fits all. He was also known as the 'stretcher' - they were hot on the obvious it seems. Doesn't pay to mess with us Smiths.

The next level is home for those just a bit too snobbish to allow them-selves to be called simply Smith and thereby associated with the vulgar hot, dirty, sweaty forges. No sir! For these were craftsmen and they stuck the name of their trade in front of Smith to make themselves look and sound more important – Arrowsmith and Shoesmith for example. No prizes for guessing their skills and occupations. But I bet I catch you out with Sixsmith. Go back further than the industrial revolution when this fair land was agrarian. Farmers used scythes and sickles in the fields – Sixsmith is said to be a derivative of both – well you could hardly call someone Scythesmith or Sicklesmith – could you? Right at the top of the tree there are, of course, the Goldsmiths and the Silversmiths – the real aristocrats of the Smith nation, damn obvious why. So, there you have it – the peasants, the snobs and the aristocrats – or the working, middle and upper classes.

There is a quaint belief held by some that babies choose their parents. If there's any truth in that theory, then I should have my head scanned for signs of life. Why choose the most common name in Christendom? And why by all that's sane sober and sensible did I not insist that the magic word 'gold' or 'silver' be affixed at the front end? I didn't choose – I was dumped. This is very feasible – the Stork is on its rounds, there are planes in the sky – fighters and bombers, and there's anti-aircraft fire from below. My theory is that I was en route to a desirable des res in the stockbroker belt, but the stork took fright – probably said something like 'bugger this – I'm dropping my load and I'm off. He did, and he was – dropped his load and off he scarpered. Me? I landed at the rear end of nowhere and became you-know-who instead of say Crispin Urquhart Skidmark-Cornplaster heir apparent to a country pile and a family fortune. Meanwhile I pass the time as 'something in the city' getting humungous bonuses and making you all greener than grass with envy. Instead I get to join the envious rather than the envied. How cruel is fate.

Fascinating isn't it that this most common of names in the English- speaking world, made of a single flat syllable – Smith – is the preferred choice of anyone up to no good. Couples married, but not to each other, book into hotels for the weekend; criminals use it as a false name and con-men as an alias. People – what has happened to your imagination? (Great Granddad Pittaway, this means you). The one appellant nobody is going to believe to be genuine in any of those circumstances is – Smith. Trust me on this – the fun I've had convincing others that it really is my proper name. On business trips, I've turned up at a hotel and said in all innocence (and honesty)

"Good evening – my name's Smith…"

The receptionist's face delivers an unspoken, contemptuous message.

"Yes sir, of course it is – how original"

Then she looks past me with an expression that says.

"Well, where is she?"

"I'm here on business" I offer.

No words – just the look – this time it says,

"Of course, you are – liar"

Oliver Wendell Holmes put it this way - 'Fate tried to conceal him by naming him Smith'.

*****

A little recapping here – I've covered the 'what' and the 'who' so that leaves the 'where' and the 'why' to come. Well, I'm going to dispense with the 'why' here and now. Why we are here and what is our purpose has taxed the minds of some great thinkers and if the likes of Plato; William James; Renee Descartes; Ralph Waldo Emerson (bit of name dropping here) and Joe Gobbo from the Boozers Arms can't sort it out I'm not rating my chances.

(A note to my dear granddaughter – no, I did not go to school with Plato). That said, perhaps the reason we can't define the meaning of life is because there isn't one – maybe it's down to us to make of it what we will and that becomes its meaning for us at least - bit of Existentialism for you there, better expressed thus.

'Meaning and morality of one's life come from within oneself. Healthy strong individuals seek self- expansion by experimenting and by living dangerously. Life consists of an infinite number of possibilities and the healthy person explores as many of them as possible. Religions that teach pity, self-contempt, humility, self-restraint and guilt are incorrect. The good life is ever changing, challenging, devoid of regret, intensive, creative and risky'

Frederick Nietzsche.

Or you may prefer the German philosopher, Hegel's theory which is that the world is moving towards an ultimate state of perfection. Got a bit to go then.

Something I don't need the help of those brain-boxes with is the 'where' – where I was born and lived for a short while. Number 14 Froysell Street, Willenhall, Staffordshire. Odd thing is that I can't recall fourteen houses in the street. House numbering seems such an obvious and simple exercise but once upon a century or more ago, houses only had names. History suggests that the early numbering was in Pont Notre-Dame, Paris in 1512. Later, Prussia developed a numbering system, and this was followed by European countries throughout the 18th century. With the passing of the Stamp Act in 1765, the numbering of houses in Britain became compulsory.

There are two Willenhall's - the other one is in the suburbs of Coventry and we don't talk about that - there's nothing to say. The Willenhall - our Willenhall was first recorded in the 8th century. A treaty signed by King Ethelbald of Mercia called the settlement - Willenhalch, an Anglo-Saxon term for 'Meadowland of Willan. It appeared in the Domesday Book in 1086 as Willenhala. We're fond of using the Domesday Book as a source of reference. It was compiled on Christmas day in 1085, completed in 1086 and delivered to King William in 1087. Literally everything and everybody in England was counted and accounted for, and the purpose? - to enhance the capacity to raise taxes for the conqueror from Normandy - perhaps that's why it's pronounced (and often spelt) 'Doomsday.' We Willenhallites certainly go back a piece. Anyhow, growing industrialisation from the 18th century onwards saw Willenhall emerge as arguably the lock making capital of the Europe. Such great names as John Harper Co Ltd; Joseph Legge & Co; Enoch Tonks & Sons dominated the town, providing work for its population aided and abetted by hundreds of smaller outfits. By the mid-19th Century there were more than three hundred independent lock makers in Willenhall, at its peak the industry employed over four thousand workers. In 1910 H & T Vaughan (founded in 1856) developed the cylinder lock, an invention of one Linus Yale from America. In 1869 Yale acquired the business of the Vaughan brothers and went on to become the most prestigious lock maker in the world. Sadly, cheap imitations from the far east marked a steady decline in the 1980's from which Willenhall never recovered.

Staffordshire was a county name with a county town at its heart. Much of it was hived off in the 1970's and called West Midlands – neither a place nor a town – just a title. There are lots of these dotted around the country – dreamt up by politicians (Edward Heath) as a means of manipulating constituency boundaries and influencing election results. We got bigger councils that needed more people to run 'em and they cost a whole lot more. A variance on Parkinson's law applies here - the number of people employed expands according to the volume of work created. (Professor Cyril Northcote Parkinson - British naval historian, gave us this adage 'Work expands to fill the available time for its completion') But I digress, back in 1940 Willenhall was run by its own Urban District Council and we lived as tenants in property owned by WUDC. It was a two-up-two-down pile. There were eight of us at the time - ten including Mum and Dad and I have learned that my mother's sister and her husband and two kids bunked with us for a short spell. That makes fourteen– must have been standing room only. Social Services would be apoplectic faced with such circumstances now. Imagine the number of boxes they'd have to tick – they'd have to keep dipping their pens in chilled water to cool 'em down. More likely we would be visited by immigration officials, suspicious that we were importing foreigners. Mentioning mom's sister reminds me that her second husband had a glass eye. He used to make us kids cringe by removing the eye, baring the socket.

The house was terraced, one of four, and they all shared a small communal yard accessed by a single entry in the middle of the block. Brick built with slate roof and a solitary coal fire range in the main living room. This basic affair provided the only source of heat as well as cooking facilities. A metal arm holding the kettle pivoted on and off the open fire. The oven lay alongside the fire and there was space beneath into which hot coals could be poached for roasting. Pots, pans and kettles would boil merrily on top of the oven or even the open fire and get burned black in the process. This gave rise to a colourful expression to describe people who criticised others whilst being guilty of the same offence themselves - 'it's like the pot calling the kettle black arse'. The whole edifice was black by nature and much effort was expended on keeping it that colour. Housewives were black-leading long before Al Jolson and The Black and White Minstrels (they would be severely done over by the pc brigade in our modern world) had the idea. There was a cellar that would have easily passed as a dungeon. It was darker and damper than the house, but the coal didn't mind. During the nightly air raids, we would all huddle on the steps of the cellar – not even the bombs could persuade us to go all the way down. People got buried in cellars and there was the bogey man to consider.

They were cold and damp places, no running water or electricity. Light was provided by gas lamps. Where gas didn't reach, candles did the job. Like most houses of their kind they were dull and dingy – especially at night. Daylight hours were treasured – you could see one another! Outside in the cobbled yard was a single tap, the only source of fresh water for the four families in the block. The water was always ice cold and crystal clear – except in winter when it tended to freeze, and a fire had to be lit near it to keep the water running. Pails (buckets to you) of water were stored indoors by some of the neighbours but I suspect they froze too. On many a not-so-cold day we kids would wash outside using water straight from the tap. There's nothing like ice-cold water for jump-starting the senses. My Kiwi convert of a brother recalls one of the neighbours' daughters cleaning her teeth at the tap using Gibbs SR toothpaste (Sodium Ricinoleate for the chemists amongst us). He says she was sort of frothing at the mouth – looking quite mad. This same girl was known to pencil a black line down the back of her legs to assimilate nylons – and she was a girl and a teenager – so almost certainly mad. Ah, some things don't change. Bit of social history – an advertisement for Gibbs SR was the first televised commercial broadcast in the UK by ITV at precisely 8.12pm on the 22nd September 1955 - the programme it 'interrupted' was a variety show hosted by the late Jack Jackson. SR was one of twenty-three contenders for first advertiser and was chosen by lottery. The first ever television advert in the world was in the USA (where else) in 1941 - for Bulova watches.

Kitchens and bathrooms weren't even in the vocabulary let alone the house – the 'kitchen' for cooking, was the range and the' bathroom' was a tin tub on the hearth. Daily ablutions were performed at the kitchen sink (winter days only), a Belfast style affair which also served to rinse laundry and prepare vegetables. The only toilet was a closet (I believe an earth closet - the invention of the Reverend Henry Moule in 1860) shared between the four dwellings and located at the bottom of the yard – and it was there for good reason – phew! That place scared the ……. er life out of me. It was dark in there – no lights- plenty of gas but not the sort one would care to ignite. I believe that in some quarters it was known as the thunderbox. Some folk referred to it as the 'privy'. The dictionary defines privy as a secret, hidden place. A misnomer if ever there was one - this foul-smelling edifice was impossible to secrete or hide. With the door closed we had to negotiate a position on the big wooden platform with a ruddy great hole in the middle. As befitting the basic status there was nothing so regal as toilet rolls, newspaper torn into small sheets served the purpose (pretentious types cut the paper evenly using scissors). Tales of what happened to people who didn't hold on to the seat and fell down the hole were more than enough to ensure that visits were kept as brief as nature would allow. I thought that they were bottomless pits. These were man-made black holes. When I told my wife of this edifice she reminded me of how, in times of yore, it was not uncommon for some people to attend to calls of nature using a sort of platform on the first floor that overhung the street below, a sort of high rise decking. Deposits were made in the street and washed away (or not) by the elements. She opines that it was likely this practice that gave rise to the term s... head' as for sure someone sometime would just have to be walking by. Yes - I know, very vulgar but you'd laugh if you saw it - you know you would, in fact you're laughing right now at the thought because you know someone to whom you would just love this to happen - don't you? The more refined souls will recoil in shock (mock) horror.

In one corner of the yard was the boiler house. A brick-built affair where each household did their weekly washing of laundry. Water had to be carried in and poured into the boiler. Underneath a fire would be lit and kept going throughout the wash which lasted virtually all day. The steam that emanated would have mocked a London fog. There was a barrel shaped tub into which washing was placed to be rinsed and possed - the poss was a large wooden dolly like affair with which the ladies pounded the laundry forcing out dirt and stains from its 'victims' aided by a soap powder. A behemoth of an iron mangle graced the yard through which the laundry eventually passed. Turning the ringer was a herculean task for the larger items. When the washing was hung out in the yard it created a labyrinth of laundry, moving in straight lines was impossible. It would take an age to get to the back door – heaven help you if you were in urgent need of the black hole. Even heaven wouldn't help if you ran through the washing, you would be shredded by a thousand curses from the launderer. Running the length of the yard and at the bottom was a high wall concealing the premises of a company called Dykes & Son Ltd – a castings foundry. High the wall might have been, but I have it on good authority that unwanted debris often found its way over – a practice I renewed at my first job but more of that later. As I remember it the wall was topped with broken glass set in concrete to deter uninvited 'visitors'. Such basic security measures are now outlawed – apparently, burglars have rights, like not getting injured whilst they're about their unlawful business. Imagine how it would be at court.

"I was on me way to break into the aforementioned premises, intending to nick anything of value when I occasioned an injury to me person on account as there was broken glass atop of the wall. Did meself a right bit of mischief your honour – couldn't go out house-breaking for weeks".

"Case proved. Damages will be awarded. It's quite wrong of the law-abiding community to think that it can go about hurting criminals – that's for the police to do when arresting them. You may be permitted to shout 'boo' or 'go away', you may even shout for Mummy, but you may not inflict bodily harm. If threatened with violence you should run away. Otherwise, if a scuffle ensues, your assailant must not be harmed in any way. Forget this at your peril - villains have human rights - not so their victims".

Lawyers will extend themselves in the defence of villains' rights but may be less enthusiastic in the pursuit of redemption for their victims - one wonders if the provision of legal aid has any bearing – and compensation of course.

*****

Froysell Street was like a side-street off the main road into Willenhall. In the other direction, I knew not where it went at the time – we didn't travel far in those days. Much later I learned that it traversed such exotic places as Lane Head; New Invention and Short Heath from where it set sail for Bloxwich a place described towards the end of the 20th century as a 'crime capital'. Well I guess they must live somewhere. On either side of Willenhall were the larger towns of Walsall and Wolverhampton (now a city). Anywhere beyond those perimeters might as well have been on another planet for all we knew about them.

I think that there was at least one street lamp – gas of course – but I can't be certain because it was never lit - maybe the old lamplighter had been conscripted. There was a war on you know. To the mind of a child it seemed ridiculous that that little old gas lamp giving off its meagre light could be seen by German planes flying high overhead. Could it really happen – a German navigator looking down.

"Achtung, zer is a light. Zat is Froysell Street, home of ze young Schmidt – ve vill bomb ze pig. Schmidt!". Did you know that the first street lamps in the world appeared in

Paris in 1667, using wax candles in glass lamps? London followed suit in 1684.

Anyway, little wonder they lost the war if they can't get the spelling of the simplest of names right. Surely one of the first rules of foreign travel is to learn the language of the country you're visiting, even if it is only a bombing raid – more so if the intention is occupation. Speaking of war and flying and Germans - during the first World War the German population had to sacrifice one of its favourite comestibles - sausages. It was all to do with the material used to make the outer skin of zeppelins. Zeppelins, sausages - what can they possible have to do with each other? Cow's intestines - that's the answer. Cow's intestines were used as sausage skins and they were also used in the construction of zeppelins and it took the intestines of 250,000 cows to make one zeppelin, so the German banger had to go. No loss in the opinion of my sophisticated taste buds - they boiled (still do) the sausages! Boiled and sausages in the same sentence is surely a gastronomic oxymoron. Tastes like foam rubber - not a proper sausage. Proper sausages are grilled or fried to a sizzling perfection.

Chapter 2

THERE'S A WAR ON – BUT IT'S OK – THEY STARTED IT

In truth, there's not a lot I recall from the war years. The roar of the planes' engines (theirs and ours) as they flew overhead was a common sound, but its significance was lost on me. I remember too, the air raid sirens - I sometimes think that many modern vocalist's model themselves on that baleful sound. Sirens of another kind continued in use after the war, apparently, they were sounded to tell the workers that it was break-time. People working in the factories were so enthusiastic about their work that if the siren wasn't sounded they'd just carry on (satire). It was heard again later to tell them that they could go back to work (which they undoubtedly did with admirable enthusiasm). Anyhow, as far as the war was concerned, I was too young to have an opinion much less take up arms. Likely it would have been different had I been born in Germany – they had the Hitler Youth and had it all not ended when it did and given that they were getting very desperate I wouldn't pledge my money on them not forming the Hitler Kindergarten brigade. Anyway, I was too busy being a kid. There's a lot to learn and there's no formal training – it's almost all trial and error. In those dark days if you were lucky and got something right you might have got a smile maybe a little pat on the back – but get it wrong and there was a pat, or two round the ear-ole. That would be on a good day – bad days saw you banished to bed without food.

There's something about childhood that has so far escaped the worthy attention of social psychologists. It is the invisible line between being willed, encouraged to do something - smile or make some (any) utterance or crawl or walk - and the audience, the instructors (usually parents and relatives), tiring of the consequences of their urgings. In the formative months, babies are pressured to speak. to imitate the inane chatter of adults - "say da-da" " say ma-ma" On it goes seeming endlessly until the poor child surrenders and yields to the pressure and dutifully mimics the utterances to the sheer delight of the performing parent. Junior got the message, talk to these creatures - it pleases them and when they're pleased you get rewards. Give it not too many months and all that changes, "will you just shut up and be quite?". Not really a question, it's a very thinly veiled threat. Same goes for walking; oh, how the baby is cajoled into standing on two legs and putting one tentative foot in front of the other. This too, appears to please doting parents and then it happens "stay there - don't move". Little tiny is likely to get stuffed into something called a 'playpen'. It's nothing of the sort, you couldn't swing a cuddly toy in one - they're containment cells - prisons. Adults! Many a kid must hope they don't grow up to be one.

*****

About this time there was normally eight of us kids at home. When I first wrote this, I miscounted and got to seven, encouraging a flippant reference to the magnificent seven - wholly inappropriate, I doubt we were Samurai material. Dad was in the auxiliary fire service and not eligible for the armed forces. He was away much of the time attending Liverpool, Birmingham and Coventry during the air raids. We certainly knew when the old man was off duty and at home 'cos he had a fine old temper and didn't miss many opportunities to give us kids a demonstration. Corporal punishment was the way order was kept then – a clip round the ear from the police, a smack on the back of the legs from mum but from dad it was special. He had a friend called Sammy. He'd give us the verbal's and ask if we wanted a bit of Sammy. Sammy was a belt, a rather thick and heavy leather belt, and it didn't take too many strikes to get to see things dad's way. Ah to have been born almost fifty years later. The United Nations Convention on the Rights of Children (UNCRC) (1989) acknowledged the rights of children to be respected and that they should be consulted on matters that affect them. I imagine it would have gone something like this.

Dad.

"do you want a bit of Sammy?"

Me.

"before I decide I need to consult with you as to the beneficial affects this meeting might have?" Dad.

"*******….. " Me.

"Ooooouch."

Now I'm probably creating the impression that the old man was a bit of a tyrant – a bully. I guess that's how he'd be seen nowadays. In mitigation, allowance should be made for the affect the trauma of attending the blitz on the Liverpool docks, Coventry and Birmingham must have had. He had been in the thick of it and had a steel plate inserted in his leg after one raid during which he was injured. We should also remember that we are the product of our generation. His behaviour then was near normal for many families – the liberal approach we see and hear so much about today would have been considered not just soft but downright unhealthy. How was a child to learn if they didn't experience suffering for getting things wrong? This was the age when teachers dealt out the cane or the slipper to miscreants. They were also very ready to launch a board rubber or a piece of chalk at an offending pupil.

We didn't know it then, but we were coming to the end of a lengthy period during which the philosophy of child rearing was summed up in the expression – 'spare the rod, spoil the child'. As long ago as the 17th century an English philosopher – Thomas Hobbes wrote about the need to curb the dangerous impulses of children with discipline and strict training. We know John Wesley for his evangelical work and as the co- founder of the Methodist church, composer of great hymns in celebration of life, love and the Lord. What is not so well known is that his mother was a fierce proponent of child subjugation. She wrote to her son on the need to break a child's will by whipping if necessary, to mould the child into a dutiful and obedient soul. Lest we judge her harshly reflect on this; she gave birth to nineteen children only nine of which survived. Nevertheless, this was an era of the philosophy that 'children should be seen but not heard.' This little homily dates back to the 15th century and is reported to have been written by an Augustinian clergyman by the name of John. In its original form and intent, it was directed at young females - I can just see the feminists steaming, kick-starting their broomsticks. Social Services, Health and Safety – they'd go into meltdown if they had to deal with such practices. But hey - lessons would be learned (that's a favourite cop out phrase trotted out when things go badly wrong nowadays). Reminds me of the lag who was asked if he'd learned anything from his spell in prison.

"Yes" says he "don't get caught next time".

The harsh reality is that violence is a dark side of human nature – a side we are ever ready to engage when things don't go our way, or we feel threatened. Between 1940 and 1945 we were living proof of man's inhumanity to man, and not for the first time in the then living memory.

Gustave Le Bon wrote in his book, 'The Crowd - A Study of the Popular Mind' - "....our savage, destructive instincts are the inheritance left dormant in all of us from the primitive ages".

Further in the old man's defence, although I don't recall meeting his parents, my grandparents, I have learned that my dad's dad was a strict disciplinarian – it's said that dad and his brothers – even grandma – could expect little mercy if the mood took him. Things were slow to change in those days, there was little incentive or motivation and I reckon it's likely that my old Dad was simply replicating learned behaviour. That's how dads ran the home – he'd seen it done – lived it. He parented like he'd been parented.

Sammy the belt, though a familiar visitor, didn't turn up every night. The dark did. As night loomed the blackout was imposed. Every single window in the house was covered on the inside with black drapes – literally black. The gas lighting was made even dimmer, but it was in the bedroom where I felt it acutely – fear, fear of the dark. Light in the bedroom was prohibited and when the door closed, and the drapes hung it was coal black. After a while some adjustment would be made, and I could at least see maybe a few feet but beyond that it remained a place where every imaginable horror lurked. Kids then, and now, have great imagination but lack the ability to rationalise. When the door was open, and I could see all four corners of the room I knew that there were no bogeymen but as soon as the door closed, darkness descended they appeared as if by magic. It's a powerful tool is the mind. I had to live with that fear for the duration of the war. There would be no calling out for help or comfort – Sammy was low on sympathy.

As I grew up and the war receded into history, I parked that fear somewhere in memory. It was a sort of agreement – it wouldn't bother me, and I wouldn't bother it. Translated that meant that I shut it out of my mind. Later, in my mid-teens, I was walking home late at night along a dark country road – no reassuring house or street lights. It brought those war-time memories back. I got home safe and sound because, of course, there were no bogeymen save for the ones in my head. I was afraid of something that didn't exist,

I learned a valuable lesson about fear. As Roosevelt said in his inaugural address in 1932.

"The only thing we have to fear is fear itself."

It wasn't the dark that I was afraid of but the phantoms I conjured up in my head – and here's the great truth – what I had created I could destroy. We can all do that.

*****

There's a war on and the family grow up in very deprived conditions. We were a poor family. Clothes-wise we got by with make-and-mend and hand-me-downs. There were no jumble sales or charity shops, the poor could neither afford to throw things away nor (much less) buy the cast-offs of the better-offs. Anyhow, clothing was rationed so we were all in it together (sound familiar?), nobody could buy new clothes.

Now, to a kid in those day, running around in threadbare gear was no big deal. My how times have changed, sometimes I could swear that kids today are born brand conscious. Anyway, threadbare clothes – ok you can get by looking shabby on the outside, but a threadbare stomach well that's something else altogether. Food was severely rationed as the merchant ships were attacked by German U-boats. Bread and scrape became the cornerstone of a staple diet. For the benefit of the ill-informed and the better off, bread and scrape consisted of a slice of bread which had been swiped over with margarine (not butter - never butter) – that's swiped, not spread, spreading used too much, as it was the margarine would be scraped off the surface leaving what had managed to seep into the bread. Spread it on and scrape it off. The margarine in question was something special – it was called 'special margarine'. I know not to this day of what it was made but I do remember that it was rock hard. Apart from its intended use it would have been good for sharpening bayonets and building houses – the Luftwaffe would never have bombed 'em down. By way of a little variety this special margarine was available as the familiar block and as a roundel. Oh, the excitement as shoppers waited, with breath held to see what shape would materialise from behind the grocer's counter.

In its natural state, it was un-spreadable. To remedy that it was usually placed on a saucer or plate and put near the fire to soften. Impatient people would simply hold it close to the fire to the same end. Now, for a long time I held that the incident I am about to recount was started by my elder sister. Doubt has been cast on that recollection in some quarters and I must protect myself against lawsuits for libel (and my lottery winnings). So, on one inglorious and memorable occasion someone who was not my elder sister was performing the warming of the margarine routine: the margarine was in roundel style and she (who was not my elder sister) held it over – not near – the fire. The fire did its work and the outer layer softened – so much that it slid off the wrapping and into the fire. We then witnessed another of its qualities – it was highly flammable. Flames spewed ceiling-wards and to us kids, it was pretty scary. Fortunately, one of the neighbours, out in the yard, heard the screams and rushed to our aid. (More likely to find out what was going on so that there'd be new material for the daily gossip). Now I don't recall exactly how this came about but at the same time, somebody came down the stairs (also not my elder sister) with the pot from one of the bedrooms. There was an unspoken understanding - nobody ever went to the thunderbox during the night. Calls of nature were satisfied using a pot stored under the bed and the contents were transported to the lavatory next morning. Anyway, someone (still not my elder sister) was presumably on their way to unload contents. They didn't get there – the 'somebody', the pot nor the contents – because the neighbour snatched it out of a surprised pair of hands and flung it on the fire. Experience is a great teacher and I learned then that putting out fires with the contents of a piss-pot is a bad, bad idea. The steam, the stench… give me the fire anytime. We're good at euphemisms - what I call the piss-pot had many aliases – pot; po; jerry; guzzunder (because it goes under the bed – goes under – get it?). These were the polite terms but behind closed doors it was the piss-pot. In later life, I heard tales of the contents of the pot being poured down on unwelcome callers at the door - namely the rent collector but I suspect this was mere fiction - or bravado. Now dear reader, whilst you have been sniggering in mock disgust I have unearthed a little- known truth. During the heat wave and drought of 1976 firemen (that's what they were called then - after modernisation they were transformed into fire-fighters) on the south coast of England resorted to attacking forest fires with effluence to save the dwindling water supply. Typical, we expound the theory, we test the theory, we prove the theory and they get all the credit. You'll find no mention in the annals attesting to the pioneering role of the Smiths in the extinguishing of fires using bodily waste. We should have got royalties.

Anyhow back to the matter in hand - that's how crises were dealt with then; no fancy frills – just direct action. No risk assessment, no calls to the emergency services, they were for real crises – bombed and blazing buildings. Seeing as the old man was a fireman it would have been a parody of coals to Newcastle – and there'd be Sammy to think about. I amuse myself by thinking how a situation like that would be handled today - a frantic call to 999 – 'somebody dropped margarine on the fire and we've tried to put it out by chucking the contents of the piss-pot on the flames'. That would need at least two tenders, two police patrol cars to blockade the street and an ambulance bringing two paramedics and breathing apparatus. The latter would have been most welcome. The largest contingent of all would be the that from TV 24-hour news (wonder if they'd send Sophie Raworth- er...anyone got any margarine they don't need?). Cameramen, technicians and reporters by the coach-load. Every minute detail of the 'incident' as it would become known, would be microscopically examined. There would be countless exclusive live interviews with neighbours.

"They always seemed such nice people - they always say hello"

Such in-depth profundity - well worth tuning in for. Then there'd be more interviews with anybody remotely connected.

"I'm speaking live (is there any other way?) with a man that once lived next door to the girl that went out with the man that sold a budgie to the father of a girl who went to school with one of the children caught up in this dramatic event".

" I mean we're all shocked by what's happened - don't know what to say"

Er... you've just said it sunshine. There would be free counselling for all and sundry affected, sorry - traumatised - by the event. A somewhat worrying trend has emerged over the past decade or so - that of third parties seeking to wallow in the grief and misfortune of others - suffering by proxy. Bound to be a Panorama special sometime soon.

Once the flames were put out there would have to be an inspection by Health and Safety and, of course, Social Services would turn up. We would all be adopted, and foster parents would be warned – 'don't let them near the margarine and remove the po from the bedroom' (Social Services would never say piss-pot – they're university educated)). Oh, and the paperwork afterwards! Say what you like about modern life, but this holds good – if it's quick and easy we're not doing enough and we're not doing it right. We must get as many people as possible involved and there must be reams of forms to be filled in – in triplicate and there must be boxes to tick and lessons to learn. But here's the magic, so long as all boxes are ticked everything is deemed to be alright. The drive isn't for solutions, rather meeting targets. Anyway, I've never seen margarine in the same light since.

*****

With the restrictions of food rationing diet was limited I guess. I don't have many specific memories of all that we ate – or didn't but I particularly remember rabbit stews at the weekend. We call them casseroles nowadays. People could ask the butcher for anything they wanted – a roast, sausage, even offal – but most often they would get rabbit. One in the eye for Harold at Hastings in 1066 wasn't the only thing the Normans gave us - they brought rabbits to our island to feed their soldiers. Anyway, the plentiful supply turned out to be a godsend to us carnivores. I don't think vegetarianism had been invented then. The downside to rabbits is that they breed like – er rabbits. After the war ended and something approaching normal service meat-wise resumed, rabbit went off the menu for many. But nobody told the rabbits and they continued to produce in gay abandon. It was said that the countryside was teeming with bouncing bunnies. So, what did a grateful country do? It introduced myxomatosis – a virus from South America (Uruguay) that was fatal to rabbits. Uruguay also won the first world cup in 1930 so that's something else to hold against them but they did beat Argentine (4-2) so I suppose we have to let 'em off that one. England refused to take part in what was considered a vulgar competition, or was it because it was the brainchild of a Frenchman - Jules Rimet, whose name the winner's trophy still bears?

Myxomatosis was a bit of a blunt instrument with which to control the bunny population. It did that alright and it achieved something else as well – it put people off eating rabbit for years. It's only recently made a comeback and is now served as a sort of speciality dish. Farmers were pleased because if there's one thing that rabbits do better than breeding it's eating – they'll strip a field of brassicas in a single night given less than half a chance. Food was then, rather basic. There was little or no fruit to be had and it was after the war ended that I made my first acquaintance with a banana, and with chocolate. Eggs? – Never heard of 'em much less seen one. There was egg powder for cooking, but it was useless for omelettes or soldiers. Oh, and there was something called 'national cheese' – the very name sounds ominous, can't recall having any but if it was anything like the special margarine maybe I should be grateful.

The war ended twice. First - Germany surrendered on the 8th May 1945. The day was called VE day – Victory in Europe. Second - Japan surrendered 14th August 1945 – VJ day – Victory over Japan. Notice how both avoided the 4th of June? ‾ I didn't mind because VE day was marked with the one and only street party I've ever attended. Trestles were laid end to end down the street, buntings hung from every window and criss-crossed the street and the Union Flag has surely never flown so proudly. Anything that stood still was garbed in red white and blue. Just where all the material came from I could never imagine – but I like to think that it was a product of the same indomitable resourceful spirit that had kept this little island going for almost six years. When something was badly needed, somebody somehow provided. It was a sight to behold. And the food! I had never ever seen so many sandwiches, cakes (all homemade of course), jelly, blancmange, ice-cream, and there was fizzy pop too – though I don't think that's what the men-folk called it, theirs was a distinct colour too. Odd, but, try as I might, no matter how much fizzy pop I drank I could not get as happy as the men. Had to be something to do with the colour I suppose – brown pop made you happy the rest just made you go to the loo a lot. The loo being any private spot you could find – no intention of missing any of the action (or food) by going home to use the hell-hole in the yard.

The day was crowned for us kids by the presentation of a bar of Cadbury's dairy milk chocolate. Wrapped in silver foil and sheathed in that famous purple sleeve this was luxury beyond measure. This edible jewel was much coveted and lovingly taken home to be consumed ever so slowly in private. How dare they allow Johnny foreigner to buy such an iconic British institution. Politicians lack national pride nowadays. Cadburys was taken over by Kraft from the USA in 2010. We refer to incompatible items as chalk and cheese - chocolate and cheese is right in there. After the takeover, politicians did what they so often do, amended the rules so that it can't happen again - stable door, horse and bolted come to mind. Meanwhile back at the party; alas the merriment had to end, as all days do, and eventually we all went home. For us kids it had been a wonderful day out, the adults spoke of a new beginning. In later years, I came to understand what they meant and to realise that things didn't turn out the way they hoped. But for now – life was good. A sobering footnote: the country celebrated VE day - it did not celebrate VJ day - don't recall any street parties. Little wonder that those that fought in the far east saw themselves as the forgotten army.

Chapter 3

SCHOOL - ENOUGH SAID

The war ended in 1945 – I was five years old, time for a monumental change in my life. Not long after hostilities ceased on all fronts I was told by my mother that I was going to school whatever 'going to school' meant it was to happen very soon. Don't remember the exact words that were exchanged only that I was told – not asked – but since it meant nothing to me why should I worry? I'd been places before – grandparents; neighbours; shops – they'd all lasted only a brief time and it was back home - same day. School was just something else to add to the list of places to go.

Oh, the treachery, the deceit: it started with being dragged out of bed in the early hours and subjected to the most vigorous laundering of the human body a young child could imagine. Washed, scrubbed, dried, brushed and polished and after seeming hours of agony I was declared fit to go. At this hour – 8.30 in the morning, what was this school thing that warranted such intensive grooming and early start? I found out of course, first it went on all day. That was bad enough but imagine my horror when I learned I had to go again the next day, and the one after that, in fact forever! One day was more than enough thank you very much. Now I know what happened to my elder brothers and sister during the day – they were conscripted into something called compulsory education and I had been dragooned into joining them. My eldest brother and sister had progressed to junior school – Albion Road Junior, a place we young guns were taught to fear. It was the 'big school' where learning got serious - apparently.

Not even the winter of 1946/47 saved us from school. Said to be the coldest for 100 years, it lasted from December 1946 until mid-March 1947. The whole country was severely disrupted, fuel and food, already scarce, became scarcer. We heard tales of ice being chipped off roads by men wielding pick-axes, but I don't remember us being allowed to be excused school - bet they made us go. Truth be told, I suspect we might have enjoyed the traditional winter sports of making slides, building snowmen and snowballing. Such frivolity would now have to be risk assessed and probably banned by the Health and Safety Czars. Winters did seem more severe then so maybe global warming is a reality. I still question the extent to which we mere mortals are responsible, though undoubtedly, we have had an input. Perhaps history will record that it was largely down to the natural evolution of the planet after all. For the record, the 1947 winter saw more snow fall (for fifty-five consecutive days, snow fell on some part of the UK), but the winter of 1963 is recorded as colder.

Cold enough to 'freeze the testes off a brass monkey' as the popular saying almost goes. I'll take odds that as I wrote 'testes' you, dear reader, read 'balls'. Cognitive psychologists will tell you that that is an example of your short- term memory, processing incoming data, and at the same time causing access to your long-term memory, which stores existing data, to make sense of what you've just read. In other words, you already had the familiar expression in your memory - all you needed was the cue - ' to freeze...' you completed the saying before reading it all and you do all of this in less than a milli-second - that's one millionth of a second - impressive. This naughty expression has a confused history. There are those that propose that a 'brass monkey' referred to the way the Royal Navy, in Nelson's day, stacked cannon balls on ships - pyramid style. First off, can you really see a pile of cannonballs staying in formation whilst the ship bucked and rode with the waves? Second off, the navy stored cannon balls in planks of wood with retaining holes. The original expression goes back to the mid-19th century and has a more mundane history. It referred to the toes or nose of a monkey and appears in several pieces of American literature. It is thought that the reference to monkeys relates to wooden carvings of the three wise monkeys to which was sometimes added a fourth with its hand covering its genitals. It was the naughty Brits who inserted the word 'balls' early in the 20th century.

*****

Development psychologists agree that the most important period in a child's life in terms of bonding and attachment are the years up to the age of seven. In the first half of the 20th century kids stayed at home with mum for the first five years - bonding and attaching (and being a nuisance). There was no such institution as a nursery school and if there had been I can easily imagine the mothers of the day bristling at the suggestion that some other woman was better equipped to look after her child. Half a century later and it seems that mums just can't wait to deposit junior in the care of another so that they can pursue a career - all in the name of equality don't you know? We are told that that is progress - helps kids build relationships - isn't that what being at home with mum was about? It is true, of course, that many do it out of economic necessity and there's also the phenomenon of the single parent family. In 1945 that was most likely because dad was a casualty of war. In the latter part of the 20th century it seems to have become a life-style choice. I wonder - can there be anything more rewarding than preparing a child for the great outside world? Sad but true - society doesn't appear to recognise, in an economic sense the real value of mothers who stay at home to look after their children. If we can fund child-minder fees, then why aren't these paid to mums who take care of their own?

The school to which I was transported daily was Elm Street Primary, founded sometime in the 1800's and losted (yes - there is such a word - ask my wife and then put it in your lexicon) in 2012. I don't recall it being an altogether unpleasant experience. The Headmistress (can't use that word now - terribly un-pc) was a Miss Dangerfield. A small middle-aged woman - although at the time I think that I would have had her down as ancient. Small she might have been, but she was of redoubtable character and had there been a Mr Dangerfield I reckon he would have had to surrender the trousers. The only teacher I can remember was a Mrs Pountney - also middle aged and of ample proportions. To be fair I don't recall much by way of formal learning, much of the time seemed to be spent drawing pretty patters with coloured crayons. I do remember there were toys to be played with and I was well pleased to be handed a lovely red fire engine. I doubt that this had anything to do with my father's war-time occupation. One - I have no good reason to believe that the school would know about that and two (the more compelling argument), psychology hadn't found its way into schools at that time - arranging something as subtle as this was way beyond the curriculum. Anyhow, I enjoyed that fire engine on a regular basis - until, that is, one sad day, when another kid got there first. I decided that I didn't really like fire engines anyway - so there – bet his dad wasn't a fireman.

I attended Elm Street Primary for two years. Not always willingly I'm told - there are tales of the steps I'd go to avoid going. Such as the occasion I hid in the pram of our youngest. It was a coach- built pram, the ones with the big underbelly and an artificial flat bottom that provided storage space underneath. Space enough to hide yours truly - but alas not good enough a hidey hole to deceive Mum. Of course, she was a veteran with kids - knew all their little tricks. 'Why Worry - Wheel a Windridge - Windriges of Wolverhampton' - that was the pram manufacturer's slogan, a neat bit of double-barrelled alliteration that lasted them for years. Anyhow, I'm not aware that the school left an indelible impression on me, but it certainly did no harm. It passed uneventfully so far as I can recall. My last day was marked by one of those incidents that demonstrate how asking the right question in the wrong way is certain to get the wrong answer. Mrs Poutney asked me to stand up in class then she announced to one and all that "Brian Smith is leaving us today. Can you tell the class where you're going Brian?".

Answer.

"No Miss".

Mrs P got a little cross like I'd disobeyed an order and insisted that I could - and should. Truth was that I couldn't tell her, or anyone else because I had no idea where I was going. Turned out that the family was being moved to a new home but in 1947 kids didn't get consulted about such grown-up matters - we just got told we were moving - even the expression 'moving-house' meant next to nothing. My pedantic point here is that I gave Mrs P the only answer possible. What she should have asked is "Where are you moving to?" That would have allowed me to say, "I don't know because I haven't been told" - and everyone would have been happy. But she being the grown-up - and a teacher to boot - and me being a seven-year-old kid, well it had to be me that was wrong, didn't it? This was my early introduction to the notion that might is right.

*****

The end of the war and my starting school combined to allow us kids greater freedom to roam. We had no fears of abduction then (no market for scruffy street urchins) and anyway, we didn't wander far by today's standards. On the main road at the bottom of Froysell Street was a little sweet shop - Chester's - the sweet range was limited but the ice cream was divine. Rich, creamy vanilla served between two wafers, known as sliders in some parts of the country. The trick was to see how long you could make 'em last just by licking. The shop also served cocoa (or was it drinking chocolate?) and sugar mixed, drinking chocolate was created by Cadbury's in 1842. Cadbury's Bournville cocoa was potent enough as a beverage, taken raw so to speak it would savage the taste buds, but whatever the mix it made for finger dibbing heaven. Further down the road was the local chippie where you could get a bag of batter bits for a ha'penny (that's half a penny - pre-decimalisation, real money or 0.20p new money). 'Oldies' often use the term 'real 'money when referring to pre-decimal currency. Now we say, 'pounds and pence' – back then it was 'pounds shillings and pence – or LSD (nowt to do with a certain hallucinatory drug). £sd – as it was more familiarly written, stood for 'Librae Solidi Denarii'. Anyways, back to the chippy, nowadays chippies skim off the bits of batter after frying fish and throw them away as waste - try selling them and the health police will have the Food Standards Agency on the case because healthy they 'aint, but back in the 1940's we looked upon them as a real treat as well as being a little earner for the chippie.

Heading towards the town centre there was a bit of wasteland called Doctor's Piece. Odd name - I'm told that the nearest anyone can get to an explanation is that in centuries past the area was home to several doctors. Not very imaginative perhaps but the logic is good. I used to play there with a school friend - Kenny Baxter. Kenny had toy cars, I didn't but Kenny happily shared. We spent many happy hours on that patch of barren land. It's long been landscaped but I still see it as it was. I don't see Kenny any more - in fact we lost contact when we moved. I guess kids don't do good-byes - maybe because we didn't fully understand what moving-house meant. It was only after the move that the reality struck. Everything and everybody changed - only the family stayed the same. There was no longer Elm Street School or Chester's or batter bits or doctor's piece or Kenny Baxter and his cars. I remember Kenny lending me his album of cigarette cards, pictures of footballers I think. So, ill-prepared was I for the move that I hadn't even thought of how I would get the album back to him - I just assumed that I would. But when we got to the new home I was upset to realise that I hadn't given it back - what if Kenny thought I'd stolen it? Then one day it simply wasn't there anymore, and I reasoned that someone must have taken it back for me - hope so.

All four families moved out of Froysell Street but I've no idea to where the others were destined. The move itself was excitement enough. There was no time for reflections - and anyway, I was only seven years of age, what could possibly have happened in so short of time to foster regrets at leaving? At the time, it seemed nothing, but later some incidents came back to variously haunt or amuse. There was the time I spilled a tin of brown paint on the stairs - when I picked it up I didn't know that the lid had been lifted and was now just resting on top of the tin. I found out when I hoisted it up into the air, miraculously the contents missed me completely, but the stairs were lavishly covered. Judging solely by parents' reaction I don't think that was its intended purpose. What makes that memorable is the I didn't get visited by Sammy - just banished to bed - another miracle I reckon. On another occasion, I drank a bottle of disinfectant - Ibcol - I have no idea why so don't ask. Maybe it was because it looked a little like beer in colour and maybe I wanted to feel as good as the men at the VE party. Many years later I tried beer - ghastly experience, awful stuff. Given free choice I would choose neither but if forced I'd go for Ibcol every time. By the way, Ibcol that looks like beer, was made by Jeyes of Jeyes Fluid fame - which looks remarkably like Guinness. Most likely tastes like it too but this one I 'aint gonna try - Jeyes Fluid that is, tried Guinness - anyone want a fence creosoting?

There is one other abiding memory I would share. Dennis, my elder brother, had the misfortune to scald his leg - badly. Not entirely sure how he managed that, but I think it had something to do with a pot of hot tea - yes, he wasted a whole pot of fresh tea! Tea was rationed then, remained so until 1952, hate to appear picky but he could have settled for just hot water surely. The scald was so bad the doctor was called, he examined Dennis's leg which, by then, had given rise (excellent pun) to a huge blister. It looked extremely angry, inflamed and painful - Dennis's face confirmed the latter. Doctor said that there was nothing else to do but wait for the blister to burst of its own volition. That would let out all the nasty goo locked inside and allow the leg to mend. The time for this event was open - wounds don't have clocks or calendars apparently. Anyhow, all that could be done was for big brother to rest as much as possible and keep off the leg. He was laid to rest on a couch (it would be called a 'chaise longue' now) and here he was to stay for the duration. I have a sneaky suspicion that he was quite looking forward to the experience. There'd be no school, no chores and preferential treatment when it came to meals. So - the stage is set. The invalid is posing, sorry, lying in state, sorry again, in pain and being waited upon by all and sundry.

Now a totally unrelated incident springs to life. Another sibling (no names – no legals) is chasing yours truly for some perceived wrongdoing. I can't imagine what it could possibly have been and anyway, they were almost certainly mistaken. The point was that they were older and bigger than me and it was another case of might is right. My flight took me into the room where Dennis was languishing, and my chaser was gaining on me I elected to run around the sofa. Round and round, we went, me just keeping ahead but Dennis was not entertained by our relay. They were still gaining - one last initiative - let's not go around the sofa - let's go over it, that would give me a yard or two. So, in mid-sprint, I launched myself across the middle of the sofa. It wasn't the best leap in the world and it didn't deliver me safely to the other side. I landed in the middle - on the sofa, on the leg, on the blister. This time the screams of pain were, I believe very genuine. The blister burst and disgorged its sticky contents. Before you round on me and castigate me for my clumsiness and whatever else, think on this: the bursting of the blister was essential to recovery - the doctor had said so. The longer that took the greater the danger to big brother. In that context, my unintended intervention was surely the proverbial blessing in disguise? Apparently not - on the contrary, I was public enemy number one. My adversary? As I recall, when they saw the outcome of my ill-timed leap, they wisely carried on running in a straight line to a place of safety. Did I get any thanks for cutting short days, maybe weeks, of waiting and suffering; for helping big brother back to normal so he wouldn't miss schooling? Not one word, I believe that I was harshly done by, don't remember how I was punished for that alleged offence but punished I surely was. Maybe I was flayed alive or strung up over the boiler in the wash-house or suspended over the black hole - whatever, I've obviously blanked it from my mind, so I never talk about it. Wonder how this works - you always remember to forget.

*****

In those early years, Christmas would have been a Spartan affair, there was little to be had and even less money to buy whatever was available. However, I do remember getting a toy submarine when I was about six. With hindsight, such a toy says a lot about the psyche of the country after the war. It chose to make a plaything for its kids out of the monster that had caused so much deprivation by the sinking of our merchant fleet. Maybe this was the establishment's way of delivering a Churchillian salute (reversed) to the vanquished. The origin of the offensive two finger gesture (palms facing in) is the stuff of myth. The most colourful version has it that the fingers represent the English archer's skill with the bow and was used as a gesture to terrorise the French. Alas, much as that appeals, the truth is comparatively dull. The earliest recording in the UK goes back only as far as 1901. It was reported as having been made by a worker at the Parkgate Ironworks in Rochdale. A newsreel was being made and apparently, he didn't like being filmed and he made an entirely spontaneous gesture that has since achieved lasting notoriety. However, further research not only suggests that the gesture is much older but also that it was far removed from being offensive in its intent. In 17th century Russia the Russian Orthodox Church distanced itself from Rome by creating an alternative ritual in the signing of the cross. The interesting bit is that the thumb and the fourth and little finger were brought together (the Holy trilogy), the remaining two were raised in the signing. Anyway, my toy submarine had a small rubber bladder attached from which air could be pumped into the toy causing it to float. Its natural state was to lie at the bottom of whatever water it found itself. That was the theory, worked out much later because there wasn't anywhere at home it could be tested. No ponds or lakes or suchlike and you can forget the bath tub and kitchen sink - they were in constant use for more boring practices.

That might also have been the Christmas that we were to have goose for dinner on the big day. The goose in question did not arrive butcher dressed and oven ready. It arrived under its own steam - goose-stepping (couldn't resist the pun) into the yard unaided although it was prodded occasionally in the right direction. Either it had no sense of direction, was plain stupid or else it was resigned to its impending fate. The plan was to kill it, pluck it, dress it; stuff it and cook it - and eat it of course. Six simple steps yes? No! My father couldn't get past first base - he couldn't kill the bird. I don't mean he had an attack of animal rights - his efforts at reconciling the goose to its lot ended up with said goose running around the yard with a broken neck and its head hanging in a southerly direction. From his grotesque position, the goose - our Christmas dinner - managed a series of indignant utterances. Were it possible to translate goose-ese into English it was probably saying " what did you do that for?" Anyhow, resistance was futile, the yard was small, the goose was one - the humans were several - goose was out-numbered and, out-manoeuvred, and eventually despatched.

Gruesome - even distasteful - as that scene may seem, through the eyes of a child not yet schooled in the sobriety and solemnity of death it was funny, black humour. Into the yard strutted this cocky bird. It spent several minutes being chased by lunging clumsy adults. And the noise they all made! Men, women and kids (not me of course) were screaming and yelling instructions and advice (the word 'bloody' was to the fore, more profane utterances were not made in the presence of women and children). The goose made its contribution - strange sort of noise, given the position of its head not surprising I suppose. The cumulative racket was not unlike a modern pop song - thinking about it, the frenetic gyrations much favoured by some pop singers (to hide mediocre voices I suspect) is very reminiscent of the cavorting of the gathering on that (for the goose) fatal night. Overwhelmed by numbers its demise seemed certain - then it broke free and ran around in circles with its upside-down head, it looked odd and funny. I am genuinely relieved that more humane practices now prevail. We were lucky animal rights hadn't been born. Easy to imagine now some scruffy drop-out leading protest marches and sit-ins because the Smiths having been unkind to a goose. A banner in one hand and a benefit cheque in the other, donated by a system he feigned to hate but one that is more tolerant of him than he of it.

That was to be our last Christmas at number 14 Froysell Street. In the late summer of 1947 we moved to 94 Essington Road, New Invention, Willenhall, Staffs. When I say moved you can ditch visions of a Pickford style evacuation - think instead of an open backed council lorry (now known as low loaders) borrowed - unofficially, for the occasion and a horse and cart. We kids were used as ballast to hold the family's worldly possessions in place on these open topped tourers. We weren't tied down as it were, so it was a rather precarious journey, punctuated by a miscellany of digs, pokes and probes as the furniture adjusted to the bumpy ride of some three/four miles. Now here's a bit of useless information for you. The slash as used in '3/4 miles' is called a 'virgule' - that's one for trivial pursuits (didn't I say that this was going to be educational?). Anyhow, I had never travelled so far - didn't know that anything, or anyone, existed outside my hitherto known world. Nothing and no one fell off and we collectively arrived at our new abode.

Whilst all of this was going on an event very many miles away was taking place in 1947, an event that would prove very significant in my life. It is this - the wonderful lady who one day would become my wife was born in Belfast on the 22 May.

Chapter 4

WE ARE DELIVERED TO A MANSION

The origin of place and street names remains an interest of mine. I've not been able to discover how Froysell Street got to be so called - maybe there was once a Mr Froysell who did good things and got a little street named in his honour. If so, he must have been the last of his line because I've never come across any little Froysells. Essington Road posed no challenge, it was (and remains) the road that leads to Essington - a place yet to be discovered and explored by yours truly. Our new home fronted onto Essington Road but was part of a development known as the Beacon Estate. Beacon Estate was, I believe, one of the first post-war house building projects undertaken by the local council. It was intended as a beacon of hope for the future, a fresh style of modern housing - the end of slum dwellings. With such a grandiose flourish, what else could the estate be called but Beacon? It was only a small estate and would eventually be dwarfed across the country by sprawling masses of urbanisation. The entrance to the estate was appropriately called Beacon Road but from there every other road was named after a local councillor. These were the days when such officials gave of their time freely for the benefit of their town or parish - attendance allowances hadn't surfaced. Probably true to say that they weren't altogether driven by a sense of altruism. I suspect a little dose of self-importance was a significant motivator. That said it still seems reasonable that their 'generosity' should be rewarded in some way and no doubt having a road or street named after them did much for the ego.

One such councillor, William (Bill) Stretton lived across the road from us in Essington Road. He was the archetypal local dignitary; a short stocky man with an awkward gait. Always impeccably turned out and topped off with his trademark homburg hat. Bill, or Mr Stretton as he preferred to be called addressed people in a condescending benevolent tone - not unkind but a reflection of his importance as a civic representative. Stretton Road was named in his honour. Now, if you're fortunate enough to have a road or a street named after you, wouldn't you want to live there? "My name is Stretton, and this is Stretton House in Stretton Road - my road" But you've got to have the name for it - much as I like the idea, Smith Street just doesn't work. I reckon that what local politicians were doing was to emulate a practice that emerged in London in the late 17th and early 18th century, a sort of reflected superiority. Following the great fire of 1666 London was rebuilt, in part, by the rich aristocrats of the day and so that the world would know of their largesse, they gave their names to their projects - Grosvenor Square; Cavendish Square; Berkeley Square and Bond Street for example. Perhaps the most notable is Hanover Square for this marks the ascendency to the throne of Great Britain and Northern Ireland by George of the House of Hanover, Germany in 1714 and all because he was protestant and England didn't want a catholic monarch. He became King George the 1st.

Maybe only local councillors could get away with such a perquisite. I doubt that there's be much enthusiasm for streets named after our MP's. Imagine the furore if a dyed--in-the-wool Labour supporter was asked to move into May Mansions or a true blue tory into Corbyn Close. Ever wondered why the Conservative party is referred to as 'Tory'? Here's a clue: the word 'tory' is a derivative of an old Irish-Gaelic word ' Toraidhe' meaning 'Robber' - enough said. Pity Tony Blair got out of politics (was he ever really in?), we could have had the Blair Bypass. You get to avoid all the complications of the inner city by going around it; master Blair was so adept at evading the consequences of his actions - they didn't call him Teflon Tony for nothing. He takes us into a questionable war in Iraq (the West wins the war and the Iraqis lose the peace) and then he's made a

Middle East peace envoy - there's a case study there and no mistake. Alas poor Vince Cable - it would have to be a roundabout so that he could change direction and still maintain that he was going the right way. It might be called Cable Island, but its colloquial name would ' the colander' - lots of escape holes/routes, each going in a slightly different direction.

*****

Anyhow, there we were, at number 94 Essington Road. And what a shock it was too - it was a mansion, a palace why - even a cathedral. Not that I knew what any of those words meant back then but they're the ones I would have used if I'd known. At Froysell Street it had been out of the front door and straight onto the footpath and the street. Now there was a long front garden (a garden - what the heck was one of those?) to traverse before encountering the front door. That was only the beginning. The front door opened into a hallway, to the left there were stairs to the first floor, on the right a door leading to the front room which had its own gas fire. This was to become the 'best' room used only on a Sunday or for special occasions. Next, also on the right, was the living room it seemed twice the size of the entire ground floor at Froysell Street. It had an open coal fire with an oven on one side - that was all it had in common with the black-leaded beast we had left behind, this one was green in colour. The living room also boasted French windows (so called because they have multiple windows in one frame), which gave instant access to an even larger rear garden - there had to be some mistake, we weren't meant to be moving into our own estate surely? But the exploration was far from finished, there was more, much more. The hallway led to a kitchen - a room specially; solely; exclusively for the preparation and cooking of food - and it had a gas cooker fitted - and a gas heated boiler for doing laundry (also doubled as Christmas pudding boiler). Still the goodies tumbled on - within the kitchen space was a self-contained larder for the storing of foodstuffs and there was a cold slab to help keep the temperature down. Oh, and there was a serving hatch connecting with the living room, so this obviously doubled as a dining room but, alas, no serving wenches. On reflection, the front 'best' room was really the lounge in estate agent's vernacular. We were becoming such snobs.

Upstairs there were three bedrooms, two that would be classed in modern sales parlance as doubles, the one at the front of the property had a gas fire just like the front room downstairs. The third room was described as a 'box' room but to the rest of the world it was a bedroom. And, wonder of wonders - there was a bathroom - with a bath (not one that had to be carried to the hearth - it was firmly fixed - and a sink, sorry washbasin. Better and better - bath and washbasin had two taps - one for hot water, the other for cold. How did they get running water into the house? How did they get hot running water into the house? Answers - in the bathroom there was an airing cupboard and in the airing cupboard there was a cold-water tank fed from the main supply outside and there was also an immersion heater, a huge copper cylinder -- the sort that gets nicked by burglars nowadays. Oh, and there was space for airing clothes - well there would be seeing as it was the 'airing' cupboard - but that was for softies. What luxury - and there a flush toilet (only cold water) - in the house, not at the bottom of the garden. This luxury was the result of the work of one Thomas Crapper who developed the modern WC (water closet) following the passing of the Metropolis Water Act in 1872. His name lives on albeit sadly in somewhat derogatory fashion. Hallway; kitchen; bathroom; hot and cold running water; flush toilet; gardens - these words were as of a foreign language – one's vocabulary was enriched beyond measure. A moment longer please - there's still the great outdoors to check. Shock - amazement - there was another flush toilet outside! Well, not outside really, there was a door in the kitchen that led to three outbuildings that were semi-enclosed. Next to the toilet, was a coal store (so no cellar then - good) and next to that was a unit that could serve as a general store or even a workshop.

The whole house was bright and light. Decorated in neutral pastel shades - cream coloured distempered walls courtesy of Walpamur, the ceilings were whitewashed. I so remember the solid balls of whitening that were crushed and mixed with water and literally slapped on ceilings using an enormous brush. Not on walls - never on walls, for it was like chalk dust when dry. Every room had large windows through which daylight flooded. The bathroom window was glazed in hammered glass designed to frustrate voyeurs. The small window in the larder was similarly glazed but with a different mandate – to dull the light whilst the window's function was to facilitate the circulation of air to help preserve food stored therein. In the hall was a small circular window - a very creative gesture - added a little character to the place.

The noise us kids made as we raced from room to room would have scared the neighbours' half to death but fortunately we were amongst the first to arrive. Is it just kids that get excited by the echo effect of an empty house? There followed the tedious business of unloading the lorry and the horse drawn cart. Us kids were used as mules to carry the small stuff and the grown-ups took care of the furniture - beds and the like. Eventually, everything was where it was supposed to be. Time, and dusk began to fall - that was the moment I discovered something magical - electricity! All you had to do was pull a switch on the wall and - hey presto - there was light, blinding, brilliant 100-watt light.

Did you know that the word 'electricity' was coined in 1600 by William Gilbert in a book entitled 'De Magnete'? Most people refer to Michael Faraday or Thomas Edison, but it was nearly three hundred years later, in 1879 that Edison perfected the incandescent light bulb. Point of interest - it is widely accepted that the British inventor Joseph Swan got there first, but it was Edison that took out patents in the USA. Swan also developed a superior bulb for William Armstrong of Cragmire in Northumberland. Armstrong was the producer of the first hydro-electricity in the world in 1878 and the generators work to this day. Incandescent light bulbs were banned in 2009 by the EU - (guess they had to have something to do after straightening cucumbers) they were replaced with 'energy efficient alternatives' - they save energy alright – because it takes 'em an age to warm up. Anyway, back to our new home; what a day - no more washing outside at the pump; no more scary visits to the 'thunderbox'; no more piss pots (sorry chamber pots - I'm university educated now); no more tin baths on the hearth. No doubt about it at all - the Smiths were going up in the world. Such was the euphoria of that first day. The war's end marked the country's new beginning - moving to 94 Essington marked ours.

*****

Essington Road went so far in a northerly direction before it morphed into Essington Lane. The road ended, and the lane began roughly at the point where the houses ran out and gave way to fields and hedgerows. The properties were a mixed bag of architectural and period design and construction. We and seven other families occupied the latest addition - 1947 style local authority built. They were of a substantial size and design and sound construction - a reputation they retain to this day. Certainly, they are superior to many of the modern bland boxes that are sold at premium prices today. Across the road were several pre-war council properties more basic than ours and lacking our modern amenities - indeed some still had only gas lighting. They had rough-cast exteriors suggesting that they were what is known as 'of non-standard' construction - that's estate agent's language for concrete. They can't say 'concrete' because nobody likes it apparently. Further down the road there was several privately-owned properties, some having been built in the 1800's. They were occupied by semi posh people. Real posh people lived in roads entirely populated by their own home-owning kind - they didn't share with the peasants, council tenants. At the other end of the road there was a row of nineteenth century terraced dwellings. Essington Road had become, in architectural terms, a bag of all-sorts.

The relatively modest population was well served by an impressive array of shops. Heading south down Essington Road there was a general store - tinned foods and some greengroceries - Bishton's. Mr and Mrs Bishton served us with a degree of disdain I didn't understand at the time - especially since they fawned over others - maybe it was a kid thing. Just a few yards further down the road was the Cook emporium - Mrs Cook was an attractive middle-aged lady running a shop not unlike Bishton's but with a more welcoming attitude. On the other side of the road was yet another general store run by a Mr and Mrs Owen - they took no prisoners. They would give credit but woe to anyone who failed to pay by the end of the week. Their name would appear in the shop window - 'Please note that Mrs Pauper of Skint Street will not be given further credit until her account is paid.' How times change - imagine the lawsuits such a notice would inspire today - customer confidentiality for starters and we mustn't forget 'Yuman Rights'. Remember, only the offended party has human rights.

A little further down the road was the local outdoor run by the Pearce family - a brother and his two sisters. They were of an age that appeared to defy mortality. This was the place to go for a jug of ale - many did - a packet of crisps and a packet of fags (cigarettes - 'fags' is so working class). A little further down from the outdoor was the local tobacconist (you ain't ever going to see the like of them again - outlawed by the health police). It also doubled as a sweet shop, but rationing meant that that part of the business was depressed.

Everyone was permitted a quarter pound (an E-coupon) of sweets per week. The ration could be split into two two-ounce purchases (a D-coupon equalled two ounces). The shop was run by name-sakes Bernard and Ivy Smith (no relation). They kept sensible hours so if smokers didn't get the tobacco fix during the day - they would have to rely on the outdoor at night. In these 'bad' old days people had the right to smoke if they chose. Not that I'm making a case for smoking - but I am making one against a nanny state that dictates. And I will add this - if you choose to smoke you must accept the consequences. Just what consequences will ensue from the latest fad of electric cigarettes is a research scientist's dream. In the centuries to come people may snigger at our strange practice of rolling tobacco in paper and then putting it into the mouth and then setting it alight, but when they get down to reading about how we made electrical versions and sucked them instead, they just might write us off. Smoking has become so anti-social that not only has it been re-invented, it's also been re-named – it's now called 'vaping' and users are 'vapers' – I can think of other words. A very real problem in modern times is that too many people abrogate personal responsibility for their actions. "It's not my fault I have cancer caused by smoking" "It's not my fault I'm obese because I eat too much" Forget fault, substitute responsibility. There's a cost to everything and he that orders the tune pays the piper.

Remarkably the road boasted two chippies - one on each corner and directly opposite each other. One didn't last long but the other - Tarbucks reigned supreme until the sad day Mrs Tarbuck departed for that great chippie in the sky - she had her chips so to speak (lest you not be well educated - that's a local expression for them wot have died). Whist she was amongst us mortals Mrs T made the best chips ever. They were fried in beef dripping to a deep golden brown "a dish fit for the gods." - (Brutus - Julius Caesar- Shakespeare) (me - showing off). People would queue for ages just to get a serving. They were so popular that when they were fried to perfection they were ladled onto a serving tray on the counter rather than deposited in the heated compartment of the fryer. They lasted for as long as it took to serve the salivating queue. There were also a couple of coal-yards in the area. Lowndes' on Essington Road and Appleby's on Lichfield Road. No central heating then me softies - everyone had coal fires. The more affluent you were, the more fires you could afford.

Imagine - three general stores; a tobacconist and sweet shop; an outdoor; two chippies, all within two hundred yards of home and two coal suppliers in easy reach. Despite the proliferation of retailers there was still room for Joey Amphlett's mobile shop. The 'shop' was a converted long-wheel based van that grumbled, groaned and ground its way along the roads. It was low down on its axle due to the heavy load it carried. Joey aimed to supply anything and everything that the local static shops couldn't or wouldn't. To round it off, at the end of the road there was island and on the other side was a pub - The Gate Inn. A volatile institution even on quite nights. I soon learned that there were some hardy boozers in New Invention and more were being imported (or should that be - deported?) onto Beacon Estate. Turning-out time (invariably referred to as 'chucking-out' time) at The Gate was often the best cabaret one could wish for - the staggering, the singing, the swearing (what a lot of novel words I learned) and the fighting. A famous psychologist - Naom Chomsky hypothesised that babies are born with an innate structure for language learning - all they need to do is acquire the language, which they do as the grow. The argument continues that children get to know the use of words before they acquire their meaning. Some of the words us kids heard from those exiting The Gate (and other pubs over time) were proof. We were more than willing and able to use those words without having a clue as to their meaning. We knew without being told that we should not ask our parents what xxxxxxx meant because that innate knowledge also told us it was a bad word. Those of us foolish enough to ask mom or dad were threatened with "I'll wash your mouth out with soap and water if I hear you say that again". Carbolic soap was all the rage then - trust me, you wouldn't want it anywhere near your mouth.

*****

The Gate Inn, and indeed the two chippies, were on Lichfield Road which headed eastwards towards Wolverhampton and in the opposite direction westwards, towards Bloxwich. The road was separated at this junction by an island forming a perfect confluence at right angles to Lichfield Road. Road, Essington Road ran northwards and to the south Cannock Road pointed the way to Willenhall. To the left of The Gate there was a little row of old terraces properties. A tale was told in later years as to how these properties were glazed and painted so as not offend the eyes of certain dignitaries passing by on a 'showing-the-flag tour'. These childlike charades are still practised by public and private enterprise. The message seems to be - 'on no account let the place be seen as it really is'. Squeezed between The Gate and these homes was a short narrow pathway set at right angles to the road. Here could be found the village post office - a tiny affair, it could only house three customers at a time. It was run by one Fred Onions. A frail looking man of some years but in that office, he was the guv'nor - what he said stood as law. There was a form for everything and every detail required by said form had to be completed. He spoke with the weight of the General Post Office (GPO) behind him. Fred was very genial to any youngster that went in to buy savings stamps. I guess he liked thrift, anyway these stamps cost 2 shillings and sixpence – 2/6d (12.5p in new money). This was how us kids saved for things – banks weren't interested in the likes of us. The GPO was responsible for post and telecommunications - a now defunct government department, those duties performed now by Royal Mail and

British Telecom respectively. Alas, Royal Mail has recently been privatised - sacrilege.

Next to the Post Office was Johnson's, a small private dairy, they delivered milk produced at Johnson's farm situated a little further along Lichfield Road in the direction of Wednesfield. It was brought to the door in huge urns. At right angles to their premises and fronting the main road was a child's outfitters and haberdashers (another type of retailer outlet you won't see again) - May Smith's. The one and only village telephone box was located here, near the post office. No one, but the super- rich had telephones in the home. Another note to dear granddaughter - there was a time before mobiles and texting. If we wanted to contact anyone we either called on them or sent a letter - how quaint, how weird says she. Here's one for granddaughter - Twitter wasn't created in the 21st century - oh no. In 1879 a series of essays were reprinted from a journal called The Saturday Review - these essays went under the title of 'Social Twitters'.

In an emergency, members of the public could use the special police call box situated on the other side of the road, opposite the GPO telephone box. All one had to do was open the door to the speaker and yell out the 'urgent' message. I am told that it was widespread practice amongst some of the unruly elements, to make use of this device, for the purpose of fun - I really couldn't comment.

Lichfield Road carried on past the only multiple retailer in the village - the Co-op grocery store. In time, I would get to know the Co-op quite well. Spreading outwards behind the Co-op was the factory of Henry Squires Ltd - another renowned lock-maker. The company has since relocated. Just a little further down on the near side was another pub - The Crown - it was said that 'them that drank in one (The Gate or The Crown) never drank in the other.' Now I consider that as, what is affectionately called 'cobblers'.

When a drinker wants a pint, he'll get it from where he can get it - thirst and taste-buds will swop allegiance if the alternative is going without.

"Go in The Crown?"

"Not me mate - I always drink at The Gate - always will".

"Well - yes I did just pop in once for a quickie"

Don't get the wrong idea - he's talking about drink.

"But that was only 'cos The Gate had run out of Ansell's bitter - wouldn't do it again".

In later years, The Crown and The Gate were joined by the Victory Working Men's Club - right next door to The Gate. Just a little later and this club made a huge contribution to the social and cultural life of the village by organising a weekly dance night. Modern stuff - rock 'n roll and all that - good times.

*****

How New Invention got its name has taxed the imagination of many a self-appointed local historian laying claim to a secret truth known only to the few. Usually ends up being a huge dollop of local folklore handed down the generations with about as much substance as a politician's promise. Never met one who knew that there are, in fact, two New Inventions - one where I grew up in Willenhall and the other in Shropshire. Two Willenhalls - two New Inventions - this is beginning to sound like a parallel universe. Of New Invention, Willenhall it is said that in the beginning the area was farmland. One of the early tenants had a problem with smoke from his chimney so he contrived some sort of cowl to cap the stack and control the nuisance smoke. Likely that the cowl was made out from Hawthorne twigs. So proud and smug was he of his fine doings that he invited others to see his 'new invention'. Over in Shropshire they tell an even more unlikely tale - there folklore has it that a local farrier was in the practice of fitting horse-shoes on backwards, in order to fool the enemy during times of war. Fitting horseshoes on backwards is hardly an invention, so not much credibility attaches this tale. It is romanced that he so fitted the horse of Charles 1 to help him avoid capture. I reckon the tale-tellers spent an awful lot of time in their equivalent of The Gate or The Crown and this yarn came about because of too much time in the company of the ale. A more plausible explanation that could apply to both is that the name is a derivative of old Saxon English. The 'vention' part may have come from an ancient word 'Fenton' a common place name that described a settlement in marshy land. The 'new in' bit would refer to a place that was new in Fenton - and there you have it - New in Fenton morphs into New Invention because of common usage. Both New Inventions were situated in fertile farmland. As a point of interest New Invention, Shropshire first gets a mention in official records in 1677.

At the beginning of the industrial revolution New Invention (the one where I once resided) found itself almost ring-fenced by coal deposits. Mines were opened from Cannock, through Wyrley, Essington to Sneyd Colliery in Bloxwich. Transporting the coal was made possible by the construction of the Essington and Wyrley canal completed in 1797 and initially used to move limestone across the county. Originally the canal ran from Wolverhampton to Huddlesford Junction in Lichfield and connections to other canals were dug. Most of these branch lines have been closed and the canal now terminates at Ogley Junction in Brownhills.

In the Midlands, a canal is known as a 'cut' - kids would go swimming in the cut. The best guess is that canals were called 'cuts' because they were cut into the countryside, sounds plausible. Now, here's a thing - remember that great delicacy made by Cadburys - the curly whirly? They may have marketing rights to the name, but they didn't create it - the Essington and Wyrley canal was nicknamed the 'Curly-Wyrley" by the locals on account of its meanderings across the South Staffordshire countryside. Around 1900 the Sneyd arm of the canal was closed. Many canals across the country were yielding to the competition from the railways. A line was constructed from the Sneyd Colliery to the wharf in Short Heath. It ran across the back of Beacon Estate and every night we could hear the train making its steady journey - back and forth. As the estate was developed that sound dimmed but my love of 'chuffers' has never waned.

*****

During the late 18th century John Wesley, co-founder of the Methodist Church, visited Willenhall but his preaching was not popular, and the story goes that he was run out of town. He repaired to New Invention where he said that he was received with civility and kindness. Wesley Road connecting Short Heath with New Invention, was named in honour of the great man and Wesley Chapel stands on the corner to this day. Wesley's liking for New Invention is marked by the Methodist Chapel on Lichfield Road although its days are apparently numbered. There's a tale about Wesley being able to read fluently upside down - that's the print not the man. Apparently, his father read the bible diligently using a finger to follow the text. The young John Wesley would seat himself opposite the old man and likewise follow the finger and the text.

Wesley was also an enthusiastic advocate of so-called 'electric therapy'. In his book 'The Desideratum' (1759) he wrote this.

'Before I would conclude I would beg one thing....It is, that none would condemn they not know what: That they would hear the cause, before they pass sentence: That they would

not peremptorily pronounce against electricity while they know little or nothing about it. Rather let every candid man take a little pains to understand the question before he determines it. Let him for two or three weeks (at least) try it himself in the above named disorders. And then his own senses will show him, whether it is a mere plaything, or the noblest medicine yet know in the world'

The ailments for which he proposed such treatment were:

'Angina pectoris, bruising, cold feet, gravel in the kidneys, headaches, hysterics and memory loss, pain in the toe, sciatica, pleuritic pain, stomach pain, palpitations and so on'

Pretty much a cure all but don't run away with the idea that it's a good plan to plug in a 13amp, switch on and hold on to the live wire - do that and live you won't be.

The worthy point that comes out of Wesley's writing here is not his belief in 'electric therapy' but his clear statement that folk should make up their own minds about things and not have them decided by others. Wonder if he applied that reasoning to religion.

In modern times, we have seen the practice of naming roads and places after people reversed. Certain 'celebrities' have made it chic to name their off-springs after the place where they were conceived - go on, reach for a vomit bag. Does make one wonder though at some of the possibilities. Imagine a child conceived in Shitterton (Dorset) or Crapstone (Devon) or Backside (Aberdeen) - Mr and Mrs Self- Important and Master Shitterton Self-Important. And if you like an international flavour, how about Phuket (Thailand)? A favourite of mine is one we discovered whilst on a family holiday in Denmark - we passed through a small town called Middlefart. Mr and Mrs Vacuous-Celebrity and Miss Middlefart Vacuous-Celebrity. Thinking about embarrassing names - how about Mr Toshiyuki Fukada? No - I haven't just made it up - the gentleman is a research scientist at the Riken Centre for Integrative Medical Studies at Osaka University, Japan - check it out. Doesn't mean a thing in Japan - what it means here depends on the state of your mind. We get around Phuket by pronouncing it Foo-kay - I'll leave you to your own devices in the matter of Mr Fukada. Here's a little extra - the Riken Institute is spread over seven campuses one of which is near Tokyo. Opened in 1931 as a research centre specialising in chemistry and physics - it's primary mandate was to develop an atomic bomb. Let's not speculate on the consequences had they succeeded before the USA. One more - Mr Jurgen Knoblich, a molecular biologist at the Institute of Biotechnology, Vienna. Mr Knoblich is attempting to grow a human brain in a laboratory. He'll sell a few of those on eBay - if it works. Another one more - Heuronyus Cock - a 16th century publisher. Okay, okay but this is positively the last - Professor Solomon Wank - he's an expert in terrorism at Tel Aviv university. On reflection, maybe Smith isn't such a bad name after all.

Prior to the construction of Beacon Estate and our arrival New Invention had grown from a tiny hamlet to a sprawling village. It's unclear whether the estate was built on former farmland, certainly there was a water tower in the corner of a field near the new houses likely used for irrigation. That said there was also substantial slag heaps but a few hundred yards away across the field that could only have come from coal mining. Dense grey clay and buried therein was a good bit of coal as we found out. Being a mining area, the underground was criss-crossed with old tunnels and I well remember the front room of one house just off Beacon Road disappearing - fortunately it wasn't too serious, and no one came to any harm. Some of the roads were prone to subsiding a little too but again, nothing calamitous - bit like speed bumps in the reverse. When we arrived on the scene there were two farms in the area - Sadler's Farm located a short distance along Essington Lane, and Johnson's Farm situated on Lichfield Road in the Wolverhampton direction. Johnson's fields ran up to the other side of the lane - opposite Sadler's. At the time, I believe that Sadler's Farm was being wound down and maybe the sale of land for the building of the estate was a part of the process.

We were living now in what could be described as a semi-rural setting. For all that, we were still in the Black Country. Arguments rage to this day as to how the Black Country got its name and how it should be defined - where it covers. Anecdotes abound as to the origin of the name. One popular tale has it the Charles Dickens described it thus on one of his visits but it's unlikely that he toured the whole region so it's not possible to agree a geographical definition based on what was probably nothing more than a passing comment - if it was made at all. What can be evidenced is that the name was first recorded in a novel called 'Cotton Green - A Tale of the Black Country by the Reverend W Gosley of Lichfield in 1840. There is also a recorded reference made in 1862 by Elihu Burritt, the American Consul to Birmingham who said of the area that it was "black by day and red by night". As to the geographical spread, there are two contenders; one that the title Black Country embraces the industrial Midlands, the other that it is defined by the coal mines that stretched across the South Staffordshire border. There is inevitably a considerable overlap since industry and mining co-existed in many of the towns in the region. Interesting to note that despite their industrial heritage neither Birmingham nor Wolverhampton are considered part of the Black Country. Interesting too that neither had coal mines, although there was some involvement in Wednesfield on the Wolverhampton border. Wednesfield gets its name from the Germanic mythological figure of Odin which, in turn comes from the ancient Norse god Odin which was corrupted by the Anglo-Saxons to Woden - the supreme god of, amongst other things war - they were big on gods of war the Vikings. Around 1100 years ago, the Anglo-Saxons defeated a Danish Army from Ireland at the battle of Woden - now called Wednesfield.

Nowadays it is generally accepted that the Metropolitan Boroughs of Dudley, Sandwell and Walsall make up the Black Country - still excludes Wolverhampton and Birmingham. If you want to upset a Brummie (anyone from Birmingham) say that they're from the Black Country. Works the other way too - call someone from the Black Country a Brummie and you'd better duck. Thus, it was that, in the late summer of 1947 we were delivered to this place. Come the autumn and I would start at a new school - New Invention Junior, located at the near end of Cannock Road, about three-hundred yards from home.

*****

The immediate post-war years were to prove memorable in national terms as well as for the Smith family. The 5th July 1948 saw the birth of the National Health Service (NHS). A symbolic opening of the Park Hospital in Manchester by the then Health Secretary, Aneurin Bevan, heralded the dawn of free health care at the point of need for everyone. Up to then it was not uncommon for workers to have health care provided by their employers, but cover did not extend to their families. Now everybody could afford to be ill. I consider myself to be apolitical, but I have no hesitation in acknowledging the NHS to be one of the greatest social advancements in the civilised world. It was brought in by Clement Atlee's Labour government despite opposition from the British Medical Association (BMA). That said it remains a remarkable fact all of a very sudden an awful lot of folk found themselves ill - unfit for work. Here's an interesting exercise - take 100 employed persons and 100 self-employed persons, then check the number of days off each group has had on the grounds of ill-health. I was once asked how to cut the sickness record of a large organisation - simple says I - make 'em all self-employed.

Currently the NHS is under siege, taking a battering. Alas part of the problem is that it signed up to the target culture. Setting targets is an American import. Has its roots in the early part of the 20th century and it is claimed that its success underpinned the rise and rise of the American economy to world dominance. One of its keenest advocates was a certain Frederick Taylor, a mechanical engineer and the father of scientific management. One of his experiments involved measuring the effectiveness of shovels - his conclusion, small shovels were best for heavy loads and large shovels for light loads. Genius - but here's the most interesting part, the only opinions not sought or considered were those of the men doing the shovelling. Opponents dubbed this school of thinking as dehumanising, reducing workers to mere machines, robots. They should visit an Amazon warehouse. Not much has changed.

Is it me - or do you find it strange too? - politicians can impose targets on anyone and everyone - but not themselves, very undemocratic. Now, since they impose targets on sectors of the public - the public should set targets for MPs - very democratic. One could be delivering on their manifestos; if they fail there should be penalties. Similarly, they should be given a budget (to replace expenses) and again penalised if they exceed. Yet another; giving straight answers, the NHS could run on the penalty income from this source alone. Anyway, how does one set targets for medics? Right Doctor Mendleg - you're on the appendix removal line today - remember to keep the line moving. Patients are loaded on a moving conveyor belt - doctor one opens 'em up, doctor two yanks out the appendix, doctor three sews 'em up and they land in a wheel chair at the end and get wheeled away for storage pending collection. If any of the doctors are too slow in fulfilling their allotted task that patient must go around on the carousel again to get another chance. Production surgery - brilliant idea. Come along Surgeon Boncebotcher - you've only got fifteen minutes to get that brain line back where it belongs - and do put it in the right way around. If they must have targets wouldn't it be better to impose them on the patient's? This is how it might work - each hospital has a quota of conditions; ailments and illnesses - for example 1,000 broken legs per annum. When its met the quota - it can do no more. Patients must either go elsewhere or wait for the next year's quota. Sorry sir - there's a waiting list for broken legs, you'll just have to keep yours a while longer. Advertisements could be placed in local newspapers to assist the public. And it has happened - per reports Walsall Manor Hospital has exceeded its quota for births - yup - more babies have been than authorised. Ladies please!

'Important Notice. The people of Walsall are advised that they are not permitted to break a leg for the next six months as the borough's quota has been reached. Anyone caught breaching this order may be sentenced to a term in a residential home where they will be cared for by unqualified staff working long hours for less than the minimum wage' and speaking no English. No pressure on the NHS or its resources - simple. Too radical I fear - don't see an invitation for outside consultancy, much less a Knighthood, winging its way in my direction any time soon.

Fascinating piece of social history for you. In the beginning of time (that's healthcare time) medicine was run by herbalists. Herbs were turned into concoctions by apothecaries (chemists to us), and it was apothecaries that ruled the world of medicine. In 1629 the Chief Medical Office at St Thomas's Hospital in London was an apothecary who was paid the sum of £60 per annum. Surgeons were paid £35 and doctors £30 (The Gardens of the British working Class - Margaret Willes). My how times have changed, herbalists are now likely to be seen as 'quacks' by many in the medical profession, operating on medicine's fringe and 'apothecaries' have converted to become chemists/pharmacists and joined the establishment.

Chapter 5

DISCOVERING OUR NEW WORLD

Prior to the building of Beacon Estate, New Invention was a well spread village flanked by Essington, Short Heath and Wednesfield and the small towns of Willenhall and Bloxwich. There were scattered pockets of terraced housing occupied by tenants and in an ad hoc sought of way there was also several post war owner-occupied properties. The village was well served with shops, chippies and pubs and it had its own post office and school. It was, like so many areas across the UK at the time, a self-contained community. To break the routine there were regular bus services that took the inhabitants to the more lavish shopping centres of Walsall and Wolverhampton. That would be for special occasions like Easter or Christmas or maybe someone's birthday. Weekly shopping for the essentials was done in nearby Willenhall - the town centre there, whilst not matching illustrious outlets such as Marks & Spencer's and Woolworths (both present in Walsall and Wolverhampton) offered a rich variety of shops, adequate for the daily needs.

Bus services were provided by Walsall and Wolverhampton Omnibus Services, owned and managed by the respective local authorities. Walsall buses were in blue livery and Wolverhampton in distinctive green and yellow. Walsall ran the number 2 service between Bloxwich and Willenhall skirting Short Heath on its way through Lane Head and Sandbeds then on to Willenhall. Bloxwich was an even smaller town than Willenhall - we didn't venture in that direction at the time. Walsall also managed the number 41 service that commuted between Walsall and Willenhall via Bentley Lane which boasted a clay quarry that was later turned into a corporation tip - that's a Waste Disposal Site in new pc English. Wolverhampton provided the number 60 service that ran between Wolverhampton and Bloxwich passing through Wednesfield on its way and the number 19 service that ran from Wolverhampton to the village of Essington.

Bus services were provided to ferry the workers to and from Henry Squires' factory or transporting them to the factories and foundries in the surrounding areas, particularly Willenhall. One special bus, provided by Walsall, was the colliers special. It ran from the bottom of Essington Road and took the miners to Hilton Main colliery in Essington. A lot of the local men worked at the mines then; the bus would be at the bottom of the road in the early hours of the morning, waiting for the miners. About half a mile along Essington Lane there were several miner's cottages, one little group, on the corner of Essington Lane and Sneyd Lane was known as' the pack' because of the layout being loosely horse-shoe shaped and all packed in together. The colliers special would pause here and pick up more miners. The bus returned early evening and disgorged the tired and (honourably) grubby miners.

Our buses then were two-man affairs (or one man and a woman - but women were restricted to being conductors only). The conductor took the fairs by issuing tickets first inserted into a punching device that perforated the ticket so that it couldn't be re-used. Buses were authorised to carry eight standing passengers on the lower deck, so it got rather crowded at rush hour. There were no passenger doors - just an open platform. This proved handy for disembarking as the bus turned a corner and avoided one being taken to the next official stop and out of one's way. The number two bus into Willenhall had one final turn off Lower Lichfield Street and into Doctors' Piece. I, and countless others, male of course, have leapt from the platform at that corner. It was easy, just a small leap backwards and the forward momentum of the bus would ensure that you hit the ground running in a forward direction. Never, never had an accident nor a near miss. But I know of many that did, found themselves trying to run faster than their poor legs were capable of; there could be only one outcome - an unceremonious collapse in the street much to the amusement of onlookers. Worked the other way too, you could leap onto the platform of the moving bus and deny the driver and the conductor of the pleasure of seeing you puffing and panting in vain as the bus pulled away leaving you ruffled and embarrassed at the stop. Nowadays, you're imprisoned in the bus until the driver deigns to release you into the wild. It's the only sport he gets, there's no conductor to chatter to. Conductors were also useful for getting the fish and chips in at break time – today drivers must make do with butties, because the bus must not be left unattended. Wise - certain bet that some nefarious so and so would nick it given half a chance - be up for sale on eBay within minutes.

*****

Interesting how many pubs featured as bus stops. The number 2 bus on its way to Willenhall crossed into New Invention and stopped at The Crown, then The Gate Inn and on to the Amery Conservative Club (a drinking house by any other name). There was respite at the next stop, it being the Wesley Chapel (there was a pub just around the corner - The Swan) but the sobriety didn't last because the next stop was Lane Head - The Bridge Tavern still stands, to the left of the canal bridge. The next port of call was The Brown Jug. Like many pubs in modern times The Brown Jug struggled to retain trade and in the late 1990's is reputed to have employed topless barmaids. An anonymous wag opined that the barmaids were as flat as the beer. Unfortunately, I was, and remain, teetotal so I had no good reason to check (damn). Anyway, it didn't last; a cocktail of moral outrage; feminism and the tiresome pc brigade nipped that in the bud (a pseudo pun there). Buses heading to Wolverhampton also called at The Crown and The Gate before proceeding to The Broadway and The Albion. The Albion tried topless barmaids too - they didn't last but the pub did - still open. In fact, it's about to be re-vamped and given a new name – The Lancaster – in homage to the famous Lancaster bomber of dam-busters fame.

New Invention was typical of many villages around the country in that a hard core of the locals resented the (enforced) introduction of outsiders. We disturbed the status quo, threatened the social balance of the village. At the time, I was too young to appreciate what that meant and how it could manifest. At seven years of age I simply took everything, and everyone as I found it and them - anyway, there was still a healthy number of the sitting incumbents that either welcomed us new arrivals or were ambivalent on the matter. One small local business that was glad to have the extra customers was Sadler's Farm - almost a misnomer because farming activities had been severely curtailed following the death of Farmer Sadler senior, he was survived by a daughter - Dorothy, and a son - Frank. Arable farming had been abandoned but they retained a small dairy herd. For a short while we enjoyed fresh milk delivered daily from the farm. It arrived by pony and trap driven by daughter - Dorothy Sadler. She was a roly-poly of a woman - as wide as she was tall. She didn't have waist - she had a circumference and she was of a most genial disposition. That didn't stop us kids for expressing great sorrow for the poor pony. The milk was carried in churns and ladled into whatever receptacle was proffered. Brother, Frank's contribution as I recall, was the shooting of rabbits. They were no longer considered as edible and the story goes their corpses found their way down a disused mine shaft. It was darkly reported that Frank would dispose of unwanted pets in a like manner. Both Dorothy and Frank died in the early years of our settlement. Sometime before those sad events, the farm had been sold to a Mr Brindley - it became known as Brindley's Farm. From then, for a while, we took our milk from Johnsons.

*****

Come late summer of 1947 and it was back to school - a new school. New Invention Junior and just a short walk down the road. I spent four years there and whilst I wouldn't describe them as blissful (bliss would have been no school at all) they passed happily enough, certainly I don't recall any disasters or traumatic events. It was a mixed school, I learned later that only the posh schools - the grammars - kept boys and girls separate. Odd that, they were supposed to be privileged, they missed out on the fun that was a mixed school. Not that boys between the ages of seven and eleven (the age at which we all got deported to senior school) had much time for girls. Girls didn't play football, or wrestling, or marbles or anything sensible. They did skipping - with ropes - and catch - catch involved throwing a ball to one another with the intention that it be caught without being dropped. Sounds simple - until you see girls throw. It was the agreed surmising of us boys that if one girl stood opposite another with the intention of throwing a ball to that other, then the direction of delivery could encompass 360 degrees. But they did give us some fun 'cos we teased 'em - why? because they were girls - why else?

It was indeed at this school that I was introduced to football. Not in any formal way - this is how it worked; the school had a playground that sloped downhill towards the road. You'd get to school in the morning or after lunch and a game would be in process. You would ask "can I play?" and the answer would likely be "alright - you can kick uphill" or "downhill" depending on whether you were any good or maybe liked by the kid you'd asked. Forget any ideas of eleven a side; nobody ever counted. If you got to school before the game started you could be included in the selection process. The selectors would be the boy who'd brought the ball and another boy he'd invited to have a game. They'd take in turns picking from the volunteers until there was none left - except four eyes and fatty and him with two left feet. There were no touchlines or goal-lines. the pitch embraced the playground which was bordered by school buildings on one side and a hedge on the other. The goals were situated in the iron fencing that separated us from the main road at one end and land that had nothing to do with the school at the other. The ball was anything that was round and could withstand our brutal assault, there wasn't much subtlety in our play just good hard punts, working on the principal that the further away it was from our goal the nearer it must be to theirs. Modern players call this the 'long ball game' - like they invented it - New Invention Junior School gets no credit. We played with tennis balls, rubber balls, even sponge balls, but never proper footballs. Rubber balls inflated and sealed under pressure were generally good, but they were vulnerable. Sometimes they got spiked by the railings in the fence (they were like Zulu spears) and other times they simply got stood on. The result was that they were rendered as not fit for purpose or, as one of the players would have it - "the ball's bost - we cor play no moo-er" Translated, that meant - "the ball has burst - we can't play anymore." Dialects and accents are important components of our culture and heritage and should be protected from the campaigners for a homogenised accent. That said there's no denying the difficulties to be found in the interpretation of some local dialects. I well remember, in later life, doing a presentation in Glasgow to a firm of accountants and it was agreed that for thirty minutes I would adopt a broad Brummie accent and they responded in equally broad Glaswegian. Fun it was - understood it was not. They 'day know wot ar wos torkin abart' especially when I told them about 'the whales in the cut'. They could only muster this response, 'Ah dinna ken a worrrd' (no idea who Ken was or from where he came - didn't like to ask). My Black country favourite has to be this little gem in response to a question as to why a certain man hadn't been seen for a few days.

"Arv bin bad - ay bin to werk - bin on the box for a wik"

It must be interpreted rather than translated - "I've been ill, have a doctor's certificate that says I've been unfit to work for a week". Everyone in the Black Country is bi-lingual - they can do local and posh - posh being something that could be understood across the county borders. Oh, and they have the habit of emphasising the letter H when they wanted to be heard as 'posh' - hotel becomes Hotel; hear becomes Hear – that sort of thing.

Anyhow, back to the football. Not surprisingly the ball was frequently booted out of the 'ground'. There was builder's yard on the other side of the road - Hough & St Ledger was the name of the firm - our ball found its way into their yard with impressive regularity. The unspoken rule was always to send the smallest/newest kid to get it back. They were big burly men those builders and they scowled and cursed a lot when asked "can we have our ball back please" something about 'bloody kids', but they never refused. We didn't concern ourselves with such refinements as penalties or free kicks or corners or throw-ins. We didn't bother with referees - that role fell to the boy to whom the ball belonged. Inevitably there would be disagreements and if ball-owner didn't get his own way he'd likely pick up the ball and walk off in a huff - game over. Naturally he'd be called a sissy - mummy's boy - some of the more uncouth elements in our midst had other names but one didn't join in - one was a bit posh now, one had just moved into a new house.

*****

I remember taking a slice of toast to school each morning to have with my mini bottle of milk (pre-Thatcher days) and I used to go through a gap in the hedge alongside the playground to eat my toast. Haven't the foggiest idea why I did that. I remember too, the army of do-gooders that visited the school. A doctor visited periodically; the routine went like this - "Come in, drop your pants, open your mouth, cough, go". On reflection, that was real production line medicine. Even better when it was injection time. Kids were lined up outside the treatment room (aka the office), sleeves rolled up at the ready. There was a steady procession into the danger zone, we would be greeted by a po-faced nurse and a very disinterested doctor. It was a well-rehearsed process - swab, jab, go - and there were no sweeties. The reaction of us kids was mixed - some came out swaggering "dain't urt a bit", some were nonchalant, trying to act tough (and failing) and there were those came out blarting – apparently, it hurt. The boys waited their turn in stoic silence (or not wishing to let anyone know that they were scared). The girls were far more animated and variously giggled nervously or got the waterworks going in advance. Some (both genders) even tried getting out of having the injection by fainting. They became the victims of a sick irony because they were hurried to the front of the queue just as soon as they 'came to'. I trust, dear reader, that it has not escaped your notice that, in the foregoing passage, I have completely avoided reference to injections as 'small pricks'.

Then there was the dentist who insisted that one's mouth would open wider, wider and wider - was he planning a walk-in check? Years later I was told that the dentists that did school visits were those that had failed their finals and this work was how they brushed up (pun intended) their skills. They seemed to work to a very simple mantra - if in doubt pull it out. Pray that failed heart surgeons don't follow a similar path. Then came the optician - what a great system for drumming up business, visit a school of 200/300 kids and you're certain to find some who 'need' specs. After one such visit they told me that I should have glasses - that was one message that didn't get back home. I'd heard kids that wore specs called 'four eyes' - didn't fancy that at all, I wanted to remain one of the boys. Spectacles would have ostracised me, I would become a 'four eyes' - banned from the footie.

Speccies did have one advantage - they were excused fighting. Apparently, there was rule or something that said that you didn't hit kids wearing spectacles. It became the practice not to do so. I say fighting, but it was hardly that - more like two kids charging each other with arms flailing like the sails of a windmill. Often eyes were closed, for protection of course, and it was rare for any serious blows to be landed - it was boyly (I've just coined the word - my wife isn't the only one gifted in this department), as opposed to girlie. Girls rarely fought but when they did they observed a strange custom. Apparently, the objective was not to land blows but to grab hold of each other's hair and then pull, tug and yank, dance around like Maoris and yell a lot. I supposed that that was why they grew their hair long. Oh, and they kicked a bit - well at least they tried, never hit each other, legs just wafted in space. That explains why they were no good at football.

I've saved the best for last - the nit nurse, or as she preferred to be known as, 'health visitor'. She carried a very fine-tooth comb with which she scoured every child's head. I mean, she dug in and ploughed her way through the hair with grim determination, I swear she left furrows in some unfortunate heads. She didn't always get nits, but she sure did always get hair. And when she found nits the unfortunate child would have their head treated with nit poison that had the most pungent aroma - no mistaking who smelled of what and why. In case they forgot some insensitive kids would chorus "you've got nits, you've got nits" - they didn't do subtlety. Immediately prior to the de-lousing she would excavate the unfortunate child's scalp. I swear that if it had been allowed she would have used blasting powder to dislodge the uninvited tenants. In an altruistic moment, one couldn't help but feel sorry for the nits. Once discovered their fate was sealed - I bet they cried out in little nit voices "we're doomed, we're all going to die". And they did. Then again, maybe there were nits with an IQ - they'd see trouble coming and evacuate to a safe place - the head of a child who had just been cleared. They would emerge from the inspection room, all smug and smiling, and walk past those waiting to go in - that would have been a small step for a nit but a giant leap for nitkind (another new word - I'm keeping a list) - apologies to Neil Armstrong.

*****

School was okay and us kids rubbed along for the most part. That's not to suggest that I didn't take advantage of any opportunity not to go. Days off for any reason were preferable to boring lessons (adults talking to kids about grown up stuff was boring). Feigning an ailment of one sort or another was common grounds for seeking to be excused. The hard part was convincing Mum - especially my Mum, she'd had enough kids to be more than familiar with our wheezes. Our acting ability, as we faked illness, would get us a part in EastEnders today. The key to success was to refuse food - a truly great sacrifice, growing kids just love eating. The rationale was that Mums knew about kids and food and eating - they had a theory - if the kids are eating there can't be much wrong with them. See how it works? Refuse food and the theory was applied in reverse- not eating, must be ill - can't go to school. Important to conjure up a miraculous recovery otherwise starvation beckoned.

I'd worked such a dodge on one occasion and wangled the day - no special reason, nothing to do with a spelling test promised for that day. Back to school the following day, missed the test unfortunately, now I've got to convince teacher that I was genuinely ill. The magic had worked with Mum, the teacher ought to be a pushover - so why was I getting nervous? Time for another plan - put a convincing story together. "Had a bad headache miss. Always prudent to test an excuse so I did - I tried it one of my classmates. " Had the worst headache in the world - took packet after packet of Phensics" He just looked - obviously impressed. Phensics were the cure-all pill of the day and came in small packets of four tablets, recommended dosage for yours truly would have been one tablet every four hours. Packet after packet would, I suspect, have delivered me to another place. I decided to drop the Phensic bit when telling teacher. As it happened, when a nervous me approached with growing trepidation, one of the school's administrative staff hurried up to her and whispered something in her ear. This served to distract her and my intended soliloquy was reduced to "Please miss me mom said I had a bad headache". She frowned but still distracted, only managed - " you missed the spelling test". I tried to look disappointed - she looked unconvinced. Some teachers were in the habit of insisting on notes from parents to explain absence. My Mum would ask if they thought that she had nothing better to do than write notes. She had a point - we were growing in number. I suppose we could have written them for her.

In those days, everything municipal was run by the local council, including education. The council took its responsibilities seriously. Any child repeatedly absent from school would get a visit from the Attendance Officer. Until the end of the 19th century education was provided free to the poor by the church. Those that could afford to pay went to fee paying schools. The cry was that every child should have a basic education - be taught to read and write. No - I haven't forgotten 'rithmatic, the one facility that everyone has, children and adults alike, is an innate ability to count. Try fiddling any so-called illiterate by short-changing them and you'll quickly find the evidence. The Elementary Education Act 1880 introduced compulsory education for all. There's an irony lurking hereabouts; prior to the act most kids wanted to go to school to learn, it was preferable to being used as cheap labour in factories, on farms and up chimneys. Nowadays many kids can't wait to escape school, and many don't wait, they bunk off. It's a paradox of significant psychological interest - the research hypothesis would be' people only want what they can't have whilst they can't have it but when they can have it, they don't want it.'

An alternative version is that we don't like being told what to do - especially by government.

The title, Attendance Officer, was typical of the time. Job descriptions did exactly that - described what the worker did. Dustmen emptied dustbins then they became 'refuse collectors'. I blame the PC intelligencia for such drivel. Here's a good one advertised by a local authority - 'Person-Centred Transition Facilitator' - no idea what the job entailed, neither, I suspect did the council. But one of my favourites must be this monster - 'Ambient Replenishment Controller and Regional Head of Services, Infrastructure and Procurement' - a Shelf Stacker - honest. There's a mercenary bit of psychology at work here - the fancier the job title, the lower the salary. The titles are often drawn up by committees now, so our Attendance Officer could be re-titled,' Juvenile Education Deprivation Enforcement Officer'. "Members of the committee - I put it to you that by inflating the job title we can avoid having to increase the salary" - motion carried. The incumbent would be so impressed with a fancy title that the salary would be overlooked. The popular name for the Attendance Officer was 'truant officers'. Truancy is defined as - 'intentional, unauthorised or illegal absence from compulsory education'. Not attending school was a criminal offence. Many of us kids thought it a crime to be made to attend in the first place.

Our truant officer was a portly man who by some amazing how managed to get about by bicycle. My sympathies were with the bike. He was possessed of a serious demeanour, like missing a day at school was a threat to world peace or dropping a catch in a Lords test against the Aussies. His was a very simple yardstick, if you weren't at school and teacher hadn't had a note from your parents you were truanting. Truth of the matter was that most parents couldn't be bothered writing notes, probably because their spelling was worse than their kids. Stroll through this logically, suppose a kid is playing the wag (that's what us kids called it - not truanting but playing the wag), that means he's absent without parental consent, is it likely then, that he'd be found at home? He'd be off somewhere with his mates engaged in extra-curricular activities. You'll have noticed that I have alluded only to the male gender in the matter of truancy, or' wagging it' as us kids would say. That is, of course, very sexist of me and it's likely that I shall get calls from the PC Militia. The one good thing about being lectured by this branch of the intellectual mafia is that it presents a wonderful opportunity for a nap. They never notice, too busy revelling in the sound of their own cacophony. The real reason for my gender bias is that, apparently, girls didn't play truant. Sugar and spice and all things cunning and devious - they had period pains! There wasn't a truant officer in the land that could counter that because they were inevitably male and didn't understand PMT and were too embarrassed to even begin to speak of it. The very mention would have produced a series of hrrmmph's and grunts and tut tuts and a hasty retreat.

The child catcher - sorry, the truant officer (I've seen Chitty Chitty Bang Bang too many times) would even call to check on sick children, that's those that have managed to pull the wool over their Mum's eyes. He'd call and insist on seeing the 'sickly' child - and I mean insist. He was no medic but if he deemed junior to be fit for school - junior would be at school the next day. The way to beat him was not to answer the door, there was only so many times he could call back. Notes would be left - ominous notes. These would be followed by letters from the council. And these would be followed by a stiff lecture from parents delivered with the back of the hand for those unfortunates caught taking 'unauthorised leave'. Legitimate cases would have Mums hopping mad in indignation - "Who does he think he is? He'll get a piece of my mind when I see him". And when they saw him - "Sorry Mr Important Attendance Officer, there seems to have been a mis-understanding" Don't get the wrong idea - they weren't scared of him (well - yes some of them were some of the time) but the real reason is that Mums were astute enough to keep on the good side of any figure of authority, you just never knew when that might come in handy. Psst - they practised this black art on their husbands - keep that to yourself.

*****

My form teacher in 1950 was a Mr Davies. He was Welsh but managed to speak English well enough for us kids to more-or-less understand - or was any deficiency down to our inability to pay attention? For one English lesson, he asked us to write an essay on how to mend a puncture. We safely assumed bicycle tyre because almost nobody with kids at our school had a car. Very few of us had bicycles either, much less any idea of puncture repairing. Fortunately, big brother Dennis did, and I'd seen him mend a puncture or two. Seemed straight forward enough: turn the bike upside down, fetch the wheel off; fetch the tyre off, fetch the inner-tube out; fetch the repair kit; fetch a bowl of water dip the tube in and drag it through the water until bubbles appear - and there's the hole. Stick a plaster on it and reverse the process - put everything back where it belongs. You will have noticed the repetition of the word 'fetch' - so did Mr Davies and he wasn't impressed - said there was far too much fetching. I now have a theory as to why I unconsciously favoured the word - at home we were constantly being asked to 'fetch this' or 'fetch that'. That, my friends, is an elementary exercise in brain-washing. Just keep using a word as often as possible and then observe how it gets picked up and adopted. The best current example is 'absolutely' - I think I've developed an aversion to it. Just about absolutely everybody manages to slip the word absolutely into absolutely any and every conversation. Personally, I'm absolutely sick and tired of hearing absolutely and I absolutely think that it should be absolutely banned absolutely. It is one the most over-used adverbs - to the extent that I sometimes doubt the truth of the statement it's used to support because it over-compensates. I think I may have logomosia - that's what aversion to a word is called.

That memory survives because I learned an important lesson that day - it's not what you say - it's how you say it. Nothing I wrote in that essay by way of instructions was incorrect but the repetitive and unimaginative language I had used damaged its credibility. Effective writers, and speakers, can deliver semi-truths and none-truths but providing they do so with a degree of eloquence and conviction, they will often get away with their inaccuracies. An extreme example is one Adolph Hitler. He got to be so good at lying to the German people he even believed the lies himself. He did, of course, terrorise them as well but make no mistake - he was a powerful orator, millions were won over by his bile and vitriol because he used language that appealed to his audiences. The enduring truth is that great eloquence or oratory, though plausible, does not necessarily equate to truth. Incidentally, interesting to note that Mr Hitler may have been influenced by a book it is said that he read entitled,' The Crowd - A Study of the Popular Mind' by Gustav Le Bon first published in France in 1895.

*****

Christmas 1950 was to be my last at New Invention Junior. In the autumn of 1951 it was to be 'big school' - whatever that meant. But, hey that was a long way off and it was Christmas. What a party we had - the school did us all proud. There was jelly, blancmange, ice cream, fruit (tinned) with evaporated milk there was cakes and buns of all shapes and tastes and there was fizzy pop with which to wash it all down. Where all these goodies came from I know not, seems likely now that they were donated by parents but I'm sure nothing went from our house. We had barely enough to live on any way. All of us kids were asked to bring a dish and a spoon, I couldn't even manage that because we had no dishes at home - never used them. We had a miscellany of plates, so I took a plate and a spoon. We had spoons, and knives and forks - we weren't savages. This was probably the first time that I had felt embarrassed, everyone else dutifully turned up with dish and spoon. I think I mumbled something to a lad in my class about not being able to find a dish, but he didn't seem to notice, or care and I very quickly forgot about it too- a plate, a dish - what's the difference, they both held generous portions of goodies.

The party started around mid-day with carol singing then came the main event - an orgy of eating and that was how we figured it would end. We were wrong - there was a magnificent surprise as a finale. Our teachers put on a pantomime - Cinderella. One of the female teachers played Cinders and the ugly sisters were our Mr Davies and a Mr Baddeley who taught one of the other classes. What a contrast they made -one a man of average height (Davies) whilst the other (Baddeley) towered well above average - over six feet which made him almost a giant in our eyes. It was the first time I'd seen men in drag and they were so funny. Scenery had been knocked up and by some ingenious means the stage was brilliantly lit. It was magical moment never experienced before or since. When we returned to school after the Christmas break I had difficulty in seeing either of the male teachers in their professional light. They remain etched in my memory as two extraordinary characters - ugly sisters - who could speak in very weird voices. I was delighted to learn that, even as I write, Mr Davies is still with us - he must be of an age. He was surely old when he taught me but then, any male wearing long trousers at that time was considered old.

My last year at junior school passed, for the most part, as uneventful as the preceding ones. But just before the summer recess there was another of those pivotal moments, the full significance of which, eluded me for many years.

We were to be given a test - nothing new in that, we'd had plenty in the past, times-table tests (I knew them literally backwards) and spelling tests - I did ok in those although, like many of my peer's I was often baffled by the perverse logic of our wonderful language. How does a young impressionable lad make sense of a language that says 'cough' is pronounced 'coff' but 'bough' is pronounced 'bow'? And why is the plural of house - houses but mouse - mice? And if you really want to confuse Johnny Foreigner try this on him 'heat' 'threat' and 'great' and to finish him off go for' breath, (breeth) and 'breath (breth). If he's still standing hit him with this one - 'her' 'hair' 'heir' 'hare'. Words that are pronounced the same such as the foregoing are called 'homophones' (your education continues). Now that sounds like a reference to mobile phones for the gay community: whoops I think I might be getting a call from the PC not-so secret police for that one. There were reading tests too and I found them the easiest of all. Apparently. the test to which our teachers now referred was bigger - more important. To our innocent minds bigger just meant more work - longer; as for important - that was like not having a ball at playtime or not being allowed to play or forgetting the toast or poking four-eyes in the ribs. School work - important? Bit of a contradiction there. We did it because we had to - they said so and they were bigger than us and they could keep us in at playtime.

Apparently, the test was the 11-plus examination. Meant nothing to me at the time and didn't for a long time after. Now I know it to have been a selection process, those that passed were eligible to go to a grammar school and get a premier education, those that didn't pass - the also-rans - would be endowed with a secondary modern version. In my late teens, considering myself quite worldly, I once commented that grammar schools were for the thinkers and secondary moderns for the doers. Message to the arrogant youth amongst us - only truly ignorant people ever think they know it all and impart smart (smug) answers, and you'll find their kind amongst both thinkers and doers. Anyway, I turned up and did the exam. When the results came out I'd passed - I think I was the first in the family to do so (creep). Honestly, I wasn't particularly moved one way or the other, but Mum was elated. I remember her telling my siblings that they would have to be quite at night because I would have a lot of homework to do. That made me popular - not. I was vaguely perturbed by reference to 'homework' but in truth I didn't really know what it meant - we never had any at junior school. One of neighbours' kids had also passed and Mum rejoiced in sharing her excitement with the boy's Mum - and anyone else whose ear she could bend.

Alas, it all came to nought. I didn't go to grammar school. I didn't go because my parents couldn't afford the uniform, which was compulsory, and all the sports gear and equipment such schools expected pupils to provide. There was a price to pay for being poor - this was one manifestation. Mum must have been bitterly disappointed, but I wasn't unduly moved at the time - I simply didn't appreciate what it all meant, at least not until I arrived at the alternative. Many years later I learned what it was that had angered Mum at the time and it wasn't just my not going to grammar school. Her sister's son, my cousin, had also passed the eleven-plus. Like mine, his parents couldn't afford the cost but help for them was to hand. Mum's parents, our grandparents, paid for his uniform and whatever else he needed and off he went. Fair? Define fair. There were two in their family, John had a sister, there were eight of us at the time, maybe it came down to numbers and simple economics.

Lest you be thinking that henceforth I harboured resentment, grudges - be assuaged. Nothing of the kind ever entered my head. First off, it was, as I've noted, a very very long time before I got to know that story: second - and most important, I wouldn't have had the life I've had. I read somewhere that someone once said that if you change but one blade of grass from the past, you will alter the course of human history. The underlying point is well made, and I would suggest that we should always be mindful of what we wish for, nothing in life happens in a vacuum, there are always consequences. There are many things I'd change if it were possible but at the core of my life has been the best family anyone could wish for, any change that threatens that is a price I would not - will not pay. Looking back, grammar school may have launched me into the rarefied atmosphere of academia and maybe I would have been successful there, but my secondary modern education set me off on a meandering trail that has seen me delve into a rich vein of interests, occupations and experiences, although it did take me while to get going. I reckon that I've had three careers so far and I'm still hankering for more. So - bitter about grandparents? Never. In their shoes, would I have done the same thing? Probably not - but that's me and it's now. I have no cognition of what motivated them at the time. Jealous of cousin? Never. Would I have taken the opportunity had it been presented? Yes - more to the point Mum would have insisted. The point is; such arguments are of the 'What if' genre. 'What if' can be finished with literally any question you wish to pose. The questions vary - the answer is always the same. It doesn't matter - it didn't happen. Life is about what does happen - not what could, would, should have happened. 'What if' arguments, in this context, must be amongst the most pointless of exercises.

*****

Something nasty happened in 1951 - I've fixated on the year although I can't find any corroborating evidence. At eleven years of age and having been taught to read I would read whatever newspapers my parents (usually dad) brought home. At the weekend, it was the (now) infamous and defunct News of the World. The story that has embedded itself in memory was about an eleven- year old boy, Samuel James Poole - being found dead. In my mind and per my logic at the time, kids didn't die, that's what old people did. Reading about the death of someone my own age made no sense and when I read further and learned that he was probably murdered - well that was off my radar. I knew a lot of kids - none of them had ever been murdered. I've never lost the horror of cruelty to children, it's one of those things I find hardest to forgive. Interesting - we were disciplined as kids, but it was never perceived as cruelty - harsh but not cruel.

*****

On a lighter note the summer of 1951 marked the Festival of Britain held in London - we had no idea where London was. Mr Davies told us all about the grand exhibition that was a showcase of all that was best in Britain, which seemed to be plenty then. None of us were likely to get to see it but it did sound very grand and important. We were told that the festivals were held every hundred years and that the next one would be held in 2051. A small group of us made a pledge to meet outside the school gates in exactly one hundred years' time. Some of us are, well at least one of us is (me) still on course and the half-way mark has already been passed. Wonder how many of the others are still making a nuisance of themselves. Too early to make specific plans but I fully intend to be outside the school in 2051 - I'll only be 110 years old. Go ahead - snigger but remember, we're generally living longer, and centurions are the proverbial 'ten a penny'. No matter how many others turn up we shall enter the school playground. I shall bring the ball - for the first time ever! I will get first pick and my lot will kick downhill. What a sight that will be. The teams will have names to mark the occasions - 'Walking Stick Wobblers -v- Zimmer Frame Arthritic. Anyone turning up without walking aids will obviously be too young to play. In honour of the occasion I hereby cordially invite Mr Davies to be the referee. He won't have much to do - he can blow a whistle if he likes and he can do the stern look and wag a warning finger, just as he did when he was teaching. Unlikely to be many goals scored due to the effort needed to get to the other end of the 'pitch' - there'll simply be no energy left to propel the ball and heaven help that lot that kicking uphill, maybe we should allow ice picks. No fear of the ball going over the fence - be a miracle if it even reaches it. For the same reason, the old builder's yard will be safe which is just as well because first, it's not there anymore and secondly it would take best part of an afternoon for a stumbling fumbling 110 plus year old to navigate passage across the road - and remember the way back.

Reflecting on those good old New Invention schooldays one mildly curious and, to you dear reader, amusing incident occurred. I have been told on numerous occasions that I sometimes behave odd, that is, different to most other people. I hotly disown the charge because we're all unique in subtle ways and this oft manifests in seemingly unusual behaviour. In short - I aint a freak! Anyhow, the incident - though trivial, didn't do my protestations any service. Up to the age of eleven and coinciding with the promotion to 'big school', boys wore short trousers and stockings - no not that sort - we weren't kinky. They were knee length and had patterned tops which one turned over at the top. Over a typical day, they would slip down frequently, hence the expression 'pull your socks up', the general meaning of which is to get oneself in order although there doesn't appear to be a definitive origin of the expression. One day I put one such stocking on inside out - long before I was aware of the concept of inside out. So, when the patterns at the top of each stocking didn't match I found that by folding the top of the inside-out one, not once but twice hey presto - the patterns matched. What an idiot you may be thinking - everyone else would have realised that the stocking was inside out and simply turned he right way. But wait, no: this was an example of lateral thinking, taking a different route to everyone else and yet still coming to a right (not necessarily the right) conclusion. A practice that has served me well in later years. My message is to never be afraid of thinking differently and don't follow the herd if you don't agree with the direction its taking.

Chapter 6

A GANG MEMBER I WILL NOT BE

By 1951 Beacon Estate was nearing completion and I'm guessing that most of the houses were occupied. There remained a sort of black hole in the middle of the estate, this was the site of a new school. The developers had unexpected problems - the huge plot kept flooding and it took months to drain it sufficient for remedial work to be undertaken and construction of the school to begin. Beacon Junior School finally opened for the autumn term in 1953 - and closed in April 1999 when it became Beacon Primary School.

We were all getting older of course, I was now 11 - big enough to go out to play with other kids from the estate. The games involved a lot of play-fighting and hunting and hiding. Somehow, we got into telling tales - very tall tales - about the heroics of our fathers during the war. I reckon that if we'd kept count it would have been that the fathers of the boys from Beacon Estate wiped out most of the German army. There were incredible shoot outs - in which our dads always won of course. An unspoken part of the game was that your dad had to have killed more Germans than his dad. Now here's an interesting fact - all our dads were army, none of us claimed to have a dad in the air-force or the navy. Yet, when playing games rather than telling tall stories, aeroplanes was a favourite. Just about every boy that ever was has run around madcap fashion with arms outstretched imitating the wings of a fighter-plane, making weird engine noises and spluttering in attempts to sound like Browning machine guns - the Spitfire was obviously a favourite. The common belief as to why the fighter was called Spitfire was its firepower but the name has other origins worthy of consideration - in bygone time the term spitfire was used to describe fiery characters. I think either or both describe the famous fighter plane admirably. The Spitfire has become iconic - sad but little is said now of its designer R J Mitchell. Mitchell died of rectal cancer 11 June 1937, he never got to see the glorious success of his greatest creation.

We never played ships - still don't know how to do that. Suppose we could have bobbed up and down and swayed from side to side but that just sounds weird and some of us would have been very sick. And we never played soldiers - we told soldier stories, played RAF and ignored the navy. That's one for the psychologists.

We'd congregate on the un-built plots on the estate. This was also where the builders kept the top soil to be spread over the gardens of the completed houses. The soil was banked high and was great for launching us as human aeroplanes. One simply jumped off the top and made like a spitfire before an unceremonious crash landing at the bottom. It was there and then that I learned a couple of things about myself although it's true to say I didn't understand the lessons at the time. First, one of the bigger boys was trying to, organise events saying that "if you jump off this bank here you can join my gang" I jumped off alright - then told him I didn't want to join his or anybody's gang. The lesson? - I wasn't gang fodder - never have been since. The second learning was much more immediate and appreciated. When hitting the ground, the lads landing on their feet jarred their ankles - I didn't. I instinctively did a forward roil and came back up on my feet in an instant. Nothing jarred - nothing hurt. I take no credit for this, it wasn't planned it just happened, it was an innate reaction and it came back time and again later to my profound advantage.

*****

It's 1951. There are now ten of us, twelve counting parents. Been here for four years. Time to meet the neighbours, well some of them anyway. They neatly divided into the newcomers and the locals. The next-door neighbours - mom, dad and four kids. We thought the kids were wimps, they thought us urchins - perhaps we were both right. The old man rose early every workday morning and you could set a clock by his coughing and hacking - 7am on the dot. He was a virtual chain smoker, un-tipped, and he worked in a castings foundry - hence the coughing. Then came the Harrisons, six of them all told. Turns out they were related to one of our old neighbours in Froysell Street. Mom Clara was a character - recognised as the official street gossip, if it went on she'd know about it and if it didn't - well there was always conjecture (that's a euphemism for making it up). Clara really had a good heart because if there was anyone in need she would organise help and this was never more evident than when there was a death on the road. Clara would ensure that everyone knew for two good reasons. One, it was the practice to make a collection to help the bereaved and Clara didn't take no for an answer - the poor family had needs. The other reason, it was the custom to draw all curtains at the front of the house on the day of the funeral as a mark of respect. It was also the custom if one was in the road as the cortege passed to pause, for men to raise their hats. if worn, and for men and women to offer a little nod of the head. Fred Harrison was a rather dashing man - tall dark and handsome as the cliché goes and sporting what the ladies would describe as an Errol Flynn moustache. Next to the Harrison's came PC Watkins - that's police constable Watkins. He wasn't the village bobby - that officer resided in nearby Short Heath - it was simply the family home, but his presence was used (and abused) by all and sundry. That accounts for all the newcomers to Essington Road. But there was a few more on the growing Beacon Estate. Beacon Road ran at right angles to Essington Road and the rear gardens of properties backed on to ours.

At eleven years of age I had no interest in girls. Having four sisters at the time persuaded me that they were a perplexing mass of contradictions and best left alone. It seemed that older lads saw them differently and for some bewildering reason appeared to crave their company. That said, my eldest brother, must have felt that he had arrived in paradise because there were girls in abundance. The corner property housed the Richards family whose daughters Joan and Mary were lively company - it was said. Two doors along and Mr and Mrs Rogers presented daughters Sheila, Hazel and Maureen - a little more reserved I understand. Had I known then what I learned but a few short years later.......well I'm not going to share that with you! The Orson family lived between the Richardson's and the Rogers', Mum Theo, Dad Ted, Michael and sister. Then Mum and daughter moved out. Poor old Ted never got it together after that. The house and garden fell into neglect.

The neighbours directly opposite had a son who used to play cricket in the back garden - on his own. He would toss a stone up in the air and, using a stick as a bat, attempt to deliver the stone elsewhere. Best part of this was that he'd give a running commentary on his performance - "And that's a fine shot heading to the boundary for four". I don't recall ever hearing him give himself out. Now that may seem an unusual way to play but I reckon he developed good hand-eye co-ordination and I wouldn't have been surprised to learn that he'd gone on to do well at cricket. Anyway, he wasn't the only one to play on his own. Occasionally, when there was no company to be had I would play football with a tennis ball in a small walled area at the front of the house. The gate to the front garden was one goal and the entrance to the outhouses the other. How does one play football alone? I hear you ask. Simple - left foot versus right foot. You think me eccentric - a man in a white coat job? Well let me tell you that that was how I learned to use both feet and when I got to play the game properly I got the better of many a player with my ability to hit the ball with either foot. Alas I must confess to a chink in my smugness - I never did get to terms with heading the ball properly. It kind of bounced off my head. But hey, I've only got one head - which side should it have been on - left or right?

Next door to the cricketer lived a family that included three sons, the youngest had an odd nickname - Spooky. No idea how he came by it, but it was not to be taken literally because he wasn't spooky in the least. The other reason - his elder brother remains one of the very few people I have met who knew at an early age what they wanted to do career-wise and did it. He told me when he was about twelve that he was going to be a teacher. He did just that. He also bred Alsatian dogs (German Shepherd they're called now - why the name change I wonder?). Speaking of odd nicknames one of the sons of their next- door neighbours was called 'Sponner'. Again, no good reason was ever discerned but it is to be noted that the word 'sponner' is how Midlanders say 'spanner' - that most useful of tools. Why bother to change the vowel is a mystery. Anyway, Sponner he might have been called but I'm not sure of the 'useful tool' tag. I remember his dad - so bow-legged that John Wayne's walk was a mince in comparison.

I recall that poor family enduring a night of tragedy - a cot death. The neighbours rallied round, my mother went - she would certainly empathise having lost a son to diphtheria when he was but a few months old. Clara Harrison went too, of course, and for all the right reasons. This would have been around 1952 I think, and I reflect now on my almost dismissive attitude to this death. As I recall there had been one or two deaths in our family - on dad's side - the deceased would have been fifty/sixty years of age. To someone of my tender years, that was old, so apparently old people died. I wasn't old, so I wouldn't die. The notion that I would get old eventually failed to make the reckoning. Now, here's the interesting part, the death of that baby didn't move me particularly either, whereas that of a stranger (Samuel James Pool) did have an effect. The baby obviously wasn't old -

but it was a baby and hadn't lived. It was as if babies didn't have an identity - a personality. Lest you think me callous and unfeeling note this; I'm telling you how it was, not how you, or I, consider it should be. Life isn't so convenient as to put all the right feelings in the right people at the right time. And note this especially - now that I have grown up I have come to value children above all others. They are, they always will be, the future. Now the death of a child moves me greatly.

I can conceptualise this now because about a year later a boy I occasionally played with - Gordon Davis - a year or so older than me, died suddenly and I was shocked. I knew Gordon - he had an identity and a personality, not like a baby and he wasn't old. Looking back, I think that for a moment then, I felt vulnerable - kids of my age could die too - but it was a fleeting moment. As a young teenager, I became more aware of the frailties of life. I recall one appalling incident that shook me to the core. Lying behind Bishton's shop was a home occupied by a man who drove one of the familiar at the time, huge coal trucks. The truck was frequently parked near the house for convenience. One tragic day the man was reversing his truck and he failed to notice that his young daughter (three/four years of age) had peddled her tricycle into his path. He ran her over and crushed her to death. There can be no more painful a death than that of one's own child - to be the cause of that death is unimaginable. The pain - the grief surely has no measure. That recollection still causes a shudder after all these years.

A few doors along from the bereaved family lived one that would also, in time, suffer the loss of their only son. The lad was stuck with another of those weird nicknames - Pugga. The silly name brigade was out again. He was an unassertive lad. He committed suicide in his mid/late 20's. Some ten years earlier he had been cornered by a gang of local lads (the indigenous lot - not the newbies) and held down and made to drink a bottle of urine. As a final humiliation, they removed his trousers and flung them up into the higher branches of a nearby tree. I strongly suspect that the poor lad was permanently scarred by that cowardly attack. Was that incident a factor in his tragic death? Possibly but neither we nor the perpetrators will ever know for certain. We shall meet his bullying assailants again later - with a very different outcome.

Near to where he lived there was a boy who had the worst case of acne I've ever seen, and it made him a bit of a social outcast. Sad really because he was a decent enough lad. On the plus side, he did, by all accounts, become a most accomplished angler. Their next- door neighbours were a tough old lot. In time, we would menace each other a few times but, in the end, nought came of it. The old man did afford us some nights of fun as he staggered along Essington Road on his way home after a good night's boozing. He and his wife would meander, several yards apart and conducting the most vociferous expletive laden conversation as they went. In summary, it roughly consisted of pledging undying love for each other - not! Giving not so constructive advice and directions as to the best way home frequently ending in ***** off. After one particularly torrid night he suffered what was called the Blue Devils - he had had so much to drink he was hallucinating. Suddenly he crouched down as if trying to hide

"They're coming after me" he wailed.

"They can ***** have you" says his dear beloved.

*****

One man I must mention though it reflects no credit on me, and many others, for so doing. Don't recall his name but, as the old cliché goes, I never forget a face. Especially one without a nose. This unfortunate man simply didn't have a nose, just two holes, which had his face been conventionally configured, would have been his nostrils. Ok so we all know what's coming - how did he smell without a nose? Do you really need help answering? One of the lads was to make a joke about the poor fellow in class and was made to explain just what he found so funny to the teacher. "He smells sir" Said teacher only made matters worse when he attempted to correct the lad's grammar. "It stinks - you smell". Reverse the verbs and you'll get the teacher's point 'It smells - you stink'. However, it wasn't an error of grammar, rather a question of semantics. Both stink and smell are verbs, and, in such constructions, I believe the first verb is called 'intransitive', it doesn't attach an object, doubtless some nerdy perfectionist will correct me if I'm mistaken (another grammatical excursion). Semantically the difference between the two words is akin to the difference in saying to someone - "you look awful" and "you don't look well" ("you stink" - " you smell"). The latter conveys the same message in a kinder way - a lesson for us all there.

It's an unpalatable truth that it is the differences in people that attract attention and those differences are often the source of cruel humour. Not so deep down I think that most of us felt sorry for him but here's another truth - laughing at someone else allows attention to be deflected from ourselves and any weaknesses others may perceive in us. Similar treatment befell a family that moved onto the estate many months after us, their daughter had what we now call learning difficulties - then she was just an oddball, we didn't really know any better. No doubt about it - New Invention's new intake was a motley collection - but so were the locals and together we often made an explosive cocktail

It's said that an Englishman's home is his castle and that he'll do anything to protect it and to a modest extent in this he is supported by the law and society. It is equally true that that same Englishman is just as protective of his territory - his patch and woe to they that trespass therein. In this regard, he enjoys less support from the law and mixed support from his countrymen. Succinctly put anything goes so long as it's in someone else's backyard. Throughout the UK there are towns and villages where outsiders are simply not welcome in the sense that they are made to feel a part of the community - at least not until they've been there for thirty years or more and then they might just get to be considered as worthy of a nod in greeting – no verbals though.

Despite our politicians being possessed of great learning, it's remarkable that this basic truth has eluded them. When organising mass immigration, they completely, and wilfully, overlooked the effect it would have on the indigenous population. Prejudice has many garbs but the one so in need of attention was that the natives would feel that their space was being invaded, and they weren't consulted, and they wouldn't like it much. But politics is essentially the convenience of the moment and the electorate the last to be considered it seems. Politicians of all persuasions have only ever considered immigration in an economic context. Social and cultural issues were conveniently overlooked. How much better it would have been if both the immigrant and the indigenous populations had been actively involved in integration. Instead what we got was 'they're here now so make the best of it'. This bit of soap-boxing leads me nicely to the fact that the residents of New Invention didn't exactly line the street to welcome us outsiders - we were trespassing. Our homes had been built on open land that they probably used to play and walk on. Once upon a recent time there was nothing between Essington Road and Sneyd Lane more than half a mile away. We were a rag tag motley collection of folk from sundry slums around the town - what was there to welcome?

Not that there was universal hostility; some were glad of the intake and some weren't and yet again there were those that were simply ambivalent. Not surprisingly the local shops welcomed the extra trade, rather more than perhaps they welcomed the traders. There were characters across the spectrum. Bishton's shop opened, I believe, in response to the potential new customers. They were a reserved couple - the Bishtons - selective as to whom they spoke reverentially. The Smiths were not among the chosen few which was very short-sighted of them because with a large family came greater spending power - at least that was the theory, but I reckon our Mum would argue the point. The Owens were mean spirited but, unlike the Bishton's, astute enough to realise the buying potential Mum had and so they smiled benignly on us - just so long as were spending - and paying. The Pearce's who ran the outdoor, were a one-off collection - two sisters and a brother, Charlie, who was the boss. They bordered on sullen at times, as if they resented being interrupted by customers. Woe betide anyone in an indecisive mood, Charlie assumed - expected - that everyone who jangled the door bell, on entering knew exactly what they wanted. Falter and you got the impatient look that said, 'make your b****y mind up'. Our namesakes, the Smith's, who ran the tobacconists and sweetshop were an interesting duo. She was suspicious of anything that appeared in short trousers, he was like an avuncular uncle, smiling a benign smile. They both realised that these nuisance kids had parents (though the legitimacy of some was questioned) and in those days, that meant at least one smoker - tolerate the kids, nourish the business. And they probably knew that sweet rationing wouldn't last forever and when it ended those pesky kids could become paying customers too.

*****

William Stretton, town councillor, we have already met. Saw himself as the big fish in small pond - well he got it half right, he would have been a challenge for Weightwatchers. Near to him lived the Sharett's - daughter Gwen and her ancient mother. Imagine Mary Poppins as the Jekyll half - Gwen Sharratt would have made a good Hyde, at least appearance wise. She was tall slender and single -

no man dared - and unsmiling. Always, it seemed she was dressed in black which suited her stern countenance. She stood tall and straight and walked in a rather military way - all stiff and proper. I had to call on her once and I recall the house being dark and dingy. I found out that they were the last family on the road to still rely on gas lighting. Half-way along Essington Road there lived an odd lady. One dark night she claimed to have seen lights in the sky, well you can see anything you like after a few drops of the hard stuff. For a while after, she was mocked with cries of " Oh *****, ******, look - flying saucers". In her defence, she always swore that she hadn't touched a drop and she would assert indignantly "I know what I saw". Well, lots of us see things, here's something to keep in mind on that subject.

'When someone looks at me and earnestly says - 'I know what I saw' - I am fond of replying- no you don't. You have a distorted and constructed image of a distorted and constructed perception, both of which are subservient to whatever narrative your brain is operating under.'

Dr Steven Novella - Clinical Neurologist and Assistant Professor at Yale University School of Medicine - USA.

That short statement embraces a profound and complex neuropsychological argument. In simple (very simple) terms it translates that it's - 'all in the mind.' Nonetheless, just because we can't prove what we say we saw doesn't mean that we didn't see whatever.

But this dear lady's best contribution came when some years later - late 1950's and she was moving-house and craved assistance from everyman and his dog. A younger brother volunteered - he was like that. When everything appeared to be packed and ready to go he said to her.

"Well that's it I think".

"No, it's not" says she - "there's still the wallpaper"

Yes indeed - she intended to strip down the wallpaper and take it with her. Now here's the best bit - she could do just that because the wallpaper was not pasted to the wall - it was held in place with drawing pins. The wallpaper was duly removed, rolled up and packed and it went with her.

The further along the road you went the more extreme the characters. There was a poor lass who always appeared unkempt and dishevelled and seemingly making regular pilgrimages to and from The Gate Inn. She and her parents were figures of fun to the local kids to whom they frequently offered advice ending in 'off'. Difficult to age but I suspect that they were retired and their daughter 40'ish. Soap, water and daughter were surely strangers supreme. Her clothes were but rags and it was likely that she had learning difficulties. Only possible mind, because she could hold a conversation albeit almost monosyllabic, but it was clear she wasn't stupid. I reckon she was the victim of the most blatant neglect. It was said that she was abused by some of her near neighbours. Given the unsavoury nature of some of them that is at least plausible. If my memory serves me well their next- door neighbours included a couple of real hard cases. One had a nickname - Nobby - I have no idea why. It was said that he could out-drink and out-fight anyone anytime. A story went around that on his drunken way home one night, someone with a grudge (there were plenty of those) bent a fence post over his head. Knocked him out cold but when he came around, he carried on home to bed to sleep the drink off - he had no cognition of the assault.

His younger brother basked in the inglorious shadow of big brother. But whereas big brother would always take things on the chin, metaphorically, little brother was inclined to whinge and threaten. When confronted, he'd think of reasons not to carry out his threats - I know, I received many. I remember too a body building enthusiast. His impressive physique compensated for his lack of height. He too would do his share of huffing and puffing but he never blew my house down. Like many who take up the pastime, bodybuilding was more about appearance than anything else. He only looked tough. He became a sort of bodyguard for a couple of bothers – wimps to the core. Good at picking on anyone considered weaker than themselves. They got that wrong a few times - as I will testify. One lout of a lad lived in Beacon Road. He was a loud-mouthed braggart. His favourite pastime was throwing stones at anyone he fancied. Prided himself on his skill in this department. Unfortunately for him I developed a strong right arm myself - didn't go down to well. He and my brother Barry had an altercation one afternoon he staged the scrap to happen right outside his own front door - just in case he needed to retreat in a hurry. He did. It came to blows, my dear brother had a ferocious temper and, suitably provoked, was giving him a sound thrashing. He broke free and raced indoors to tell his dad that "them Smiths had set about me". I was merely watching - big brother didn't need mine or anyone else's help. Well, cry-baby certainly called that moment wrong - his dad gave a clout round the back of the head and told him to go and fight his own battles, definitely not, like father like son'. He never bothered any of us Smiths again.

By and large, I rubbed along with this band of anti-social types. There was friction from time to time, but they didn't actively seek me out for aggravation. But to most rules there're exceptions. Some of the locals were born troublemakers and, as we were newcomers, that was reason enough for us to be targeted. I believe one of them was related to Lilly Powers - a formidable woman but one who always looked kindly on yours truly as I became good friends with her sons. This relative was a different pile of bricks - he looked for trouble, and usually found it. My elder brother was on his way to night-school on one occasion and had cause to run to catch his bus. The lout jumped out of the hedgerow as brother passed and attempted an assault - he got short shrift and brother got the bus. Strictly speaking he wasn't a local, he lived in Short Heath – the next- door village to New Invention. One family of local yobs made it their intention to rule the kids in the neighbourhood. It was they that were responsible for that poor lad being made to drink urine. They had it in mind to treat me with similar contempt. Suffice to say that never happened. I think they worked it out – I would give them battle.

*****

I didn't know it then, but I was about to leave a period of childlike innocence, even naivety for a much less pleasant world. As children grow out from under the parental control in terms of conduct and discipline so certain characteristics independently within the child develop and flourish. Some are virtuous and commendable, others less so - indeed some are downright evil - as the Pugga incident illustrates. Children that are dominated at home often harbour suppressed anger and resentment. Rarely do they have the courage or character to resolve that with the source, rather they seek to bully and intimidate the perceived vulnerable in their peer group - they are replicating learned behaviour. Bullies always choose their victims on the basis that they (victims) are lesser human beings - ones for whom a certain contempt or resentment is appropriate. We were a poor family, apparently considered by some as less worthy. Hard times were coming, in more than one way.

Chapter 7

TOO MUCH WEEK LEFT AT THE END
OF THE MONEY

When we moved to 94 Essington Road in 1947 there was nine of us including Mum and Dad. Dad was now working for the council as a driver. He always kept his earnings close but I'm guessing it didn't amount to a king's ransom. He gave Mum a weekly housekeeping allowance, again, amount unspecified. It was the way that domestic finances were managed then. The liberal notion of handing wage packets over may have been practised by some but certainly not in this household. So, whatever meagre sum was available, Mum had to feed and clothe us as well as taking care of the bills. There was never enough to go around. Rent was collected at the door every Monday, the first working day following payday which was always on a Friday. Oh, so often the rent man had to call again - and again, which didn't please him because that would eat into the collection time of another round (area). On most of those occasions it was simply a matter of pretending not to be at home - the law calls this 'keeping house' - an almost quaint description for people who try to avoid creditors by not answering the door. It couldn't always be deployed, partly because repetition dilutes - makes it less believable and partly because the eagle-eyed rent man had spotted signs of life on his arrival. That was when one of us kids would be sent to say Mum wasn't in - he would ask,

"Are you sure?" and on one such occasion this question caused infant (not me) at the door to yell out,

"Mum, he says are you sure."

What a clever rent collector he turned out to be. He didn't

press the matter because he reasoned that there was really no money, so why waste time arguing? Instead, deploying cunning psychology, he went on his way knowing full well that Mum wouldn't dare try that scam again. We shouldn't forget that he had this and similar experiences a hundred times a week most likely and he had a simple rule - don't believe any of them. The truly remarkable thing about the rent collector is that he went about his work on a bicycle with a leather cash bag hung over his shoulder. Everybody knew who he was - everybody knew what he was carrying and yet I never recall hearing of him being mugged - different times, different values.

After the rent came gas and electricity. Apparently, we kids were told often, neither were free.

"Switch that light off - turn that fire down - I'm not made of money"

I also learned that money didn't grow on trees - actually, I don't think I ever thought that it did - adults, parents especially can be quite odd at times. There were no collectors involved, consumers paid as they went along - pre-payment meters were universal. One penny a go - that's 0.417p in the new funny money - push the coin into the slot and turn the dial - a clunk and gas or electricity were available. Often Mom didn't have money for the meter, so we went without and meandered around in the cold and dark. Gas was supplied by the West Midlands Gas Board (WMGB) and they were old hands at the task, the supply was never cut off. The Midlands Electricity Board (MEB) on the other hand were, like their industry, relative newbies and the supply was frequently cut off because of problems at their end. Mom would get really annoyed if, when the power failed, she put money into the meter only to find out that there was a power-cut. She took to peering out of the window to check if the neighbours were also in darkness. It was a sure fire away to learn who, amongst the neighbours, was financially compromised. It was prudent to keep a good supply of candles at the ready.

The meters were checked and emptied regularly, an event greeted with much joy because there was always a healthy payback. The householder got a modest wedge of cash handed back - in the form of penny pieces of course. This odd ritual perplexed yours truly - why did they give you money back when you've paid for what you have used? Both WMGB and MEB employed a practice still in operation today for those that have prepayment meters. Consumption is estimated, and the consumer's meter calibrated accordingly. It's then a matter of pay-as-you-go. Now, if the consumer doesn't use all the gas it had been estimated he would, he would be due a refund because he's paid for gas he hasn't used. It's amazing how the balance is always in the supplier's favour. They invariably finish up with more of the consumer's money than entitled. That's a novel version of an interest free loan. If you have one of those meters check it out right away - you could be owed hundreds of pounds.

Things we didn't have to worry about then included water and house insurance, or to be precise contents cover. Water was paid for by the council as landlord, owner occupiers paid their own. As for insurance, nobody really had anything worth stealing - well we didn't for certain. I think that if we had been visited by burglars in those days it would have been to make a delivery. Little was spent on clothes either, partly because they were still rationed and partly because there was no money available anyway. By now we were getting by on hand-me-downs - sometimes from within the family, sometimes from outside.

*****

Food shopping was exciting. During the week, it was a case of buy as you need from the local shops but once a week -

Saturday (following payday) Mum would take us young ones on the bus to Willenhall, we were the original mules. A number 2 bus ride to Doctors' Piece, a short walk along Lower Lichfield Street, down the alley that connects with the market place and then on to Conway's Butchers. No fancy joints but no rabbit either, some cheap boiling beef, sausage and a ring of black pudding then along the market to the grocers. The grocer in question was Mum's uncle (Nan's brother) - Uncle Billy Parker to us, although he was really a great uncle.

Ever wondered why they're called grocers? The term goes back to the 14th century when merchants generally specialised in one commodity. One group however, traded in a wide range of dry goods (spices, pepper, sugar, cocoa, tea, coffee) and they bought in bulk and were effectively, wholesalers. The French term for wholesalers was 'Grossier' which, in turn was a version of the Latin word 'Grossarius'. Circa 200 BC the Romans invaded Gaul (now France) and taught them Latin, over time the French corrupted the word then, in1066 the French (from Normandy) invaded England - didn't teach us French but the merchants from Normandy gave us their names for trade including 'grossier' which, in turn we corrupted - and, following that meandering semantic tale, we emerge with our word - Grocer.

Uncle Billy's shop was on the edge of the town centre in, opposite the Central School where big brother passed his daytime hours. The shop was a large timber single storey construction. Behind it lay Willenhall railway station, the means of commuting to such far flung places as Wolverhampton and Birmingham and then along came a guy called Dr Beeching and gave the station one his famous chops - and it disappeared from use. Interesting, they killed off the railways, so people took to cars and the authorities got to hate cars and tried to get everyone back on the trains. By way of incentive they made public transport so expensive that it was cheaper to use the car, so they penalised car drivers with exorbitant parking fees, yellow lines, red lines and – another cash cow – bus lanes. Staying at home seems the sanest course of action.

But, back to Uncle Billy's. The shop had an aroma all its very own. Almost everything on sale was bulk supplied and had to be cut, carved, weighed and packed. Butter and lard were patted into small half-pounds portions to order; cheese was cut in similar fashion only it couldn't be patted so there was often a tiny added wedge to make up the weight - hence the term 'make-weight' when someone or something is added to make up a number. Biscuits, flour, sugar. tea and dried fruits were all sold 'loose', that is, they were weighed to order. Everything gave off its own unique aroma and they all blended to create a curiously welcoming odour. Suitably laden we would head for the number 41 bus stop, because it was nearer and head home. As a teenager, I was occasionally trusted to go solo to Uncle Billy's. With a list, of course and strict instructions to get only that that was on the list. Mum must have had an account there because I never carried cash, beyond bus fare - trust went only so far apparently. It was on such a journey that I experienced another of those contestable issues that saw age triumph over sense. I got on the bus at the bottom of Essington Road and proffered what I knew to be the exact fare. The conductor (we had such a luxury then) asked where I was going "to my uncle Billy's" I replied. He laughed, and very condescendingly, said - 'no sonny, which stop are you going to'. The other passengers then enjoyed the 'joke' and laughed with him. But he - they - were wrong. He asked the wrong question, and that's why he got a wrong answer. I labour this point because the fault prevails to this day. For a host of reasons (fear, embarrassment and downright lazy speak) people frame questions badly and then complain bitterly about not getting the right answers.

When Uncle Billy ceased trading, Mum switched allegiance to the Home and Colonial Store in the Market Place. Home and Colonial began in 1883 and expanded by acquiring other grocers such as Lipton's. It changed its name in the late 1920's to Allied Suppliers and in the 1970's was taken over by Caversham Foods. In 1981 the business was again the subject of a take- over, this time by Argyll Foods and in 1986 Argyll merged with Safeway's. After a period of underperforming, Safeway's was bought out by William Morrison's which remains one of the big four food retailers in the UK. The term' grocer' has all but disappeared, but I like to think that when we now shop at Morrison's we're still at the Home and Colonial grocers.

In those, days grocers weren't into bread or milk. These were the province of specialist traders. Following the demise of Sadler's farm, we got our milk from Johnson's for a while. I suspect that the Sadler's dairy went out of business. Bakers delivered bread door to door to order. Prominent in our area was the Co-op from Walsall & District Co-operative Society and Scribban's Bread which may have come from Smethwick. That's the nearest I can trace the brand and certainly there wasn't a baker of that name locally. Mum got our bread from one of the general stores, usually Bishton's because it was the first shop we reached. In 1955 Rank Hove, McDougal set up Mother's Pride bakery and that became the bread of choice. Sliced bread hit the shelves in the mid-1950's and was an instant success. Manufacturers could get more slices out of a loaf than the average housewife, so loaves went further. There is some dispute as to the birth of the sliced loaf, some reports claim that it celebrated its 50th birthday in 2011 but I know we were indulging long before 1961. There's also evidence that, in the USA they were slicing bread in the late 1920's. In fact, it is said that in 1943 the US government banned the practice because it was a waste of resources. Sliced or unsliced, there's little to beat the end of the loaf – the crust, fights were fought to secure the coveted crust. And the notion that posh people cut off the crusts and threw them away, eating only the soft white middle, was considered an abomination - and a bit girlie. We were known to eat the inner soft bread, nibbling it at the end to preserve the outer crust and to make it last. This was to be savoured at the end - always save the best for the last.

*****

Saturday was market day in Willenhall. Located between the two cinemas, the Dale at one end, the Picture House at the other. It was a thriving market packed with stalls selling just about every conceivable item - from fresh fruit and vegetables through linen clothes, household wares, hardware and the latest miracle product that was guaranteed to do the impossible. One stall holder had a pitch under the clock tower. He sold general merchandise, which is one way of saying whatever he could get his hands on - mostly bankrupt stock - allegedly. His sales patter was brilliant, I swear he could have re-sold coals back to Newcastle, convinced the Arabs they ought to buy more sand for the deserts and Eskimos would have returned home with sledges laden with ice, convinced that it was about to be rationed.

I watched him sell hair cream to a mesmerised crowd once, completely beguiled by his commentary.

"'Ere missus - want your old man to look like Dennis Compton?"

Dennis Compton was a cricketing legend of the day. He and his brother, Lesley, played test cricket for England. He also advertised Brylcream - the preferred hairdressing for men. In those days those serving in the RAF were known as the 'Brylcream boys' on account that they always had shiny hair. In the posters, Compton was made to look suave, sophisticated, worldly. A hard act to follow for the gathering around the stall.

" 'Ere - this cost me a bloody fortune to get it into the

country. They don't want it in you know - the Brylcream boys - can't stand the competition. But today I'm gonna do you lot a favour. I'm gonna treat you. I could get £5 a tub in London on my life. But I ain't gonna ask yer for a fiver, nor a fourer - not even £3 - 'ere - snatch me bleeding hand off and give fifty- bob (£2.10.0d). C'mon missus - he's worth it ain't he? Do the washin' up for a month if you treat him right. 'Ere - you mister - fancy showing your old woman a news man? Cor, I bet she's got one already."

And all the time the tubs of hairdressing were flying out of his hand as he kept up a relentless patter of outrageous claims and cheeky innuendo. In a way, I reckon he and his kind were the original spin doctors - making everything appear anything but what it was, and, getting the public to pay for it to boot. Years later I saw another market trader with similar skills. This one could stack a dinner service and a tea service onto a carving dish and literally juggle that lot with one hand whilst giving a running commentary on the number of pieces in the stack, the quality of the china and the ridiculous price he was asking. There was also the Del boys – they literally opened a suitcase and peddled whatever was therein – perfume for the ladies to magic cleaning compounds to wrist watches. Markets have become more subdued affairs these days, the characters have long gone.

*****

Sleeping arrangements at the Smith residence were uncomplicated. Mom and Dad took the box room; the girls had the front bedroom - with the gas fire! equality my.... elbow and us poor boys had the cold stark back bedroom. That arrangement didn't last because as us boys came to outnumber the girls an exchange was organised - we needed the extra space - the gas fire was, of course, incidental. Beds were the priority, no room for anything else. Clothes were hung on the floor unless they were jackets or coats and then they performed as eiderdowns. On cold winter nights, the beds would be heated by bricks that had been in the oven for a while, wrapped in a towel or a piece of laundry they were a great comfort to cold feet. We were beginning to realise that we weren't as well off as some, but it didn't really bother us - we simply got on with our lives. At night, we lads would sometimes take it in turns telling stories and mine were always about places of plenty. No idea what dear sisters did to pass the time between shivering in a cold bed and the bliss that was sleep.

As can be imagined seeing as there was so many of us, a little sibling rivalry flared up on the odd occasion. Never inspired by me of course but my brothers and sisters could be so unruly at times. They did their best to involve - even implicate me in their carryings on but as you've probably guessed I did my best to remain aloof. That didn't always work because they would get physical. During one moment of rough and tumble I was pushed against the wall, I fell on an electric socket, one of those old Bakelite affairs that protruded from the wall. I hit the socket leading with my left hand, the socket shattered, and I got a nasty gash - still have the scar to this day, a rather neat little crescent shaped souvenir. That's the best part - the worst of it was that I was a fraction of an inch away from the live wire - and eternity. That would have been the end. Under legal advice I refrain from naming the culprit but if you really want to know, take a peek at the comments that will appear when this tome hits kindle and company. Honestly, brothers - sisters, I don't how my Mom put up with them at times.

To balance the books, I should also report that we managed to play together quite nicely at times - at least us younger souls did. A favourite game was shops. Stock came from empty cartons and packaging ultimately destined for the dustbin but here enjoying a respite. We charged proper shop prices when we knew what they were, otherwise we simply made them up. We used pretend money - on account that none of us had any - wouldn't have spent it in our crummy shop if we had. We acted out the parts too: "can I pay you next week?" "No, you haven't paid last week's bill yet" "That's the last time I come here to shop" - "Please yourself" As you will gather, we were hot on customer care back then. The dialogue wasn't made up - we were repeating what we'd heard in local shops, particularly Owens - it had been said to some of us kids many a time. Back home we would go with the bad new and likely get blamed for not 'asking right'.

Of course, play with sisters (girls) could only go on indoors; to have done so outside was to risk being seen by other lads which was to risk - no it wasn't a risk, it was guaranteed certainty - being called a 'sissy' and that usually ended in a fight. It seems that boys learn how to fight over girls at an early age. In the great outdoors girls played hopscotch for which grids could be seen chalked onto the pavements far and wide, Boys on the other hand, were much more sensitive to the environment and contented themselves in playing marbles. Any old manhole cover would do and if one wasn't to hand then a rough circle scratched in the ground would suffice. A boy's favourite marble was his, 'shooter' - few would risk losing that in a game. Most marbles were around half an inch in diameter, but some came twice that size - they were called 'popties', I know not why. Girls also did skipping, solo or teams of three - two holding the rope and the third jumping it (rope) in the middle. Us lads thought that that was definitely very girlie - until that is, we found out that boxers, even heavyweights, did skipping as part of their training. We would never, never even dream of calling Rocky Marciano (world heavyweight champion) girlie. Honest mister it wasn't me - it was him. Marciano was an exceptional boxer. He held the world heavyweight title from 1952 to 1956 and retired, undefeated after forty-nine bouts. He was just thirty-two years of age and a very smart man - get out whilst on top. Bet he didn't spin tops though. Both sexes enjoyed spinning tops though us boys were rather more aggressive. Simple pastime - spin a top on the path and then whip it with a piece of string tied to a stick. The top would fly through the air, then land and carry on spinning.

*****

A growing family, in size as well as numbers, and only one wage coming in meant that times were hard, very hard. There was no such event as breakfast, partly because there wasn't the food to go around and partly because we timed getting out of bed to perfection. There was just enough time (sometimes barely that) to wash, get dressed and leave for school. We had school dinners, paid for by the local authority, but back home at teatime and it was typically a couple of slices of bread and margarine - yes, still that war time special. It was now softened by being placed on a plate and heated over the kettle. We had no choice, with two toilets in the property there was no need for the er...pot.

Financially things eased for Mum when first my elder brother and then sister left school and found work. Kids finished so-called compulsory education at fifteen then - there was no incentive to keep them any longer and there was a desperate need for labour. The war had cost hundreds of thousands lives of Britain's youngest and finest. Their places in the workforce had to be filled as quickly as possible. The up-side of that was that there were jobs aplenty, unemployment, especially amongst school-leavers barely existed. My elder siblings were thus able to contribute to the family budget and what a difference it did make. We were many leagues away from being affluent but at least we were heading in the right direction.

Come the Saturday shop and we fared much better. The supply of basic foods was improving, and cheap cuts of meat could be had to order. We would cook slices of cheese in the frying pan so that it would spread out and go further - tasted good too. Sausage, black pudding, eggs and tomatoes (not tinned - too expensive) made for a mouth-watering meal. Then there was draft pork (pork belly to our colonial friends across 'the pond') served with broad beans and peas, the liqueur from the pork would be drizzled over the vegetables - heavenly. The cheap cuts of meat were great for boiling and Mum made some great stews. The eating extravaganza climaxed with a superb traditional roast dinner on Sunday. Monday saw the return to Spartan rations. We made sandwiches out of almost anything - golden syrup; Nestlé's condensed milk; honey; dripping - if it could be spread on bread we spread it. We even had lard butties - went down ok with a little salt and pepper. These were inexpensive goodies and at least gave us some variety. Lard, the cooking fat of the age, was also said to have been used by some lads as a hair cream. Never by us - cold water was the hair conditioner of the day. Oh, and we made toast - that meant sticking a fork in a slice of bread and holding as near to the fire as was comfortable. Sometimes the bread fell off in to the fire. I was retrieved and if scorched, the black would be scraped off to make it edible. On good days, we got to toast crumpets and pikelets this way too - funny thing, we had them the wrong way around. What we called pikelets are now called crumpets - when did that happen? Truth is we had a grill on the gas cooker in the kitchen, but it cost money to toast this way - so coal fire it was. Potatoes suffered the same fate; too expensive to bake them in the oven so we chucked them onto the fire. The rule of thumb was that when they turned black they were done. Again, the black stuff was scraped off leaving a crispy skin and a soft inner - just the way they should be.

Chapter 8

I'M (NOT) IN THE ARMY NOW

As quick as the improvement in the family fortunes came so it ended, at least for a while. My eldest brother now having reached the grand old age of eighteen was conscripted into National Service. This was the fate of all able-bodied lads of that age save those that could wangle a way out - not a facility available to many. Only men working on the land (farmers); down the mines or serving in the merchant navy were exempt. Conscription had been allowed to lapse after the end of the first world war but was -re-introduced on the 27th April 1939 in response to the rumblings coming from a bellicose Germany so we weren't altogether unprepared. Interestingly it was brought back to life by the Secretary of State for War - Lord Belisha, he of the Belisha Beacon fame - he was then Minister for Transport. Belisha Beacons were introduced in 1934 and the first one appeared in Wigan on the 4th July 1935 - rather took the gloss off American Independence Day.

Conscription, or National Service as it became known as, was originally for eighteen months. It was extended to two years at the outbreak of the Korean War in 1951. All young men aged between eighteen and twenty-one could expect to be 'called up' for service. It ended in 1957 when it was decided that those born after 1st October 1939 would not be called to serve. That meant that, apart from my eldest brother, who was a clear candidate, my second elder also got the call - his birthday being February 1939. Mine being the 4th June 1940 (remember) meant that I did not get to serve Queen and country. Which of us benefited most from that remains debatable. Eighteen -year olds were generally quite malleable but by then I had developed something of a defiant streak that would not have squared with army discipline. That said, about a year later I had a yen to join the Royal Marines, I liked the prospect of an all action lifestyle. Wasn't to be - they rejected me because my eyesight wasn't 100%. Seems the school optician might have had a point. The army recruitment tried to tempt me into other regiments, but it was my turn to do the rejecting. I'm flattered to have been told by my dear wife that I would made a good marine. Very single minded and when I focus on a task, nothing else in the world gets a hearing.

*****

Anyhow - the big school. Up to this point school had been ok most of the time - even fun, and I'd managed to learn a thing or two. Enough to pass the eleven-plus at least. So, I, not unreasonably, assumed that the 'big school' represented a mere change of venue, the teaching and learning would go on pretty much the same. Wrong. wrong. wrong. Apparently, school, and learning, now got to be serious - not fun. What nonsense this was. The warning signs, missed by yours truly until it was too late, were evident in the preparation. Big school meant new clothes and new shoes - rationing and finance permitting. Why the need to dress up for school? Never done so before - why now? At eleven years of age I was allowed to launder myself of course, however there was the matter of mother's inspection before one was passed fit. This check involved the yanking and stretching of ears to make certain they had been scrubbed to standard (do dirty ears impinge the ability to hear? That was not my experience to date). Necks, knees and elbows were next in line. Apparently, one could grow spuds in the average boy's neck - that's boys mark, not girls, seems they were more inclined to cleanliness. That was Mum's conclusion and I feel sure that it had nothing to do with her having been a girl herself. My simple mandate was that if you couldn't see it why wash it and now that I was to be draped in long trousers and long-sleeved shirts that left only hands and face - agreed?

All kids share one single ambition - to grow up. A mark of a boy's transition in those days was to swap short trousers for long ones. Short trousers terminated at or near the knee and were the mark of a child. They weren't good for the knees when one fell over - it was a case of skin on gravel or concrete or tarmac. Whatever the surface the knee always came second. Grazed and bloody knees were as common as head lice. Now I'd like to tell you that long trousers eliminated such injuries - and so they did for the most part - but instead of bloodying the knee they frayed the trousers. You will doubtless be as dismayed as I was to learn that damaging trousers was a greater sin than wounding knees. I had it on good authority that trousers cost money - knees did not and there was clip round the ear to reinforce the message. Such a materialistic outlook. Ever wondered why 'trousers' is plural? They're only a single item after all - two legs you say? Well a jacket has two sleeves so why isn't it/aren't they called jackets? The answer is to be found in Medieval times. Trousers, or what passed as trousers then, were indeed two separate coverings - one for each leg, they were clipped to a waistband to keep them up. Over time they evolved into a single garment the name 'trousers' was retained - and passed on to all similar apparel - pants; shorts; knickers; pj's. Spectacles are an issue - they're a single unit so should be spectacle - it's the two eyes that do it I reckon. On that theme - why isn't brassiere brassieres? Think I'll walk on - leave that one with you.

Some of the less affluent kids got their long trousers as 'hand-me-downs' from an older sibling. We couldn't afford even that luxury - sibling was still wearing them! Of course, kids continue to grow - trousers do not. At some point the end of the trouser leg began to rise above the footwear. When the gap exposed socks the teasing and tormenting would begin.

"Has someone died in your family?"

"No "

"Then why are you wearing your trousers at half-mast?"

Long trouser aside (they did feel odd at first although I admit to feeling very grown up)) all the other apparel was the familiar standard issue - shirt, jacket, shoes and socks. No uniform - only the posh grammar schools had uniforms and no ties - at least they weren't obligatory. New shoes were a real problem. They were tight, and they pinched, and it was uncomfortable to walk. They need breaking in I was told and the only way to do that was to wear them, walk in them. Wearers of new shoes that pinch and hurt can easily be spotted. They walk on the soles only, avoiding putting the heels to ground. This creates a curious sort of mincing gait and attracts much ridicule to the unfortunate wearer. There is an unwritten rule acknowledged by all kids of a certain age; if you see something in one of your peers that is odd, weird or even slightly amusing, then you are duty bound to draw his or her attention - and as many others as possible - to the defect. Laughing at the discomfort of others allows us to conveniently overlook our own shortcomings.

*****

Short Heath Secondary Modern was the big school. Short Heath because that's where it was; secondary because that's what it was and modern - well I have no idea. The building was old, and the teaching methods were traditional so nothing modern in sight. And quite why it was called the 'big school' alluded me until I realised that it was an oblique reference to us kids growing up - learning what the grown-ups called important stuff. The school itself was - is - modest even small by today's standards. I guess there would be about three-hundred kids attending and probably twenty or so staff. Teachers knew almost all the pupils and we certainly knew every member of staff. I look now at the sprawling comprehensives, or academies as some have chosen to be called, attended by thousands of kids and staffed by hundreds. Even the staff don't know each other. Over the past three or four decades we have become obsessed with size. If it aint big it aint beautiful and it won't work- big is best - means more pen-pushers, sorry - managers - are needed. I wonder what the digital equivalent of a pen-pusher is called - how about keyboard-clapper?

To get to this place of learning was literally a straight walk of about a mile and a half from home to school. Down Essington Road, cross Lichfield Road, cut through the entry to the row of terrace house, traverse a piece of wasteland, over the railway bridge, follow the path alongside the embankment littered with trees over the main road cut through the Croft, cross Bloxwich Road and finally there it was - Short Heath Secondary Modern School. During mild and dry weather, this was not an unpleasant walk but come the rain, the snow and the cold - ah then one would wish for an overcoat at least, scarf and gloves would be good. We had no such luxuries, if it rained and we got wet, we dried out at school - eventually; on a bad day we'd be just in time to get another soaking on the way home. There were no boots or wellies to protect feet from snow and ice. Chilblains was a common complaint, and as anyone who has suffered knows, they can be intensely painful.

A modest encampment. The school was built on a slight embankment, the main buildings, comprising classrooms and offices fronted the road and were at the high end. The remaining classrooms ran parallel at the lower level. The two were joined together by the hall which doubled as a quasi-gymnasium. Playgrounds were on either side of the hall. The hall shielded one playground from the morning sun which made it ideal for creating ice slides in winter. What fun we had on those slides, fun that's likely denied kids now because of them risking limbs and falling foul of Health and Safety. The configuration of the school was, in effect, a 'H' block. We were 'H' block long before the Prison

Maze in Belfast or that curious Australian tv programme (Prisoner – Cell Block H) - hard to call which was worse - the storylines, the acting or the scenery. The school also boasted two prefabricated outbuildings that served as classrooms.

There were two concrete playgrounds separated by the school hall. Beyond the buildings there was an expansive sports field, a small part of which had been taken over by a couple of brick- built air raid shelters. The field curved off in one direction to run at right angles to the classrooms and up to the main road. In the other direction, it gave way to the school garden and a rough track-cum-lane that ran parallel to the sports field and led to a coppice that extended from the school boundary to a minor road maybe a mile or so away. The coppice was skirted on one side by our old friend the Essington and Wyrley canal. This is a suitable point at which to make a confession of sorts. In my early teens and whilst I attended this place of learning, I was prone to demonstrate a naive belief that I was invulnerable. This is the thing - I can't swim yet I walked across the canal, head under water. Why? As the chicken - to get to the other side. The nearest bridge was miles away - walking across seemed the obvious thing to do. Still had to wait for my friends to catch up - they did the sensible thing.

With its landscaped frontage of green lawns, the school was not an unattractive sight. In later years, I often saw reference to 'copse' rather than 'coppice' and wondered as to the difference. There isn't any - copse is simply a more modern name for what is a small wood. However, the original name 'coppice' dates back to the late 16th century and describes the act of coppicing. Coppicing is the practice of cutting trees back to their roots, cuttings were needed as poles, and to encourage new growth. Pollarding, on the other hand, is the act of simply pruning, usually higher up the trunk, the objective being to restrict growth. The areas where coppicing was done was called a 'coppice', but you worked that out already I guess.

*****

Big brother was my escort on that first day - he'd gone through the process a year earlier. On arrival, all newbies were herded into the school hall. There wasn't one smiling face to be seen - us kids didn't look to happy either. The staff were stern and officious, treating us as if we were an intrusion. This was so very different from New Invention Junior. Finally, when all newcomers had been corralled we were all ordered to the back of the hall, there was around fifty to sixty of us. Some of the teaching staff were gathered on the stage at the front. Then our names were called out in two batches of between twenty-five and thirty. The calling stopped, and the chosen ones were told to follow the member of staff who had alighted from the stage to lead his or her class to their form room. The set up was simple. The school had two streams - A and B. Kids were to attend for four years starting at eleven years of age and ending at fifteen when they would be ejected into the world of work. At eleven one was either in 1A or 1B; at twelve years of age it became 2A or 2B and so on. The A stream was for the bright kids the B stream for the rest. I started in 1A - well I had passed the eleven-plus.

Comprehensive schools were introduced in 1965 as the preferred alternative to Selective schools (grammars). The notion was that everyone started out equal as admittance wasn't based on academic achievement whereas entry to grammar schools depended on passing the eleven-plus. But since all those attending grammars had passed the same exam weren't they starting out as equals? Tut tut, how very un-pc of me. The social perspective on comps versus grammars is an interesting comment on the mass mindset. Grammar schools have always been held up as bastions of privilege for the indulgence of the better off. Secondary and later comprehensive schools were/are seen as essentially working class. Utter tosh - first off, our neighbour's son and my cousin did not come from 'well off' families and second off many of my contemporaries at Short Heath Secondary Modern came from fairly well- off middle-class families. Doubtless there were a few 'in-betweeners' like me but most kids were at the school their ability prescribed. One perspective of comprehensive schools is that they dumbed down learning to the lowest level of performance - grammar schools did the opposite. In truth, there has proved to be some very fine comprehensives.

My name was called, and I had to walk the length of the hall, all by myself, in new shoes that pinched and squeaked at every tread. As names were called alphabetically most of my class were already assembled at the foot of the stage. They looked very well turned out already I felt like the poor relation - despite shiny squeaky shoes. We were herded together by our chosen form teacher Mr Ernest 'Nozuk' Morgyn. He was called Nozuk because he had the habit of tilting his head back and thereby raising his chin when he addressed a class. This resulted in his nose assuming greater than usual prominence -nose had morphed into Nozuk over the years he had been at the school.

He led his flock from the hall to the first of the two pre-fabricated classrooms. He introduced himself in a formal but not unfriendly way. We were the 'A' stream apparently, the smarter part of the intake although all accept yours truly had failed the eleven plus. The 'also-rans' made up a 'B' stream. Mr Morgyn told us that the school was divided into four houses each being named after the most notable of a species group. That gave us Dolphin; Eagle; Lion and Oak houses. Each house was marked by a distinctive colour - Dolphin was blue; Eagle yellow; Lion red and Oak green. I was put in Eagle. A points system was in operation administered by the teaching staff. Points were awarded for commendable work and lost for poor work and bad conduct.

Anyone earning twenty-one points or more in a week would appear on the Headmaster's commendation list and anyone losing eleven points, or more would be on a report list for which sanctions applied.

So much of this would not be tolerated in the 21st century. For a start, the gender sensitive brigade would frown on the use of the term 'Headmaster' or 'Headmistress' - they're Head-teachers now or simply Heads. In the same vein, the terms chairman and chairwoman cause much wincing and grimacing - nowadays we refer to them as 'chairs'. So, when attending a meeting one must talk to the chair - they used to commit people for less. The points system too would be frowned upon - favours the clever children, makes the rest feel inferior - unhealthy competition between pupils. What a curious paradox then that these schools that are so anti-competitive fight hard to get to the top of the leader board when it comes to examination results. Competition between schools is apparently ok but between kids - not ok.

Back to Nozuk - sorry Mr Morgyn - he then proceeded to lay out the timetable for each week. We were going to do Mathematics, which, as far as I understood at the time, was simply a posh version of Arithmetic which I had done at junior school. It took a little while but eventually the defects in that thinking became apparent as we trespassed into geometry, trigonometry and algebra. No more 'if I have thirteen apples and I give five away and eat three - how many do I have left'. There were English lessons - that was fine, just like the old school - well almost. Geography was good, and History looked set to carry on from where New Invention Junior left off - naming and knowing the dates of a seemingly endless procession of English monarchs. Art was there and there was talk of a potter's wheel - whatever that was. Music lessons were on the agenda too - I just hoped that they would be an improvement on the New Invention version. At junior school, there had been a scarcity of instruments and I had been offered the triangle!

The triangle is surely not a musical instrument. Has anyone - ever heard of a solo composition for the triangle - Mozart's triangle concerto? Of course, not because you can't play a tune on the wretched thing - so how can it have anything to do with music? The triangle is nought but a Barbie doll coat-hanger.

There were some new subjects too: Religious Education which turned out to consist of the telling of bible stories and making us all wary of the wrath of God. Science was on the agenda and here an experience that would have the PC battalions spluttering in their righteous indignation. Boys would study general science - the internal combustion engine (motor cars - ladies), how to generate electricity and play around with Bunsen burners. Were these teachers serious? Would they allow a bunch of budding teenagers to play around with naked flame? Things were looking up - there could be some fun to be had here. Whilst us boys were learning 'men's' stuff the girls were to learn biology - proper girlie stuff we 'men' assumed. Boys and girls were separated again when we were assigned to woodwork classes and the girls to learn about domestic science. Quite right too, can't have little girls messing around with all those sharp tools like chisels and planes and saws. The rationale was obvious - prepare them to be able to look after the home, the family and - most important - a husband. Put another way, they were to learn about just the most important and underrated role in society. There was space on the timetable allotted to Gardening - no idea what that was all about. Finally, there was to be regular PT lessons - that's Physical Training, or as it became less affectionately known, physical torture. I can confirm that boys and girls were segregated. Reason enough when a girl actually asked – how do you play cricket? I was still shaking my head in despair days later.

All the foregoing was to keep us occupied between the hours of 9am to 3.30pm. There would be fifteen- minute breaks mid-morning and mid-afternoon. Lunch was from 12 noon to 1.30pm. That was to allow for those that had to go home to get fed.

*****

Every school day began with a morning assembly in the hall attended by all classes and teachers. It was a story, a hymn and a prayer session only there was more than one hymn. An assembly a day for four years has resulted in the words and tunes of many hymns lingering forever in memory. Such assemblies are frowned upon now in this alleged secular society but as I reflect on those days I realise that they contributed to a sense of belonging. For short while each morning we weren't a motley collection of gender, streams and classes, and staff - we were all together - one school. The religious part of the proceedings over Mr Statham would embark on a short report, righting wrongs and cautioning against bad behaviour. This led conveniently to the points report. Any pupil on the commended list and be suitably praised. Those unfortunate enough to appear on the reported list would face an inquest as to the cause followed by retribution of some sort. Repeat offenders could expect the cane. I regularly appeared on both lists, perplexing the Headmaster considerably but I never got caned.

I well remember one special assembly in February 1952. It was called very suddenly, and a very sombre air presided over the affair. We were told that the King (King George V1) had died. It didn't seem to mean much to us kids. He was a remote figure that we heard about on the radio from time to time and maybe read about in the newspaper - assuming we'd bother to read such grown-up material. Paradoxically we all knew what he looked like because he was on all the coins and stamps. There is this too, we spent entire history lessons learning about dead kings. We may not have been much moved but some members of the staff certainly were. I can still see the delectable Cherry (Cheryl)

Wilkins shedding tears. Cherry Wilkins was a blonde bombshell, she taught the girls biology, she taught us boys lust, only we didn't know what that meant.

Our current Queen's coronation was set for the 2nd June 1953 (notice how they carefully avoided the 4th - again). I believe the entire school was charged with creating a coronation folder. We did get a bit excited about that, it was a chance to do our own work rather than be told what we had to do. It was then that I learned that one cannot use pictures of the Royal Family without express permission.

*****

Once a month and on a Friday afternoon there would be house meetings. House members from all four years would convene in one room. The house master would tell us how many house-members had been commended and reported during the past month and how important it was to do better than the other houses. No doubt they were getting the same message. It was considered healthy competition. Then they would get down to the important stuff - details of the inter-house games. The four houses played against each other at cricket, football and netball (girls only). At the end of the academic year there would be the annual sports day when all four houses competed at track and field events. Winning a cup for the house was the supreme objective

I didn't take to Short Heath Secondary Modern. Maybe it was the size - small by today's standards but larger than New Invention Junior: maybe it was because there was more of everything and everybody - classrooms, pupils, teachers: maybe it was being separated from my friends from New Invention Junior – although some did make the journey, they were in the B stream: maybe it was because everyone seemed so stern and serious or maybe it was those painful new shoes.

It took some time for me to realise that, although all the above had some bearing the overwhelming reason for my discontent was the growing hostility visited upon the Smiths by our peers. It came to the surface rather dramatically, and very unexpectedly, in the boy's cloakroom which doubled as a changing room for PE. I was standing at one end doing nothing in particular; there were three other lads at the opposite end, I didn't know them. They started to make nasty comments about me and my family. I didn't know what to make of it - didn't know them, hadn't done anything to them - hadn't even spoken to them - ever. My simple instincts told me to get out of there - away from them. Three of them - one of me - welcome to the world of the bully. As I turned to leave the cloakroom a plimsoll slammed against the wall right next to where I was standing. It had been thrown with force by one those lads and I have no doubt but that it was intended to hit yours truly though I know not why. They sniggered and smirked provocatively.

This turned out to be one of those pivotal moments when a significant part of character is shaped. Without a moment's thought, I picked up the plimsoll and hurled it back with equal force. It wasn't aimed but had it been the aim couldn't have been bettered. It hit the lad in the middle right in the er. credentials. He collapsed slowly, clutching his groin and, at first silently, then he howled in agony and made some impressive gyrations on the floor, a sort of early break-dancing. His two confederates looked ashen; clearly this was not the response they had anticipated. I made my way towards the door, passing them, they made no move towards me but one of them said something like:

"You've done it now. If he has to go to hospital, you'll be in trouble"

I just stared back and said

"You started it" and I left.

That ought to have been the end of the matter. Likely that some of you out there will say the lad got his just deserts and that's pretty much how I saw it. Alas, not so the instigators. The injured party gave an award-winning performance for the benefit of a teacher searching for him and his cronies because they were late for their next lesson. Of course, his version had been suitably edited. Apparently, he didn't throw the plimsoll he merely passed it to me because he thought it might be mine. Wouldn't be surprised to learn that he made his way in the law or politics when he left school.

The incident was reported to the headmaster, one Percy Edward Statham. He ran that school of that there was no doubt and he was a strong disciplinarian. As was the way then, corporal punishment was the prime mover in maintaining law and order. I was summoned to his presence. He was about 5' 10" tall and ramrod straight with a bit of a pot that was well accommodated by an immaculate three-piece suit. He had a roundish face, piercing eyes, a hooked nose and thin lips, his well-oiled hair was flattened against his scalp and parted on one side. I could tell that this wasn't going to be a pleasant encounter.

Seemed that there was no defence. I had thrown the plimsoll that had hit the boy.

"Is that not a fact Smith?"

"Yes but...."

There were no 'buts'. Apparently, if things were as I claimed - they threw it first - then I should have reported them to a member of staff. A 'snitch' a 'nark' a 'tell-tale' - that would have made me very popular with the other kids and what, I wondered would any teacher make of a lad that says

"Please sir, Johnny Snotball threw a plimsoll at me"

Cringing little wimp methinks. This sort of thinking prevails to this day - retaliation is severely frowned upon. Nevertheless, it remains an instinctive human response. It is natural to want to act in one's own defence. It is my opinion that such a reaction is but a manifestation of the 'fight or flight' response - we choose whichever course of action is deemed most likely to protect and preserve our wellbeing.

Even if I could have articulated such profound (for an eleven-year old) thoughts at the time I fear the outcome would have been the same. Guilty as charged - it was the numbers game, there were three of them and one of me and they corroborated each other's version. Punishment was to be summary - six of the best. If ever there was a misnomer, six of the best would be it, the best it most emphatically was not. What it was, was six strokes the of a cane across the palm of the hand - three to each hand. The cane was long and thin so that it swished through the air on the downward stroke causing great pain. The victim is expected to extend each hand in turn so that the enforcer may inflict maximum impact, in tacit acceptance. Well, I couldn't prevent the, punishment but I could deny satisfaction - I wasn't going to be a cry baby. I took each of the strokes without flinching or even batting any eyelid. Now here's the interesting part: I do believe that I earned Statham's respect for the way I took that caning. After the last stroke, he looked me in the eye and simply said " Go" and he said it quietly. I nodded and walked away.

I suppose it could have been worse - the public-school version of caning the backside sounds altogether more uncomfortable - and humiliating. Schools were allowed by Common Law to use corporal punishment to maintain order. The view was that staff were acting as surrogate parents for the duration of the child's stay at school. In other words, had the child been at home, parents would have probably done the same thing. Remember Sammy the belt? Some teachers in my experience emulated parents in other ways - like hurling blackboard cleaners at offending pupils. These were about six inches long and an inch and a half wide and had a wooden base. They were guaranteed to get attention should one be unfortunate enough to be on the receiving end. Disturb a teacher in mid-scribe on the blackboard and the missile heading in your direction could be the chalk. Some parents of my acquaintance were handy in the throwing department - reckoned it saved walking and talking.

Corporal punishment in all schools that received any degree of state funding was banned in 1987. Coincidence or otherwise this is about the period that teachers began to lose the initiative in classroom control. At the same time that teachers were losing the right to discipline, growing liberalism was telling everyone of their rights, so far so sound but the message was incomplete, there was no reference to responsibility. Claiming one's rights demands acceptance of the other, responsibility. Maybe they could have learned something from the Poles. Poland banned corporal punishment in schools more than two-hundred years ago, in 1793 and I don't think that Polish schools have become havens for anarchists.

I said at the start of this little anecdote that it was a pivotal moment. It was indeed, and in two important ways. First off, taking the issue to those three bullies (for that's what they really were) spread amongst the first-year pupils and the notion that I wasn't easily scared was born. That had an interesting consequence; there were those that thought better of chancing their arm against me and there were those that saw me as a challenge, someone to be brought down and many tried. The second way in which the experience had an influence was my realising that by not letting anyone see that they had caused me distress I could retain my self-respect and, where appropriate, deny any assailant satisfaction. I became well practised at keeping a straight face. Now. Statham wasn't a bully - he was simply a man doing a job, maintaining order in the time-honoured way. The three lads were bullies. Bullies need to sense, to see, the fear they think they cause - they feed off it, deny them that and you're on the way to beating them.

It's often argued that bullies are cowards, that's too simplistic and not always the case. Many are repressed and can only discharge their anger at the more vulnerable. It isn't the fight that they want, it's the venting of pent up feelings and they won't get that pitching against someone who's likely to give a good account of themselves. In those circumstances, the likely outcome will be increased resentment. Domineering adults, particularly parents, are often the cause of the development of bullying traits. Conversely there are those kids that get no discipline at all, they're allowed to have their own way - they're spoilt. When they don't get their own way, they lash out at the most vulnerable. The lasting solution is to teach us all respect - respect for our fellows and for ourselves. Such lessons begin in the home and should be expanded into the wider social spectrum at school. The one thing bullies do not have is self-respect and if one doesn't have respect for oneself it's difficult to have it for others.

*****

The school has a surprising number of budding fight promoters. These were boys who would busy themselves carrying messages like

"So, and so wants a fight with you" or "do you fancy a fight with so and so?"

The unwary fell for this by saying things such as

"Tell him I'll fight him any time" or "I'll fight anybody".

The match-maker would then scurry off to relay the response to an unsuspecting opponent. "so, and so says he'll fight you any time" Wouldn't take too many messages before the intended opponents were wound up to the point of having a scrap. And our beloved promoter? He'd have a ringside view. They weren't hard to find - all one had to do was to ask one simple question.

"How many fights have you had?"

The honest answer was always - none. They liked watching other kids knocking seven bells out of each other but had no stomach for the pastime themselves - they might get hurt. You might think then, that in answer to the simple question they could just lie and say "hundreds". "In that case, they would be told

" You go and fight him - one more won't make any difference".

I was propositioned by these guys on countless occasions. Truly, I never fell for it - I didn't like fighting, certainly not for the fun of it, but I'd stand my corner in self-defence anytime against anybody. Many times, I was accosted by kids who had taken the 'promoter's' bait. I always tried to walk away but eventually the idiot would either push and shove or, worse, throw a punch - now it was self-defence and I would nail him. I can't remember how many fights I had at school, but it was a lot and I never lost one. In all truth, I tell you this, I never started a fight, but I finished many. Don't run away with the idea that I was some sort of gladiator - I won for two good reasons. One - I was a natural southpaw - I lead with my right hand. That made me appear to stand sideways to my opponents making it harder to hit me where it might count. Every kid I came up against led with his left hand - the classic style. Surely, they were standing sideways to me so how was being southpaw an advantage? - you ask. Simple - they all stood that way, I got used to them - they never got used to me. Two - the second reason - I would never ever give up; I hadn't started the fight, but I was going to finish it - I was simply downright obstinate. Instinctively too, I knew that the day I lost a fight would be the day the bullies would take over. My life at school would have become unbearable.

A few pages could be filled with tales of my boyhood scraps but that would focus undue attention on but a small part of my life at school. That said I will indulge just a few such tales. There was the occasion when I was walking along the school corridor to find that suddenly the way ahead was blocked by three grinning yobs who had decided that "you aint going past". They then proceeded to tell me what they thought of me and my kind using compost language. There was a big lad, in the middle he was doing all the talking, he was flanked by two minions who repeated his utterances such as parrots might. Apparently, they were going to teach me a lesson and put me in my place. The gang-master made his move, in a split-second I responded, we lunged at each other; the other two were just idiots but the big fellow - he was trouble. My advance took him by surprise, maybe I was expected to turn and run, anyway whatever went through his version of a mind caused him to suddenly stop and then take half a step backwards. I literally ran into him; he lost his balance and fell backwards - I helped him on his way by tipping him over the wall that separated the corridor from the playground. The playground was a concrete affair and lay several feet below the level of the corridor - hence the wall. My would-be assailant looked decidedly scared as he went over, doubtless anticipating the long fall and possible injury. However, he couldn't see what I could see - over his shoulder I saw that we were directly opposite the huge heap of coking coal used to fuel the school's central heating, it was banked high up the wall. I dropped him in that heap.

There are varying types of coke - coking coal is essentially coal that has been baked to remove most of its undesirable impurities. Once coked the coal becomes hard, grey and porous but it comes in small pieces rather than great lumps more commonly found with coal. As a matter of interest, the idea of making coke goes as far back as the 16th century but came to the fore in 1709 when Abraham Darby used it in the manufacture of cast iron. I digress - the pieces were small, light and airy, most unlikely to prove injurious to anyone falling on them. I would have gladly explained all of this to the descending bully but, one; I didn't know it then and two; I strongly suspect that it would have been of little interest to him, particularly during his descent. My intended tormentor was far too preoccupied howling like a banshee (according to Irish legend, a fairy woman who wails when someone is about to die - very apposite) as he landed in a most undignified fashion and struggled to extract himself. Pride and reputation severely dented along with his desire to do yours truly harm, he slunk away. As for his cronies - they ran off to tell a prefect of my dastardly deed.

Prefects were 4th year pupils proposed and elected by their peers and were supposed to act as a liaison between pupils and staff. They could report kids who had done wrong to the teaching staff who would then take appropriate action. Apparently, I had thrown a boy over the wall onto the playground for no reason - the prefect had two witnesses. Guilty as charged and six more of the best from Mr Statham. Didn't I realise what might have happened had the poor boy not landed in the coke? I protested that I knew it was there and that's why I 'turfed' him over and anyway, he started it. I got a caution as to the folly of being insolent. It didn't occur to me until much later, Statham parked his car next to the coke. The thought of my adversary landing on his meticulously maintained pinkish/reddish Standard 8 two-door saloon must surely have crossed his mind. That boy never bothered me again and the 'witnesses' gave me a very wide berth.

*****

As I've noted, I fought in self-defence - never for the joy of fighting but I did once get caught up in that nonsense. True to animal instinct it mattered to many boys at school who was the best fighter; once established said boy would become the 'cock of the school'. He didn't always have to fight for the honour, sometimes a mere physical presence would suffice. Such was the case at the start of my time at Short Heath Secondary Modern. The acknowledged cock of the school was a very big, strong lad: he was also rather benign - even affable and to the best of knowledge never had a fight with anyone. It was assumed that his mere physical presence warranted the crown. Those wretched fight promoters did attempt to match me with that guy - didn't work because we sort of got along, friends. But, when he left school, a contender for his replacement was put forward - and so was I. We weren't eleven-year old kids now - we were fourth year fourteen/fifteen- year olds - much bigger and stronger. The not too cunning plan was that the two of us would fight to settle who was top dog. I wanted nothing to do with such a gratuitous gesture, but the other lad was a little keener, and he accosted me one afternoon. He said that there were some who were saying that I was cock of the school, but he thought that he was, so we had best sort it out. To that end he struck a pose in front of me and flung a couple of punches which I dodged. The futility of such a fight made me cross and his attempts to hit me only aggravated the situation. I responded in the only way I knew how at the time and I didn't miss, I knocked him to the ground a couple of times. He seemed to get bored with having to get up only to be knocked down again, so he just gave up and said, "you can win" and just like that I became cock of the school. Curious to report, the fights dried up about then - at school anyway.

Pugilism wasn't altogether crude and vulgar. There were unspoken, unwritten rules - never hit an opponent when their back was turned; never hit an opponent when they went down; never kick an opponent under any circumstance and never, never use a weapon of any description. There was a moral code to our fighting. Sadly, it has all become nasty and vicious - devoid of morality. There was honour in our winning, now there's just winning. We didn't know it at the time but our conduct in fighting was following the so-called Marquis of Queensbury Rules. How historical reporting does distort - the rules were written by John Graham Chambers in 1865 and were to apply to boxing - it wasn't enough to win one had to do so by observing rules of conduct. John Douglas, the Marquis of Queensbury, was a keen boxing fan and merely endorsed the rules but that was enough for him get the credit.

There was one incident not covered by Queensbury Rules - they assumed that no male would ever hit a female. Girls were considered the weaker and fairer sex; not at all suited to fisticuffs. I had five sisters, so I knew well how annoying girls could be. The incident I am about to report involved a girl to whom the normal courtesies did not apply. She went far beyond annoying. She was related to the family that ran the famous chippie at the end of our road. Apparently, she didn't like me or my family - she described us all as 'scum'. A strong opinion for someone I didn't think any of us had ever met much less interacted with but that's the way of prejudice. She began by name calling and when that got no response resorted to poking and slapping - she even spat, disgusting little creature. Her slaps got harder and were accompanied by cries of "you can't hit a girl". I can - and I did, and she landed in a shocked heap on the floor.

I was neither proud nor ashamed of hitting her. She got what she deserved. What was interesting is, whilst I might well have expected the powers that be to descend on me in some measure- after all, fighting was frowned upon but boys hitting girls was unheard of, nothing happened. There was no summons to the Headmaster's study and no six of the best. The simple reason for my escape was that nobody reported the incident despite it happening in full view of several pupils. I gathered later that the consensus was that she asked for it; that she went too far in her abuse and provocation. I'd do it again in self-defence, turning the other cheek just gives the bully another target. But I've long since learned that there are other, more subtle ways of putting offenders in their place - and they're more satisfying because they endure. I could, of course, now seek shelter behind the PC propaganda on gender equality.

Fighting wasn't always inevitable. Sometimes more subtle ways of dealing with bullies was more lasting and rewarding. In my fourth, and final year at school I recall an incident involving some second-year boys and a fourth-year bully. He was demanding that they share their sweets with him and they, not unreasonably, didn't see why they should - at least until he threatened them. Now it so happened that I had about my person a roll of sherbet looking sweeties - not unlike the old 'fizzers'. They were not sweets - dear me no, they were laxatives removed from home for the benefit of a certain unpleasant individual - him - the bully. I had seen him at work in the past and I thought he might benefit from learning a lesson. I invited him to try some, he took about four. The prescribed dosage was one every four hours. Bully boy missed the whole of the afternoon lessons, he was glued to the toilet bowl. I suspect that he lost a lot of weight that day and what he wasn't going to do to yours truly. It was all talk, he knew well that I'd stand up to him. I was cock of the school, he didn't bother those boys again.

I must not leave you, dear reader, with the impression that me and mine were vilified by every kid at the school for that was not the case. Indeed, the villains were in the minority but here's the thing - you remember the ones that hit you - not the ones that didn't. Most of the time most of us kids rubbed along okay. There were some good sorts too - they may have been better off but they didn't flaunt, and they didn't put the less fortunate down. What was interesting about those that did was that they were our kind - working class. So much nonsense is propagated about class, particularly by those seeking an advantage from their posturing, rather than any lasting reform. They have it that the so- called working classes share a common bond, that they reject the idea of a superior ruling class - we are all equal. All I will say here is that it was the off-springs of many of this enlightened working class that would have us Smiths as inferiors - some equality. As the Russians found under communism it is that some are more equal than others. Haven't heard of a social order yet that didn't establish a hierarchy of some kind. Consider this. *'They call me a tyrant.......one arrives at a tyrant's throne by the help of scoundrels.......what factions do I belong to? You yourselves. What is that faction, which, since the Revolution began, has crushed the factions, and swept away hireling traitors? It is you, the people, it is the principles of the Revolution'*

Maximillien Francoise Marie Isidore de Robespierre.

Robespierre was leader of the French Revolution (1758). A tyrant who sought to rid the land of tyranny – by tyranny, how ironic. That bit of history was repeated by the Russians in 1917.

*****

School wasn't altogether heavy going, there were some fun times. I recall the food fight that ended the Christmas celebrations at the end of year three. We were housed in the science laboratory for our feast of sandwiches, cake, jelly and blancmange. We gorged fit to burst and when we could eat no more we surveyed the left-overs. I was for taking as much home as I could sneak out and whilst I was trying to come up with a plan a slice of fruit cake slammed against the door inches from my head. Was history about to repeat itself? I remembered the plimsoll affair. But no - my 'assailant' was hooting with laughter and that's why he took his eye off the ball so to speak and that, in turn, is why he got hit in the face with a sandwich that had been dipped in blancmange. Mayhem ensued, missiles made of food skimmed through the air. Enter one not-to-impressed member of staff. Exit some very sheepish boys but only after we had cleaned up. I did manage to find some un-launched cake to take home.

Old newspaper was the preferred toilet paper of the day for many at home, but schools took a more sanitary line. They provided proper toilet paper, not that anyone would guess because there was rarely any to be found where it was most needed. I had hatched a plan to remedy that shortcoming and at the same time teach a rather unpleasant youth a lesson. He'd spent several weeks making snide remarks aimed at me and within my earshot. I knew that if I challenged him he would simply deny that what he had said was anything to do with me and I couldn't prove otherwise. He was, he thought, being very clever.

My father frequently suffered with pain in the lumber region. One of the many medications he tried in efforts to relieve discomfort was a product called Thermogene Wadding. It was a pinkish cotton wool like material that had been impregnated with a pain-relieving ointment and the idea was that it should be taped over the affected area in order that it's soothing properties could be released to ease the pain. There were several such ointments on the market and they all shared one common characteristic - they used heat to draw the pain out. They burned – Thermogene Wadding burned.

Lest you be thinking that I've suddenly lost the plot allow me to connect the school's lack of toilet paper with my father's choice of medication. I took some Thermogene Wadding to school. I waited for my intended victim to make a visit to the toilet. I had already removed the toilet paper, I followed him in, discreetly. Sure enough, up went the plaintiff cry

"There's no ****** toilet paper".

" Don't worry" says I, "I've got something that will do the job." I passed the wadding under the cubicle door.

"It's pink and it stinks - I'm not using that".

Such ingratitude!

"So, what" says I," it will do the job and anyway, there's nothing else."

The wadding was then put to a use for which it was never intended. There was a moment of relief and then, an anguished cry

"My **** is burning".

It burned for the rest of the day - and beyond I presume, I didn't follow him home. We were not in the same class, but I have it on authority that my victim experienced difficulty in settling in his seat at every lesson. I like to think that I invented bum-burn long before vindaloo curry hit the streets.

Chapter 9

SCHOOLDAYS – BEST DAYS OF YOUR LIFE – REALLY?

Overall, the staff at the school were decent enough. They did a difficult job with an oft trying and reluctant, albeit, captive audience. Discipline was quite good, due in no small part to the ever-present threat of being sent to the Headmaster. Mr Statham ran the school with an iron fist; when he wasn't teaching, he prowled the corridors, monitoring each and every class and I suspect that it wasn't only the kids he was watching. He was the epitome of firm and fair, likely he had his favourites but it's certain they were chosen based on their work ethic. He certainly had no time for prima donnas.

'Jack' Gee taught history and had problems pronouncing the word 'meteorological' - he was what would be called today 'a safe pair of hands'. J R Morgan was a rugby playing teacher of English and music. The latter came as a surprise; he was asked to cover one lesson for the regular teacher and what a revelation. He coaxed a disinterested group of 30 mixed gender early teens to sing together. I was inspired by his conducting of us singing the Hallelujah chorus from Handel's Messiah in descant. I've loved that music ever since. 'Zac' Howarth was a replacement science teacher. A diminutive man he had little control of his classes which often descended into farce. His only sanction was the school's points system. The customary practice was to award one point for commendable work whilst poor work or bad behaviour would cause the loss of a point. Extremes in either direction could warrant two points but that was rare. Zac exceeded those standards by a country mile; as the class slipped further and further out of his control he would raise the points lost, six being his record. Of course, by then the challenge was to see how far he would go so kids played him up deliberately to lose points and see if they could get him to set another record.

I scored a maximum (six) during one lesson when an experiment went wrong. The lesson was about electro-magnetism or something similar. I don't think I was fully engaged but I do remember that iron filings figured on the menu. To get myself more involved in the proceedings I decided to run a little experiment of my own. I wanted to learn of the outcome following iron filings being dropped down the back of a fellow student. To preserve objectivity my chosen subject was not to be made aware of the test. I leaned across the table (science laboratories didn't have desks) and carefully deposited the iron filings down the back of the lad immediately in front of me. Turns out I chosen a bad subject. Any decent kid would have wriggled and scratched a bit maybe and threatened me with "you wait till playtime" but that wasn't he - the one I chose. He was a good-looking lad (one reason to dislike him), always very well turned out (and that's another) and very popular with the girls (a hat trick). He was also a bit - no, a lot - of a show-off. In a huge over-the-top response, he did a hand stand right there in the middle of the laboratory to shake out the offending material. Zac could hardly miss the acrobatics. Naturally curious, he asked what was going on and my experimental subject, creep that he was, told him - "Smith's put iron filings down my back sir"

Under other circumstances I might have gone for denial but apparently, the look on my face was enough to condemn me - guilty as charged. "Lose two points" said Zac. I argued that I was conducting an experiment - "Lose another two points". I muttered some threat to the circus act "And you can lose another two points". That was six - I needed two more for the record. I tried, oh I did try but Zac wouldn't budge past six. Turns out that he would have to explain to the Headmaster what had happened to warrant such draconian punishment, and this would be as good as admitting that the class was a little out of control - not a good testimonial to effective teaching. I reckon that some of the staff at least, were as afraid of Mr Statham as many of us kids. Many moons later, I fell foul of Zac again, (can't remember what for - probably nothing really) but here's the interesting bit - he didn't order me to lose points, instead he gave me lines, that exercise whereby the offender gets to write the same line out x number of times. 'I must not fool about in the science class' - to be written 1,000 times!! Recall that I said that I sometimes behaved a little differently to the rest? This quirky characteristic surfaced again here. Zac got his 1,000 lines alright - but my version which was to write the line at the top of each page and simply put the mark signifying ditto (") all the way down the rest of each page. I only wrote out the sentence in full four times. I call that original thinking - Zac called it dumb insolence. Mr Statham agreed with him - there was no trial, just summary punishment, six of the best.

Zac and I had a thing going now - each time he felt the need to punish yours truly (usually for no good reason of course) he would come up with a novel punishment. Once he chose a hymn entirely at random, it wasn't a familiar one and it had umpteen verses - no chance, too boring - hand held out at the ready. On another occasion, he ordered me to learn the 17 times table and report back to him after school to recite. No need to wait says I - and I did it there and then. He wasn't to know that I was more than handy with numbers, mental arithmetic especially, that left him speechless and got me off the hook. Well - one can't let authority win all the time.

I liked Zac really, he was decent guy, but he just couldn't control hormone raging adolescents. I did not like Mr Davis, teacher of, amongst other subjects, religious education. He taught the subject with an air of smug superiority but no real conviction. I reckon he belonged to that band of adults that saw religion as a means of maintaining the social order, even a tool of suppression. Anyone stepping out of line was quickly stamped upon - metaphorically. Davis didn't like me either, he was a professional middle-class teacher, we were largely working -class kids. Those that aspired to better things and looked the part he encouraged. I represented the ragamuffin also-rans who would never amount to anything remotely important. He never missed an opportunity to try and humiliate and embarrass me in class. He once referred to the beggars in Jesus' time as, 'Garbed in rags, unkempt and unclean'

"You'd be at home with them wouldn't you Smith?"

As a child in secondary school in the mid 1950's there was nothing to be done other than to ignore such taunts, at least as best as one could. The worst part of that was that it gave incentive and impetus to some of the kids, albeit a minority, to do the same. But my reputation with my hands did much to deter direct confrontation with fellow pupils. It cut no ice with the teaching staff and anyway, one could hardly fight teachers. Nevertheless, that's very nearly what happened one dark day. Davis asked me a question to which I didn't know the answer. "Not listening were you boy?". I was sitting on the front row and he came and stood right in front of me and continued his haranguing and then, without warning delivered the hardest slap across the face I've ever had. It stung like crazy and hurt like hell. As I got over the shock I was consumed with rage. I jumped to my feet sending my chair clattering to the floor, the desk was shunted forward a foot or more. The class fell silent - they were as stunned as I had been. With fists clenched like they had never been clenched before I said

"'Do that again"

By now he'd backed away, I think with hindsight he realised that he'd gone too far. He made no effort to come forward which was just as well because I knew; he knew; the whole class knew - had he done so I would have hit him. The silver lining in this dark cloud was that Davis never ever bothered me again.

That was the first time I had been literally slapped by a teacher, plenty of cuffs around the back of the head but administered with no real force. It was to happen a second time, at the hands (great pun) of one Miss Bishop. She was a teacher with whom boys had not much contact, her teaching role was to instruct girls in the noble arts of knitting, sewing and embroidery, very un-manly pastimes. Our scheduled teacher was indisposed for some reason and Bishop was the stand-in. There was no lesson plan, she was making it up as she went along - what else could she do at short notice? For whatever reason, my mind wasn't on whatever she was going on about - teachers call this 'not paying attention' - a point loser for sure. Not on this occasion; I was brought back to the land of the living abruptly and dramatically by a stinging slap to the side of the face. No warning, no words - just the slap. Not as hard as Davis but it got a like response. Shocked and hurt I jumped to my feet, my hand on the desk lid. Bishop simply retreated to her position at the front of the class. It was her turn to be startled by my reaction. I recall lifting the desk lid and then slamming it down with one of heck of a bang. I stared venomously at her; had she been within reach I would likely have lashed out.

It wasn't long after this event that I had that run-in with the mouthy girl who did get her come-uppance. After Davis and Bishop, it was a case of third time unlucky. Given that I had no track record with Bishop it was hard to understand why I had been punished in such a way. There were others in the class equally guilty of drifting off - why was I singled out to be used as the example? Turned out to be fairly obvious - sisters; Bishop taught girls, I had two sisters at the school at the time in the lower years. The Smiths didn't measure up to her tastes and standards. She'd had to put up with the girls and now here she was faced with one of the scruffy brothers, proved too much of a temptation. She never spoke to me again whilst I made a point of glaring at her in dumb insolence whenever I passed her in the corridors. As the lesson ended and we exited the classroom I muttered, rather loudly, to a companion "Easy to see why she's a Miss". She heard me but didn't rise to the bait. She would have been about fortyish at the time, unmarried - she was then, a spinster - on the shelf. That status carried stigma then. Say what I said today, and I'd be sentenced to re-education classes (that's pc-speak for brain-washing).

*****

Derek Bolton wasn't much of a PT teacher in that he didn't exert himself, preferring instead to watch us kids suffer. That said we were happy enough most of the time playing games; football, cricket, rugby, hockey but jumping up and down making like stars and bending to touch one's toes was more of a chore than exercise. Bolton was into belittling the less able and the less fortunate. I fell into the latter category: he once asked everyone to remove their pumps (plimsolls) and perform in stocking feet. I had holes in my socks, my mother had neither the time nor the resources for regular darning, clothes got mended as and when. Our illustrious PT teacher seized on the spectacle of my holed socks to say

"I didn't say barefoot Smith" and then rejoiced in his own humour.

I was in the third year then and my reputation had been made so not all the other kids joined in the fun - but there will always be the few. On another occasion, we were playing cricket, and everyone was to get a chance to bowl. To encourage greater accuracy Bolton removed the bails and put a two shilling (ten pence) on the middle stump. The deal was that anyone who could knock it off would get to pocket the money. My turn to bowl comes along; he mocked that he could put a whole bag of two- shilling pieces on the stumps and his money would be safe because look who's bowling next. His taunting made me angry and I ran like a demon and hurled the ball with all the force that I could muster in the general direction of the opposite wicket. The poor batsman flailed like an out of control windmill, by sheer chance the ball clipped the bat and took off at a tangent. The money was safe alright but the window the ball went through was not. I cared not - it shut him up. Bolton would have had to explain the broken window – happy happy days.

In my third-year Bolton got married and left Short Heath Secondary Modern to take up a post elsewhere. I mourned his passing like the devil mourns the loss of Holy Water. His replacement was a Mr Slack, an ex-RAF PT instructor. He was as different to Bolton as chalk is to cheese. Whatever he asked us to do he did first - several times. Three to four-mile cross country runs had always figured in our programme. The point of this exercise eluded most of us, running after a football, a bus, a girl (a girl?) and the likes had point and purpose - a football so you can kick it; a bus so you can get on it; a girl - no idea! But running away from somewhere so that you could run back there seemed like an exercise dreamt up by a committee - spend a heap of time and energy running in a great circle and finishing back where you started. We would run out of the school gate, down the lane and into the coppice and alongside the canal until we came to Wood Lane where we would veer left and head on back to school. That was the prescribed route: those of us lacking the incentive for such an arduous task would simply run alongside the canal until we were out of sight of the school and the cut a diagonal path across the coppice to the road leading to the school gates. That knocked about a mile and a half of the journey. A steady walk would see us join up with the worthier souls who had run the course and we would all enter the school together.

It had been easy to fool Bolton because he only ever came as far as the school gate to see us off, he would simply await our return. Unfortunately for us slackers (clever pun coming), Slack was made of sterner stuff. He not only ran the whole course with us but backtracked countless times to gee up the backmarkers. He must have run at least twice the distance as us, he later enlightened us that in the RAF, twelve -mile runs were the norm. On my first outing under this new and worrying regime I had no choice other than to run the course. When we got back to school Slack spoke in admiration of my efforts, apparently, I had come in in third place, along with the swots (first and second - the same pair, they never took liberties) he said that he would recommend me for the inter-school's cross country run later in the year. I knew nothing about this event, but I figured it was a whole lot longer than our three to four miles. If ever I needed a cunning plan I needed one now - to get out of this race. Welcome centre stage - a twisted ankle - okay, it wasn't really twisted but for all his guile Slack was no doctor. A suitably penned note from parents and an exaggerated limp did the trick.

On those days when the weather deemed it unwise or unsafe to venture out PT was conducted in the hall. Not much fun as few of us were into gymnastics and anyway, we had very little in the way of equipment. There was horse, a pommel, a vaulting box and miscellaneous benches. Good old Slacky tried to make these sessions challenging and enjoyable. He did this by having us arrange all the apparatus in a single line going all around the perimeter of the hall. Then he set us off one by one, the exercise was to use each piece of equipment as intended - vault the box, walk the bench and so on - and get all the way round without falling off anything and touching the floor. Note to teachers, make learning fun and kids will do (almost) anything.

Art was taught by 'Dirty Dick' Webster. It was rumoured that he earned his nickname on the back of some nefarious conduct with the ladies. That's the thing with rumours - when they stick they stick forever and nobody troubles about evidence. I do know this, he was a mean man to anyone he didn't like, and he didn't like me. On dry summer days, his lessons would transfer to the coppice where we would be encouraged to draw trees. I was rubbish at the task. What I saw with my eyes got lost in the transfer to my hands because of permanent roadwork's in the neural highways. On the other hand, given what passes for art now I'm inclined to the view that my creations were surreal interpretations and properly assessed they may be possessing considerable artistic merit. Alas I remain thwarted by ignorance. The art-room boasted a potter's wheel upon which, and under severe cajoling I produced a pot - genre ill-determined. Webster was not impressed and consigned my effort to the tip. One day, in the millennia to come, some young aspiring, ambitious archaeologist will be excavating a site where ye old Short Heath Secondary Modern school is said to have been. The plot has long stood as an abandoned brown site but soon it will house the new droid manufacturing station. He or she will suddenly yell out "I've found a pot". The team will all gather round excitedly and debate the likely uses of my pot - for it will be my pot. Not fit for drinking from, unsuitable for storage - "aha" blurts one bright spark "they would use this under the bed at night to pass their waste". The learned professor would frown intelligently, as they do, "In that case it's what they called a piss pot". One of the underlings, eager to impress would chime "I say, isn't there an ancient tale about a family that tried to put out a fire with the contents of a piss pot?"

Webster was late for a lesson on one occasion and some of us got a little bored. To pass the time productively and bearing in mind that this was an art room with many of the essential accessories, pots of paint; brushes and cleaning rages, we decided to get creative. The concept was modern art, splash paint around in random fashion and let the experts cluck in-depth interpretations in the customary meaningless jargon. So, that's splashing around sorted; next where to splash and who is to do the splashing. Answers: anywhere and everywhere and four of us frustrated Picassos. Modus operandi? Dip rags in paint and hurl them at each other - art should be liberating. One of the 'artists' got over-excited and let go of a paint- soaked rag that some amazing how found itself attached to the ceiling and refused to come down. I hate being sexist (I don't really) but the guilty chucker was a girl - I say no more. Our look-out gave us the pre-arranged coded signal "Dirty Dick's on his way". There was much scurrying about, mopping, scrubbing and cleaning and generally restoring of order but the rag on the ceiling continued to defy gravity. That is, until Webster entered the room and then, as if on cue, rag fell to the ground. He couldn't miss it and when he looked up he couldn't miss the great red splodge on the ceiling.

Sensing that this was the mere tip of the proverbial iceberg his eyes roamed the rest of the room taking in every detail. We were rumbled - he was livid. His face went the colour that was a perfect match for our unintentional redecoration.

"Who is responsible for this?" he thundered.

There was no movement - no sound and it would have stayed that way had he not threatened to keep the whole class in detention. Only one thing to do - own up. I did, and the other three followed my lead.

"Smith - I might have guessed that you'd be involved"

My being involved made his day. He could (and did) ridicule my work any time but it was never grounds for punishment - at least not the sort he had in mind. It was to be the familiar six of the best. Webster was, to my knowledge, the only staff member to carry out his own corporal punishment, the others sent the miscreant to the

Headmaster. There we were - the four musketeers, lined up in front of the class. This was to be a public flogging. He placed me at number four. In truth, I was more than a little blasé - just get it over with. But Webster wanted more than his pound of flesh, before delivering the blows he demanded that each of us admitted that we were 'a stupid fool'.

"Please sir, I'm a stupid fool". He intended to humiliate us in the process. Villain number one said it then blubbed even before the cane landed - he howled after each stroke. The other two cried quietly hoping no one would notice. Then it was my turn; Webster taunted me

"The ringleader no doubt. You're useless as well as stupid. What are you?"

I said nothing.

"I said - what are you?"

Nothing. This went on for two or three minutes, it seemed much longer. Realising that I wasn't going to speak it was hands out time. Statham would hurt when he caned but it was always controlled. Webster caned me in an uncontrolled rage and it hurt like never before. He obviously wanted a reaction - he got nothing. I'd had almost four years of attempted bullying and fighting my corner and the one thing I had always denied any adversary was the satisfaction of seeing me rattled. My reasoning was that I should not let them see that they were getting at me, I would deny them that. I gritted my teeth and kept my face as straight as I knew how. Webster got to give the me the cane, I gave him nothing and that made him even madder. The best part was that he'd chosen and delivered the punishment, he couldn't give more than six strokes of the cane, I don't know why but more wasn't allowed. He couldn't admonish me in any other way - he'd made his choice. For the record, I have no complaint about being punished for what I had done - it was as the saying goes, a fair cop. The guilty should not cry foul when their misdeeds catch up with them. It was the personal spite that I railed against.

*****

Round is the word that best describes Mrs Bailey, teacher of music. She was round of body of head and of eyes. In retrospect, I must admire her devotion to duty for she so very valiantly persevered in her attempts to teach a most disinterested class (classes? - I doubt she fared any better with the rest of the school). It was a misnomer to call the lesson 'music' for there was not a musical instrument to be found – that is discounting the piano which was for her exclusive use. Better to call them singing lessons for that's what they were, and that explains why they were so unpopular. These were not the day of talent shows and Simon Cowell, nary one of us had the slightest interest in learning how to sing, certainly not quaint old folk songs and polite versions of sundry shanties. Pop singers of the day were largely crooners – Frank Sinatra style. Oh, for a crystal ball, within a few years Rock 'n Roll exploded on an unsuspecting world and all of a very sudden it seemed every teenage boy wanted an electric guitar. Couldn't sing a note? Tone deaf? No matter, they had gear that could amplify the voice, the louder the better. Talent was sacrificed on the altar of commercialism.

One fine day, I did deliver unto Mrs Bailey a shock which I kind of hoped would help her see me in a different light. Big brother was, at the time, serving in the army and was based in Germany, part of the British Army on the Rhine (BAOR). Every Sunday lunchtime the BBC Light Programme broadcast Two-Way Family Favourites during which requests would be played for serving soldiers and their families. Mom wanted to have a piece of music played for brother. The piece she chose was called 'O Lovely Peace' apart from liking it she didn't know anything else about it and I was charged with making enquiries of Mrs Bailey. Having recovered from the shock she informed me that it was from the oratorio Judas Maccabeus by Handel. It had been written in honour of the Duke of Cumberland to celebrate his victory at the battle of Culloden - 16 April 1746). I relayed the message faithfully, the request was sent, and the music played. It's a beautiful piece of music – it remains a favourite.

*****

Our woodwork teacher was one Mr 'Soapy' Joe Hudson - Soapy after Hudson's soaps, a prominent manufacturer at the time. I don't think Soapy was a proper teacher like the rest, he didn't have a teaching qualification. His knowledge, skill and experience were his qualifications and none better. He only taught woodwork. He was a World War 1 veteran - the story went that he had been a victim of mustard gas and had lost a lung.

His was a workshop, not a classroom, as you would expect there were no desks, but work benches laid out in two rows that ran the length of the shop. At the front was a blackboard fixed to the wall, that at least was in keeping with the classrooms. Now there's another banned word - blackboard, out of respect to someone's/anyone's -well actually no one's in particular, perceived sensitivity, they must be called chalkboards. Our capacity to invent offence knows no bounds; they had been blackboards for decades and then along comes some intellectual terrorist who asserts that the term 'black' is derogatory to - er well black people. There's an anecdote doing the rounds that a barrister appearing at the Old Bailey asked the presiding judge to alter the description of the charge against his client; yes, you've guessed - the charge was blackmail. The judge is said not to have been impressed by this example of pc nonsense. All very academic now because they - blackboards/

chalkboards - have given way to whiteboards - now just a minute, isn't that...?

In Soapy's day it was a blackboard, not any blackboard but Soapy's blackboard. It was different to every other in the school because written across the length at the top were Soapy's golden rules. The chalk-work was impressive, every letter was evenly drawn, couldn't have been printed better. All in capital letters for greater emphasis and refreshed on a regular basis to keep them pristine. The snow- white lettering was neatly underlined in yellow. Anyone and everyone that entered this workshop was committed to abiding by these rules - non-negotiable.

Woodwork lessons were something of a paradox for me. I liked the smell and feel of wood, even liked working with it but liking didn't translate into ability - or skill. In short, it was far from my best subject. I started out with good intentions but rather like art, something got lost in the translation of what I could perceive and what I could achieve. Soapy was never impressed, even with my finest efforts. He chopped up some dolls house furniture I made because "I could drive a coach and horses round these mortise-and- tenon joints". For the purpose of administering summary judgement on sub-standard work, Soapy kept a small axe handy. He wielded it with relish on anything that offended his standards; he was the proverbial mad axe man. My ability to challenge him didn't end there. At the far end of the work-shop there was an old (ancient) treadle lathe; Soapy explained most carefully how this appliance should be operated. The piece of wood to be turned was fixed to the spindle and the treadle depressed to ensure a clockwise motion. If the treadle bar was raised and not depressed, the spindle turned in an anti-clockwise direction. Thus, the wood would turn with the chisel and likely snatch it out of the operator's hand: there was only one way it would go - in a high arc overhead. Anyone in close proximity had seconds in which to retreat to safety or get chiselled. Soapy always aimed to stay in close attendance to ensure such accidents didn't happen. But...as any sportsman will attest, we all take our eye off the ball occasionally. Soapy did when I was at the lathe. The chisel fully cleared two work benches before it crashed to the floor inches from some unfortunates, foot. I was impressed with the distance - I was also removed from the lathe.

*****

Usually we were allowed to take home our creations and some kids were justly proud of their efforts. Mine kept the fire going. Whilst us boys were woodworking the girls would be doing Domestic Science - cooking, they too were permitted to take their offerings home which was only right and proper since they had to provide their own ingredients. When my sisters joined the Smith procession to Short Heath Secondary Modern we often enjoyed the fruits of their culinary escapades. When they anxiously asked what, it was like we would answer.

"it was alright".

As the weaker sex, it was felt unwise to fill their heads with too much praise and they were sisters after all.

The induction of every new woodwork class began with a study of Soapy's golden rules. Inductees would stand by their allotted workbench as each rule was solemnly read out by the master himself and was accompanied by a meticulous detailing of the dangers said rules were designed to avert. They were Soapy's version of the Ten Commandments, (I'm sure there were more than ten). Over time we got used to them and familiarity weaved its customary web of contempt as they were frequently breached - out of Soapy's sight of course. Then comes the day that Soapy is late starting the lesson, he'd gone to his woodshed to replenish supplies for the task to be undertaken that day. He was late, and we were restless; agile minds were looking for a suitable distraction to pass the time. "Why don't we change them rules" offered some mischievous soul. "He won't notice until he comes to preach to the next lot of newbies" Excellent idea - now all we need is some volunteer (make that idiot) to bring about the recommended changes.

Yours truly was nominated and seconded for the role and in the face of such support I accepted. I took my stool to the blackboard and set to the work in hand. 'Tools must never be thrown but passed by hand' became 'Tools must be thrown and never passed by hand' 'Use the mallet when chiselling wood' became 'Use your head when chiselling wood ' - you get the idea. My classmates were very vocal, instructions and suggestions poured forth and some of them were rather naughty. In making the alterations I had to work slowly and carefully which demanded concentration at a level not ordinarily associated with fourteen-year old boys unless, of course, it was a crucial shot in a game of marbles. Marbles were important - lessons were not. Anyhow, so deeply engrossed was I in my work that the sudden silence failed to register. Not so the 4 x 3 x 1 (that's four feet - three inches - one inch) that made its presence felt on my backside. Apparently Soapy had stood watching me for a while before launching the strike on my person. He was not impressed with my efforts. I had to stay behind, it took over an hour and a half to restore order to Soapy's satisfaction. Next time I saw those rules they were once again done in his own not-so-fair hand. The blighter had rubbed off my lettering.

I liked old Soapy - he was a character; he praised reluctantly, ridiculed readily yet there was never any malice and believe it or not, I did learn much from him, not the least how to handle tools correctly. That I had failed to impress him was made clear when, after reviewing my latest offering, Soapy gave me my first career advice.

"You will likely get a job wheeling smoke out of a factory in a wheelbarrow - and you'll let some fall out"

The work that had led to this sage prediction was the making of a coffee table. It was to have four legs, staves at the top and bottom and a hexagonal top. What happened was that try as I most certainly did, the legs refused to conform to a uniform length - the table wobbled. So, I shortened first one and then another. The table got shorter and shorter and nearer and nearer to the floor. Soapy asked me if I was trying to make a rug. "No sir, it's a coffee table" says I. He looked at me over the top of his spectacles "If I put a cup of coffee on that table and if a fly fell into the coffee the poor insect would get seasick" and that's when he gave me the job reference. The coffee- table? It was dismantled and placed in the scrap box and I was left to ponder - smoke wouldn't be heavy - would it? Soapy retired at the end of that year and was replaced by a Mr Ditchfield - or Dishwater as he was re-christened. A humourless man who took his work far too seriously. Seriously enough to retrieve all the pieces of my ill-fated effort saying that "something could be made from this". I can hear Soapy's ghostly voice - "Firewood". I truly can't recall what happened to that would-be coffee table except that it didn't make it - it never became a coffee table.

Chapter 10

JUST GETTING BY – OR LATENT DISILLUSIONMENT?

I didn't do as well as I could/should have done at senior school. Several reasons may be conjured up in explanation; the culture shock after leaving friendly New Invention Junior school; bullies; intimidating staff or just plain old adolescence (that's an odd expression – think I'll leave it in). The latter is probably closest. At around eleven years of age the conscious mind really kicks in and starts its work in earnest; up to then all of life's experiences have taken a direct non-stop route to the unconscious. There they set about moulding the character - for better or otherwise. Early adolescence sees kids begin to make conscious decisions about what's happening drawing on the perceptions created by experience – 'I can't do this'; 'I'm no good at that'; 'I'm better than the others'. These seeming unbidden feelings rise to the surface and influence our every deed. There is this too; I was what has been labelled by some social scientists, a late developer. That put me at odds with many of my peers in certain respects, but I doubt I was alone in being so labelled. Anyway, I was in esteemed company, Winston Churchill was a late developer and he did rather well. I proffer this too - developing late means that one stays younger longer (the theory is good even if the logic is dodgy).

Whatever the reason, or reasons, I began my secondary education in the A stream - form 1A. I did not distinguish myself academically and in year two I was relegated to the B stream - form 2B. A year is a long time to a twelve-year old and probably because I was settling down in several respects, my results improved significantly. Nonetheless, the school was loth to promote me back to the A stream and

I moved on to form 3B in my pen-ultimate year. By now I was getting really switched on and the end of year results couldn't be denied - back to the A stream went I, ending my secondary education in form 4A and top of the form.

I performed above average in all the key subject - Mathematics; English; History; Geography; did well enough in Science and PT and even improved my grades in Art. I stood still in Woodwork; Music and Gardening weren't assessed. Maths was taught in the final year by none other than Mr Statham, he proved to be an exacting and demanding teacher - but a damn good one at that. I recall one lesson during which he had spent time explaining and demonstrating a mathematical formula. He then put us to the test by giving a question to work through. Whilst we all worked silently at our task Mr Statham walked up and down between the rows of desks pausing to look over the shoulder of each and every one of us. Many are the kids who have broken into a cold sweat at his presence - with good reason if they were staring at a blank page. I wasn't offering anything of the sort, I thought I knew what was required and was beavering away - Mr Statham spoke.

"You're going about this in a different way; you won't get the right answer, but I will be interested to see your conclusion" - and he beamed as he spoke.

He was right of course, I did get a different answer. So why the smile, the encouragement? I didn't get it right away - it was because I was working and thinking and seeking the answer in my own way. That's how knowledge advances, not by simple repetition. That was another example of me thinking and acting differently from the rest. Alas I can take no credit for this for it was not a calculated act, I was only doing what came naturally.

Our English teacher at this time was one Agnes (Aggie) Neal. Outside of school I guess she would have been called a middle-aged frump. She was no more than five feet tall, well rounded with a permanent unsmiling expression on her face. She wore her hair short and parted, not a solitary hair was out of place. We would take bets that it was a wig but that was never proved. I shall always remember her for her attitude to handwriting, it had to be " Nice and round and upright". She (rightly) presumed that if anything was written down the intention was that it could be read. She would surely faint if she could see my scribble now - sometimes even I can't read what I've written! She was a master of crowd control, never knew any kid play up in her lessons. Being late was a cardinal sin warranting a full explanation and apology. Two lads from my class were late for one lesson. We all knew why; they'd been mis-behaving with a new girl in the coppice and she had reported them to Statham. They were late because he was meting out punishment both verbal and physical. Aggie demanded to know what they had done to warrant Statham's intervention and make them late for her lesson. They couldn't tell her what they'd been doing with that poor girl; whether she guessed or not we couldn't tell but she really made those lads squirm. Us very worldly fourteen to fifteen -year olds knowledgably opined that dear old Aggie wouldn't have understood if they had told her. She was a middle-aged spinster, what on earth could she possibly know about er.... you know what.

The last lesson on a Friday afternoon was English Literature, or more precisely reading aloud. Class members took turns to read section of the chosen book. I loved that lesson, as always Aggie kept everyone quiet save for the reader. Some were good at reading others not so, many stumbled over pronunciation and the observing of punctuation. Not their fault of course, they - we - were there to learn but it did spoil the flow of the story. By this time, I was an avid reader of anything and everything that came to hand and I not only loved reading out loud, I was good at it - Aggie said so. The last book we read was Children of the

New Forest by Captain Frederik Marryat, set in the time of the English civil war. I loved that book, so I was thrilled recently to receive a gift from my lovely, wonderful daughter (she is - really), it was a book entitled The Forest by Edward Rutherfurd; the forest being the New Forest. Reading it revives those happy memories.

My introduction to gardening was a revelation - I enjoyed it. Gardening was introduced into secondary schools in the 19th century so that boys might learn how to grow vegetables and fruit to supplement the family diet. Mr Wright, our gardening teacher, kept a mixed patch. There were flowers, shrubs, trees, vegetables and bees! Yes - he kept bees and it's thanks to him that I lost any fear of these amazing insects. Towards the very end of my time at Short Heath Secondary Modern I was one of a small group, four in all, chosen - yes - me - chosen - to erect and glaze the latest addition to the school garden, a greenhouse. I was introduced to the art of bastard trenching and couldn't wait to get home to ask Mom if she knew what it meant. It's an ingenious and simple practice. Imagine, you have a large area of garden to fertilise (spread muck on and dig it in): mark the area out in squares - now dig the first square out to one spade's depth (called a spit), load the soil into a wheelbarrow and take it to the end of the plot. Here comes the clever bit - chuck the fertiliser into the hole you've created and turning to the next square dig that out just like the first but this time, throw the soil on top of the fertiliser in the first square and so on to the end of the plot. There is no apparent reason for the practice being called 'bastard trenching'. Everyone knows that the word bastard describes an illegitimate child - born out of wedlock - but a wider definition is 'not genuine' so I reckon bastard trenching wasn't genuine trenching - elementary my dear Watson (Sherlock Holmes never actually used those words). I could hardly wait to get home to demonstrate that I could use a naughty word without getting into trouble. "Mom - do you know what bastard trenching means?" "It means a clout and a bar of soap to wash your mouth out if you say that again". How was I to know that they called it double-digging? Nearly cost me my dinner. Mr Wright got me into trouble again (unintentionally I hope) with a little pearl of wisdom offered during one of his lessons. He said that there was only one thing worse than a man's pocket and that was a woman's handbag. Appears that women don't agree, at least not the ones to whom I've been foolhardy enough to quote this manly wisdom. You wouldn't get away with it now Wrightie - your utterance would go viral on social media, you'd be suspended from duty pending an enquiry and you would certainly be investigated by the thought police. Your assets would be checked for substance - 'outraged' doesn't sue anyone if there's no money to be had. The money's not important they say grandly (then give it to charity says I), it's the principal. Principals are great if one can afford them.

Year two gave me one of those enduring funny moments that continue to make us laugh years after the event. It happened during one of the morning assemblies. There weren't enough seats for all us kids, so the drill was that the fourth year had seats at the back of the hall and the rest of us sat cross-legged on the wooden floor. As usual Mr Statham was the master of ceremonies, so everyone was on best behaviour. He was delivering a stern message about some issue I don't recall - being on best behaviour didn't mean that we were always listening. He paused - for effect; it was still and quite - no movement, no sound. Then - it happened, a high-pitched whine; at first it was inaudible to most of the assembly, it steadily increased in volume and depth until it could be heard by one and all. A lad squatting one row in front of me and to my left, had farted. He tried hard not to and that's what prolonged the fart's life and caused the whine. Sitting cross-legged on the floor is not the best position from which to control a fart - quite the contrary. It built up to a crescendo amplified by the general stillness and quietness of the occasion. In fact, it seemed so loud, so powerful that one feared for the wooden floor -

splinters and all that. His desperate efforts to stifle the fart failed abysmally. Then came the smell, rancid about covers it. Now, whatever you do, don't laugh, smirk or smile - that would-be suicide. Bite the bottom lip and stare straight ahead - on no account look at the kid next to you, that would be fatal. Then the aroma gently wafted over, no doubt about it - the perpetrator was rotting on the inside. Not one member of staff moved a muscle and Mr Statham, after a longer than planned pause, simply carried on. The sophisticates amongst you might consider that I would have been better advised to use the term 'breaking wind' rather than fart. Sorry, breaking wind spoils the affect. Fart is one of those words that raises a laugh anytime anywhere - but not in lifts I'm told.

*****

Quite why the girls toddled off to study biology whilst us boys dealt with general science was never explained to us. Not that we cared, we were studying the internal combustion engine - motor cars and its common knowledge that girls know absolutely nothing about cars - they haven't got a head for mechanical things. That was the creed of the era. There is some proof still however; they don't watch Top Gear. Anyway, whatever biology was (we had no idea) it was almost certainly very girlie - and therefore, boring. At least until the day some of the girls let it slip that they had been learning about the 'reproductive system' apparently, that was teacher speak for sex - well it's what they told us. We were all between thirteen and fourteen years of age at this point and some amongst us were tuning in to the notion that girls could be rather interesting although specific reasons eluded us. This is the age at which boys (and probably girls I suppose - never asked any) pretend that they know all about sex and girls and boys and things.

So, it was that a cocktail of 'experience' and hormones provoked some of us lads into querying our exclusion from

sex - sorry biology - lessons. The argument was cogent –
surely, we had a right and a need to know about sex - sorry,
the reproductive system. Nobody asked us why we felt that
need; good job too because I seriously doubt that we could
have cobbled a decent answer between us. At this point I
should explain that the girl's biology teacher was female,
blonde and very attractive - Cheryl 'Cherry' Wilkins -about
thirty which would have been old for anyone else but for her
it was just right. It was said that many of the lads fantasised
about her - not me of course, late developer, remember. I
asked one of them if he did, "cor, not half" me - "so what do
you do?" him "you know" me - "not until you tell me" him
- "don't you know - it's like, well you know". Jeremy
Paxman would have roasted him. But I digress, to our utter
surprise the teachers accepted our protest and promised a
lesson switch.

To our continued surprise the girls didn't object. Poor
innocent souls - just wait till they're one hour into the history
of the internal combustion engine; of course, we told them
how interesting and exciting that was - even for girls - and
how we wished they hadn't altered the timetable at that
point. But we would, of course, have to accept the teachers'
decision. So, adopting our reluctant faces we trudged (make
that raced) off to the delectable Cherry Wilkins and sex -
sorry biology. "Good morning boys, may I say how nice it
is to have you for this lesson, the first of many I hope" We,
the drooling goons, nodded and smirked our agreement. "I
thought that today we should look at the reproductive
process". The slobbering of my peers was embarrassing - it
was only sex - sorry biology after all. Then it all went very,
very weird - Cherry had us all gather round her table at the
front of the classroom. She produced from one of its draws
a small board of wood, a scalpel and a frog - a dead frog!!
You won't believe what she planned to do with that frog -
that dead frog. It was spread-eagled on the board and pinned
- literally - by its legs. She was going to slice it open - she
asked if one of us would care to operate. Didn't she realise

that that would mean touching the thing with our bare hands? Oh, but it did get worse - the frog was sliced open so that we might examine its innards. More than one of the assembled felt certain that, if they did as the lovely Miss Wilkins suggested, it would be their own innards that would be on show.

What had this to do with sex - sorry reproduction? Miss Wilkins identified and explained the reproductive organs in some detail; there was also reference to the mating practice of frogs. One brave soul ventured an anxious comment " We don't do it like that do we Miss?". She was not about to enlighten him. The remainder of the lesson passed in a haze of bits of frog and stifled retching. Cheerful, charming Cherry Wilkins sallied on, disregarding our discomfort- no not disregarding - relishing it. "Look closely at this" "Anyone want to feel this?". I swear she was playing with the frog and with us. The bell rang - end of lesson. "I do hope you boys have enjoyed your first biology lesson. We must see if we can do it again – soon". Cheryl Wilkins, you were gorgeous but if the price of ogling you is participating in the dissection of frogs and the likes, we the boys from form 3B will go celibate for the afternoon.

We joined up with the girls for the next lesson. They were eager to learn how we had got on; to a boy we shrugged shoulders and said it had been ok. What did you do? they asked. Sex and stuff, you know. We were squirming, and they knew it and then they could contain themselves no longer. They began howling with laughter. You had to watch Miss Wilkins cut open a dead frog - we know because it was all set up. It was too: this is how it went. The girls told us that their biology lessons were going to be on sex. Us indignant boys said that that wasn't fair, why couldn't we have lessons on sex? The girls told the delectable Cherry Wilkins who had a word with our science teacher. The plot was hatched, the girls were sworn to secrecy. Oh, the treachery - girls - 'sugar and spice and all things nice' pah -

humbug. Miss Wilkins? I would never ogle her in the same way again. Note to all kids - don't trust grown-ups when they readily agree to anything.

It was many years before sex education was to become a part of the national curriculum. I would share this little anecdote following its introduction, on the first fumbling and stumbling attempts to formally teach junior kids the subject of sex. A female teacher was presenting to a mixed class of eleven -year olds. Despite the assumed innocence of the class, she was not wholly comfortable with the subject. But, it was early days and no doubt it would get easier over time. She had got to the point of explaining contraception as practiced by males. She avoided explicit terms, seeking refuge in broad generic type language but did manage to say that they were often referred to as 'French Letters'. The class were getting lost amongst the long words and verbosity and their puzzled looks told teacher that she was losing them. It's a universal classroom law - there's always at least one in every group that will burst the bubble and say the right thing in the wrong way. The 'one' on this occasion was a tousled haired " lad sitting at the back of the class. His eyes lit up at the term French Letters, the penny dropped "Miss" he called out "are French Letters the same as johnnies?". She coloured crimson - the kids all laughed. More importantly, they learned something, though not in the manner outlined in the teacher's lesson plan. In case you're wondering – the boy was not me – it was not!

Of course, sex education wouldn't be complete without a caution about 'sexually transmitted deceases'. That's what they're called today, we didn't call them anything because we didn't know of their existence, they went by the names of 'venereal decease' (VD) and 'gonorea'. We have the PC battalions to thank for the name change - seems that VD or gonorea are too explicit so they have to be replaced with something more innocent. My how sensitive we've become in the 20th century - they've been venereal decease and gonorea since the beginning of time. It was the condition, not its names, that got people of old worked up. In the early 18th century they had a marvellous remedy for VD. It was called 'snail water'. The ingredients were -

.... *a pound and a half of wormwood, ground ivy and thistle, half a pound each of pennyroyal, juniper berries, fennel and aniseed. These were mixed with three ounces of cloves and cubebs, eight gallons of spring water and spirit of wine and* - (here's the best bit), *six gallons of snails and three gallons of earthworms.*

The gardens of the British Working Class - Margaret Willes

I believe this deadly concoction was meant to be consumed (no idea how many this single brew would serve)- there's no empirical evidence that it cured VD, but my money is on it killing the patient. It was surely a caution against promiscuity - a reckless night of passion and then snail water - the sensible vote goes to celibacy.

*****

My final year at Short Heath Secondary Modern was significant in several ways in terms of my development. My academic results improved dramatically, and I was promoted to 4A. What's more, to my great surprise I was nominated as a school prefect. I suspect that Mr Statham was behind this, for certain it would have gone nowhere without his blessing. I wasn't elected. Clearly, I lacked the popular support amongst my peers, but I had at least been nominated - that was more than most. An even greater surprise came when I was asked by Aggie Neal to do a reading at a special event. This is what I read to a distinguished audience of parents, governors and dignitaries from the local council.

The Merchant of Venice - Shakespeare.

To those of you not familiar with the story Antonio - a Christian - acts as guarantor for a loan made by Shylock - a Jew. Antonio is very anti-Semitic. He and Shylock share a powerful dislike of each other. A condition of the loan is, if it defaults, Shylock shall take one pound of Antonio's flesh. In this scene, Shylock is asked if he really intends to invoke the condition and if so, what he intends to do with his pound of flesh.

Act 3 - Scene 1

Shylock

"To bait fish with. He hath disgraced me, hindered me half a million, laughed at my losses, mocked my gains, scorned my nation, thwarted my bargains, cooled my friends, heated my enemies, and what is his reason? I am a Jew. Hath not a Jew eyes, hath not a Jew hands, organs, same dimensions, senses, affections, passion? Fed with the same food, hurt with the same weapons, subject to the same diseases, healed by the same means, warmed and cooled by the same summer and winter as a Christian? If you prick us do we not bleed? If you tickle us do we not laugh? If you poison us do we not die? If we are like you in the rest, we will resemble you in that. If a Jew wrong a Christian, what is his humility? Revenge. If a Christian wrong a Jew, what should his sufferance be by Christian example? Revenge. The villainy you teach me, I will execute, and it shall go hard but I will better the instruction"

Shylock is asserting that he will take his pound of flesh and, rather bitterly, saying what he will do with it. The message is that he (Shylock) will do as he would be done by. The play was written towards the end of the 16th century and already the Jews had suffered centuries of abuse - abuse that was to climax in the holocaust some three-hundred and forty years later. They didn't use the term 'racist' then. In the First Folio (a collection of some of Shakespeare's plays) The

Merchant of Venice is classified as a comedy, but it is its anti-Semitic theme for which it is best known - and 'my' speech says it all.

Not a long speech you may think but surely a powerful one, as relevant today as it ever was. I was so nervous that evening, I held the book up so that no one could see my face but as soon as I started reading I forgot all about the people watching and listening and read it fluently, faultlessly. Applause from the audience and beaming smiles from Aggie Neal and Mr Statham - that was a good night.

*****

Sport was another area where I blossomed in my final year. The four school houses competed each year in football, rugby and cricket for the boys and rounders and netball for the girls. Hockey was shared but not mixed. Likewise, athletics offered events for boys and girls - not together of course, the poor dears had to have a chance of winning something. Point of interest - much to the chagrin of many in the USA - rounders is the forerunner of baseball. The origins of the game may be found in the late 17th/early 18th century when something called 'stool ball' was played, this morphed into rounders and was a popular game for both sexes. The term base-ball was first used in a rhyme by John Newberry, a children's author, in 1744. The game was taken to America by the early settlers and the name 'baseball' adopted. Possibly because it has been regarded for many years as a girl's game in the UK, some of our American cousins would disown the connection. After all, in the USA, it is primarily a male sport and has a macho image. There is some slight redress for the Yanks in that netball sort of emerged out of basketball but there isn't much history to the division since both games came out in the 1890's. Basketball was devised by a Dr James Naismith at a YMCA centre in Springfield, Massachusetts in 1891. One Martina Bergman-Osterberg brought a version to a female physical training college in Hampstead, London in 1893 and this became known as Netball.

We boys did give rounders a go but it's surprisingly difficult to hit a ball hurled at speed with a small round bat. Don't let on that I said this, but the girls were rather good at it. It was that the school was into team sports. There were no facilities, nor instruction, in individual games. For the most part I had, in the past, simply turned up and did what I was told - games were on the menu in PT. But now, I was taking a more pro-active interest. I was full of running, boundless energy and blind faith in my own survival. During a rugby match I would rampage round the field, fearlessly tackling anyone that had the ball. Alas, flying tackles were not allowed I was emphatically informed, shame because I was rather good at them. At football, I was useful because I could use either foot and as long as I was on the pitch I'd play anywhere. When it came to cricket seems I had to learn that, as a batsman I should not see every ball as destined for the boundary and as a bowler expect every ball to take a wicket. All of us boys were drilled in the mantra that the hockey stick was not a weapon.

On sports day, there were loosely four versions of each sport representing the four school years. As I recall, the first and second years didn't have a javelin tournament. I stunned our housemaster by volunteering for the sprint events; hurdles and throwing the cricket ball. I have no idea from where came the latter, never heard of it being replicated anywhere else, pity because it would make a great Olympic sport. Offering my services was a sign that I was growing up fast - in some regards at least. In general school play I had learned that I was as fast as some of the nominated runners and lobbing the cricket ball from the boundary had proved what a good right arm I possessed. I didn't win anything, but I didn't disgrace myself either. I came third in the 100 yards' dash (not meters - we hadn't been conquered by the EU then); fourth in the 200 yards' sprint and fourth again in the hurdles and I managed to rattle the corrugated tin roof of the bicycle shed with the cricket ball, a straighter line might have proved a winner. My off - centre throw was nought when compared with some poor lass from the senior's javelin team. Dear old Soapy was acting as master of ceremonies and so that he could see and be seen he was standing on an upturned wooden (soap?) box, well out of harm's way he must have thought. The javelin slammed into the box. Soapy was unmoved, well, for a man from the trenches of World War 1, what else would one expect?

Lest it be that I have spawned the notion that I had suddenly become endowed with great sporting prowess allow me to return you to planet earth. My abilities in every regard were what I would describe as merely average to good - not outstanding. What I did have in great abundance was energy, enthusiasm, commitment and a no surrender philosophy. Where some flagged if things were not going well I stuck doggedly to the task. Immodest of me to say so but I have sometimes reflected that had I fallen in with a proper coach perhaps I could have had some success in the sporting world. However, I temper this with the knowledge that I was probably one of many. It was sport, football that exposed that quirky fallibility of mine of seeing things different from most. It was Monday morning and a group of us lads were re-living moments from the weekend's football. One kid said that so-and-so had missed a penalty - no, I interjected he didn't miss it, the goalkeeper saved it - I was ridiculed unmercifully. It's the same thing, idiot they almost chorused. Well, I beg to differ - missing would be to miss the target - he didn't. He hit the target, but the goalkeeper prevented a goal so, the penalty wasn't missed - it was saved. Later in life I turned this logic to advantage for examination candidates. The outcome for exams is not pass or fail but pass and not pass (this time). Failure is giving up. Some will doubtless argue that I am being pedantic, engaging in a pointless exercise in semantics. I stand by my opinion.

*****

My schooldays are coming to an end. What will I miss? School dinners for a start. When I see, what kids are offered today, I almost feel sorry for them - anything with chips or baked beans or a limp looking salad. We were treated to a proper traditional cooked dinner - meat, potatoes and two sorts of vegetables and lashings of gravy. This was followed by pudding - fruit pie or steamed pudding covered in custard or milk puddings - rice (the most likely) tapioca, macaroni. Not all on the same day - there'd be one pudding per day. The word 'pudding' has faded in use as the more sophisticated 'sweet' or 'dessert' is preferred. Sheer snobbery - those words convey nothing when compared with good old pudding. There was no menu - no choice, anything one didn't like was simply left on the plate. The meals weren't cooked at the school, they arrived in large vacuum sealed containers and were doled out by dinner ladies. What we had was unfussy unadorned basic but balanced meals. I still prefer them today - I don't want to eat art on a plate; I don't drool over the creations offered by MasterChef. Not that I don't respect their work, it just doesn't tingle my taste buds.

For some of us this was the best meal - sometimes the only meal - of the day. Plates were routinely cleared regardless of what had been served - hunger had it over 'don't like that' every time. I guess that's where and how I got to eat vegetables that, given a choice, I might well have rejected. We were hungry then - maybe fussy eaters aren't really hungry. There was often a second pudding to be had because not everyone liked the offering. They had already been served so by the time the 'seconders' got them they'd be cold. No matter - still grub. Milk puddings were inclined to congeal, they were served with a spoon placed in the dish and this acted rather like a lollipop stick so that when the spoon was lifted the whole contents came with it - you got to choose, lick it or bite it. School dinners were good, I've been a fan of traditional English food ever since. Don't even think of tampering with my menu by introducing that ghastly curry stuff.

These dinners had to be paid for and it was a Monday morning ritual for dinner money to be collected by the teaching staff. Some of us, the poor ones, didn't have to pay, we had free school dinners. That stigmatised us and led to much taunting by some of those who had to pay. Why should they have to pay, and we get it for nothing? Other kids went home, they didn't sponge - why didn't we go home if we couldn't afford the dinners? You have to wonder where some of the expressions and opinions came from, I suspect their parents – in our part of the world, their socialist parents.

I may not have made prefect, but I did get to be milk monitor, it was my job to ensure that the little one-third pint bottles were ready for dispersal in the hall at break-time. Being a monitor wasn't entirely new. I had taken my turn in being a class monitor in the third year. That involved, amongst other things, ensuring that all inkwells were full. Each desk had an inkwell inset and the school provided pens - with nibs. No ball-point pens back then, and they are ball-points - not biros. Biro is a brand name. Ball points were the brainchild of two Hungarian brothers, Laszio Biro (a newspaper editor) and Gyorgy Biro (a chemist). They developed the idea whilst working in Germany but fled to Argentina in 1941 where they patented the ball point pen in 1943.

Filling up inkwells presented a wonderful opportunity for a little prank. We would roll bits of blotting paper into tight balls and drop them into the inkwells. Soak up the ink and clog the nib, likely to cause the creation of blots in the user's class books. A jolly good way of getting some deserving souls into a spot of bother. Us ink monitors couldn't be blamed, we were only supposed to top up the ink, not inspect, much less, clean out the wells.

There wasn't much by way of extra-curricular activities at Short Heath Secondary Modern. Fourth year kids got the opportunity to go on a week's camping trip but that had to be paid for by parents so that was me and mine out. In this we weren't alone, several kids couldn't go, some like us because parents couldn't afford; some because parents wouldn't afford (it's a school trip so the school should pay) and some because some parents weren't prepared to let junior go off on a wild soiree with a gang of hooligans - they trusted their own of course but the others... Those of us left behind were to be subjected to ad-hoc lessons according to teacher availability. Most of the time it was a case of "read your books". I got to thinking how unfair that was, three quarters of our number were swanning around a camp site in the glorious countryside, cooking sausages over a camp-fire and singing 'Gin gang goolie' and getting a Hi de Hi start to the day. That's what the happy campers told us: wet grass; bumpy ground; creepy crawlies; snakes and having to dig your own toilet in the woods is what we told them - made a few of them hesitate. But we still got lessons. On the plus side, there was the look of disappointment on the boys' faces when they found out that girls went to a different camp-site, far far away. May the good Lord have mercy on their lecherous souls. Anyway, I'm thinking of the injustice and its Friday, the last day - we were out playing cricket (the girls - netball). The bell rang to mark the end of one period and the start of the next -"read your books" time. Zac Howarth was to be the man in charge. That was until yours truly decided to lead a revolt. I argued that as the happy campers were having fun, so should we and I proposed that we stayed out in the field and continue our game. Motion seconded and carried - game on. I think that Zac was privately relieved because I was allowed to get away with that little naughty.

*****

There was little in the way of school visits. There was

neither the inclination nor the funding for such indulgencies. We did get to visit selected industries, the motive being variously educational and vocational. We were fourth year kids (never referred to as students) we were being readied for discharge on an unsuspecting world. Industry was still struggling to fill the void brought about by the losses of the war. Secondary schools were producing the raw material - we were scathingly referred to as 'factory fodder'. I recall two such visits, one to Ductile Steels Ltd and the other to Henry Squires & Sons Ltd.

Ductile Steel was founded in 1915 and was situated in Sandbeds, midway between Lane Head and Willenhall. Ever curious about the choice of names be it people, places, roads or businesses I discovered that the name Ductile was chosen because it described what the company did which was to turn rolled steel into wire. Ductability is the ability to deform under tensile stress. That visit was indeed an education, I learned of one industry I didn't plan to enter. Whatever they were paying the men operating the furnaces wouldn't have been enough had it been multiplied a hundredfold. The heat from the furnaces would toast bread at a hundred yards I swear. In summary, the foundry was dirty, noisy and dangerous.

Henry Squires & Sons Ltd is more transparent in its name choice. Henry Squire was the third generation of the Squire dynasty that began making locks at their factory in Lichfield Road, New Invention in 1780. Henry was a staunch supporter of John Wesley's Methodism, likely that this explains Wesley's warm reception when he arrived in New Invention, and the building of the Methodist Chapel a few hundred yards further along Lichfield Road from the Squires' site. The company has recently decamped to a new location in Willenhall. Touring the foundry was much less daunting than the Ductile factory; noisy and dirty still but not at the same level and not really dangerous. As we completed our tour and were on the way out, our guide handed each of us boys a tin-opener. I took mine and happened to glance back, on the side of the crate containing our gifts, in bold paint, was the word 'rejects'.

Leaving school for good meant that it was unlikely that I would ever again visit the shops that pandered to our childlike tastes and meagre resources. There were two such shops, one at the corner of the Croft that brought us to the main road with the school on the opposite side. They sold anything that could be bought for a penny or half-a-penny and that was not governed by rationing. Typically, that would be, liquorice. liquorice wood and a lemony flavoured dip that turned the dippers finger yellow after the fashion of nicotine, it was called 'kali'. The folk that ran this shop knew exactly with whom they were dealing - troublesome kids, but the business was worth the aggravation. They were firm and stern and would summarily evict any potential troublemaker.

The other shop, further along the road and on the same side, run by the Bright sisters was altogether more accommodating of a little mischief. They were elderly (by our standards) and always seemed to be nervous whenever a bunch of kids entered the premises. It was fair to say (though cruel) that they were bright by name but not by nature. That may have had something to do with the silly things we would ask for - penny sticks of lamp oil being a favourite. "Oh, I don't think we have any of them. What colour are they?" Naughty but, it seemed to us at the time, harmless fun. A side of this I did not like was that some kids used the distraction to help themselves to goodies - shoplifting - stealing. A joke was a joke, but stealing, that was going way too far. Never did it. But now I must dent the halo, on the way home, back along the Croft, we passed a garden. In this garden were fruit trees, apples and pears. I confess to nipping over the fence and indulging in a little scrumping. Scrumping is defined as 'stealing fruit from an orchard or garden', the word first appeared in the English language during the 19th century. Scrumping as defined by us kids was simply helping oneself to fruit growing on trees - it wasn't stealing. Stealing was taking things from the Bright sisters or breaking into someone's home and taking their possessions. Scrumping wasn't stealing - it was just scrumping. Anyway, most of the fruit would be allowed to fall to the ground and rot – surely scrumping and eating it was preferable.

Chapter 11

MOM'S INCREDIBLE WORK-LOAD

Whilst us kids were busily enriching ourselves at school, life at home carried on much the same. It was tough and there were frequent periods of deprivation. At least we were buoyed up by school dinners. I could say Mom did her best but that wouldn't be the half of it - she performed miracles. No matter how meagre she always managed to conjure up something to eat. In despair, sometimes she would give us one shilling and sixpence (1/6d) (that's 7.5 pence in new money) and send us to the chippie to get roe and chips. The irony is not lost, what was then considered as a cheap alternative to a decent meal is now not only acceptable, it is even sought after, but it will cost a lot more than 7.5p - in the region of a couple of pounds. Adjusting for inflation one 1/6d in 1953 is now worth £1.83 - so still a cheap meal. Appropriate here to introduce an act of affrontery. Fish and chips, we all agree, is a traditional English fare. The French insist they created the fried chip - hence 'French Fries' but the Belgium's will argue that they were frying them towards the end of the 17th century. It appears that the word 'French' was attached by British and American soldiers during WW1. What say you then, to the claim made by the Italians that the dish was brought to England by Venetian immigrants and cite a reference in Charles Dickens' Oliver Twist? Records show that fish and chips were first served by a family called Malin of London, in 1860 although this is contested by a family called Lees of Mosley, Manchester. Whichever of these two was first, we deny the Italians - they've got pasta, pizza and spaghetti.

Sometimes, around mid-week when the money had run out, Mom would take a bundle of goodies to the pawnbrokers in Willenhall. They had a shop next door to Samuels the jewellers in Lower Lichfield Street. She'd get a few 'bob' to last to Friday (payday) and redeem the items on Saturday morning. Pawnbrokers were then what payday loans lenders are today, revile them at will but they don't survive without meeting a need. I asked Mom why they had three balls outside, she was irritable.

"I'll give you three balls if you don't shut up"

I didn't pursue the subject. I now know that the three balls were simply the way of telling the public what business you were in - generally the masses couldn't read then so written signage was out. The idea of three balls was borrowed from the Medici family. They were renowned Italian bankers around the 15th century. Pawn-broking is probably the oldest form of secured lending, there's reference to the practice in 5th century China. It came to England with the Norman conquest, although there had been an earlier attempt to set up such an enterprise by the Bishop of London in 1361 - didn't succeed but the Norman version survives to this day.

It wasn't just money worries - Mom had an incredible workload. She laundered for fifteen - no washing machine, only the benefit of an indoor boiler. On wash day, there was a never-ending procession of laundry hung out to dry on a line that ran the length of the garden, it was conveyor belt washing. Now, had she married one William Blackstone she could have had the first washing machine made for the home. Couple of snags - he hailed from Indiana USA and he designed and built it for his wife, in 1874. That monster of a mangle travelled with us from Froysell Street, I think it was turning that mangle so much that gave Mom such a strong right arm, handy for clouting miscreants, my brothers and sisters. She ironed with a flat iron heated on the gas ring of the cooker, one would be heating whilst she ironed with the other. The luxury of an electric iron was many years away although the concept wasn't new. A man called Henry Seeley from New York patented the electric flat iron in

1882. Monday was wash day, like it had always been. Washing was almost all Mom could manage on Mondays - run her own laundrette. I say almost because she still found time to keep the house tidy and prepare meals - no, she didn't find it, she made the time.

Not surprisingly us kids were press-ganged into doing our bit. Gender equality came to 94 Essington Road long before it became fashionable. Brothers, sisters - made no difference, we all had to perform. I've scrubbed floors on my hands and knees using only a cloth and a scrubbing brush - mops? - they'd be for wimps. The working classes didn't do carpets so bare boards it was, it was these that had to be scrubbed. A square of linoleum usually lay in the middle, cold to the feet but preferable to splinters. Hearthrugs were hand-made affairs, a piece of sacking, some old clothing cut into small strips and a bodger - a decent rug could be made quite quickly. Handy with a duster too and I remembered to lift every ornament to dust underneath - had to, she'd check. I enjoyed wax polishing furniture, there was the lovely aroma of Mansion polish and the shine it produced. The hall floor consisted of red tiles, these had to be polished with red Cardinal. That not only demanded excess elbow grease, it was also very severe on the knees.

We had a coal fire in the living room and one of us boys - never the girls (revert to sexism when it suits), would be charged each evening with chopping firewood and bringing in a bucket of coal so that the fire could lit first thing in the morning. We got to do the lighting sometimes, to get the fire roaring quickly it was widespread practice to screen the open grate with a sheet of newspaper thus trapping oxygen and encouraging the fire. When this worked, it worked well but it could easily go wrong like when the newspaper ignited. One could easily set the house on fire and there's no piss pot to hand now - they were so 'yesterday'. We did manage to set the chimney on fire a few times. Standing outside and watching flames spew out of the chimney pot is pretty scary, and all because the chimney needed sweeping. Surely, we had a 6/7-year-old that could be spared for an hour or so? Actually, looking at the size of the chimney, I think it might have been a tight fit.

*****

Friday was payday, Saturday was shopping day, Sunday was the day to volunteer help Mom with the Sunday dinner, usually a traditional roast. The volunteering bit was more to do with being chief taster than contributing to the work. Simple tasks were allotted like shelling peas, broad beans or slicing green beans. There was a special rhythm to shelling peas - one for the colander, one for the mouth, one for the colander... and so on. I also got to sample raw vegetables such as carrots, cauliflower and the hard, white heart of cabbage. I ate raw potatoes too, but I learned later that that isn't healthy. Those that I didn't scoff were placed around the joint in a large roasting tin and cooked in the meat juices. They were the best. When joint and roasties were cooked. they were removed from the baking tin so that gravy could be made with the meat juices to which was added the water in which vegetables had been cooked, and plain flour for thickening - that's proper gravy. Another dish Mom excelled at was a boiled dinner, a cheap boiling joint of beef or bacon, corned beef (which was inexpensive then), poached fresh fish (also cheap) or a tine of pink salmon (never the best red), this would be topped off with lashings of parsley sauce.

Mom made a mean apple pie, no fancy frills just cooked apple in a short crust pastry, exactly how they should be made. She made jam tarts in the same fashion - wonderful and her fruit cake was divine. However, in my considerable opinion Mom's best dish was custard tart. She made them in a large dish and after cooking the tart was sliced into generous portions. I have never tasted a custard tart that comes anywhere close to Mom's - and I've tasted a few. Sunday was the day we ate like kings, or so it seemed.

Our diet may have been basic, but it was obviously healthy because we were rarely ill - genuinely ill that is, we were ever ready to fake it to get out of school. When we were out of sorts, some simple patent- medicine was called upon. Colds and stuffed up noses earned a rub down with Vic's vapour rub, still going strong today. Strong is indeed the word that best describes its fragrance - capable of clearing a crowded room in seconds. A cut or a badly grazed body part was treated with Germolene ointment to fight infection. It too had a pungent pong but at least it could be contained under a dressing, it also is still available. The treatment of fevers (high temperature) was left in the safe (metaphorical) hands of Alfred Fennings, a chemist from Cowes on the Isle of Wight. He created several over-the-counter cures for a miscellany of ailments, opened his first shop in London in 1840. Little Lung Healers; Cooling Powders and Fever Mixture were the ones with which we became most familiar. Little Lung Healers were exactly that - little, about the size of a pin-head, the box they came wasn't much bigger. Cooling Powders were mixed with water and drunk, tasted like chalk. Worst of all was Fennings' Fever Mixture, it tasted like nothing on earth, the sort of concoction one would drop into the punch bowl, when no one was looking of course. The dosage for a kid was a couple of tablespoons full, enough to de-scale mouth and throat. Oh, to be suddenly afflicted with dysphaglia (swallowing difficulties). Did any of these medications work? Maybe - maybe not but there was always the placebo effect. Fennings was no quack, his medicines were still selling more than a hundred years after he created them and when he died in 1900 it is said that proceeds from the sale of his products went to certain charities. I do concede that some of the cough mixtures we were made to take weren't wholly unpleasant, but the recommended dosage was more than sufficient.

There were a couple of remedies that were almost instantly effective. Our youthful indifference to boring stuff like infections left us exposed to - well, infections. I had many a boil-like blister on fingers and hands. Mum would make a mixture of glycerine and borax, bind it round the infected digit and you could lay real money that within a day or two the blister would burst, recovery quickly followed. The other cure-all was much less pleasant. Present with a chest infection today and you'll likely get antibiotics and/or an expectorant to aid breathing. Less serious cases warrant a liberal layering of Vic vapour rub. This has a pungent pong and was/is good for ensuring that one was left in relative peace and quiet. Back in the dark ages of my youth there was the evil that was Kaolin poultice. Kaolin was a thick gooey substance that had to be prised from a tin. It was heated up and spread over a piece of cloth easily a foot square - and then came the best (worst) part, this over-sized hot dressing was slapped on to the chest of the ailing party. It stank, it burnt, and it was uncomfortable. Did it work? Of course, we swore by it - it was the only way to ensure the experience wasn't repeated.

Prior to the creation of the NHS, treatment for sundry ailments rested either in proprietary medicines (as made by people like Fennings) or by a more mysterious rout - 'ye olde wive's' tale'. Those wonderful old customs and practices of ill-defined origin and sometimes doubtful effect. My favourite was the cure for a nose bleed - the key of the door down the back of the neck. Not just any key mark you - a rim lock barrel key, four to five inches long. Remarkable as it sounds, there are (unconfirmed) reports of this working. To those that believe, the word 'coincidence' doesn't compute. At least one of the do-it-yourself remedies enjoyed popularity (even notoriety). Hot stout - I have it on authority that a much-favoured cure amongst adults was a bottle of stout heated up and drank. It was considered to be medicinal - well that's what they said. In that case, why weren't children given it? They had to settle for hot lemonade. Pleasant enough in its own right but a curative? Doubtful

The NHS was introduced on the 5th July 1948. Everyone had a doctor (GP) to whom they could refer. Ours was a first in several ways - our first doctor of course and also the first time I saw a coloured man - an Asian. Dr Singh had a council house in Sandland Road (Bob Sandland - local councillor) on the Beacon Estate. His surgery was the front room. Being an educated man and a doctor there was no question of racism and he was much liked and respected. Years later he came into some money and had built a large detached house and separate surgery on Cannock Road. I didn't have to see him very often which was probably just as well. Taking prescribed tablets was okay, you just swallowed - no after effects, but some of the concoctions put together by the local chemist, as prescribed by the doctor, and served in brown bottles were an affront to anyone's gullet. Getting it down and keeping it down was a challenge. I developed a theory that medicine tasted vile so as to act as a psychological encouragement to recover, the alternative was to have to take more of the evil potion.

By far the worst thing inflicted on us kids then, was the daily dose of cod-liver oil and malt. It was thick and gooey and resembled the dregs from the sump of an engine that was not often cleaned. If the sight of it was off-putting it was nought compared with the taste. it was positively disgusting, revolting. One tablespoon per day was the dosage, only its slimy inability to adhere to the inside of the mouth ensured that it went down, it slid under its own volume. Had it been required to be held in the mouth for even a second, I guarantee that it would have re-emerged as projectile vomit. I am assured that some kids actually enjoyed this glutinous offering.

Having gardening lessons at school nudged me subconsciously into helping Dad with our plots - front and rear. Here I learned that Dad had talents of which I had been unaware. He designed and developed a wholly functional back garden. First, he laid a path of broken flag stones (crazy paving) the length of the garden and across the face of the house giving easy access to and from the French windows. Then he landscaped the first third, there was a lawn with floral borders to the right of the path and flower beds to the left. Heightened privacy was achieved by planting privet hedges at the boundary on both sides. The remaining two thirds of the garden were given over to growing vegetables. The two gardens were separated by a rustic trellis with an archway over the path. Climbing roses were planted along the trellis and we had a magnificent display every year.

We grew most of the popular vegetables: peas; beans (runner and broad) carrots; parsnips; cabbages; cauliflowers; sprouts and, of course, potatoes. Here I learned something else, never to grow potatoes in the same plot in consecutive years. It was called crop rotation, whatever potatoes took out of the soil wouldn't replenish in a year, it would take two at least. So, it was spuds to the right one year and to the left the next. The origin of this practice is found in the 14th century. The lord of the manor owned the 'common fields' - families in the village were allocated strips of land in these fields annually and usually one field was left fallow. Family A might grow potatoes one year and the next, when the strip was rotated to family B wheat or some other crop would be grown. A strip of land was measured at sixteen and a half feet in width and a furlong in length - a furlong equals two-hundred and twenty yards and there are eight furlongs in an acre so a family with four strips was working half an acre - virtually by hand. This style of crop rotation was entirely coincidental, the peasant farmers didn't really understand the need for replenishment anyway, that was what the fallow field was for. It was only in the early 18th century that the merits of the concept were reasonably understood and the recognition that fallow fields were idle fields. Lord Townshend of Norfolk introduced a four-field crop rotation system by which four different crops simply rotated one field at a time in a four-year cycle. One of the crops favoured by Townshend was turnips and, unfortunately for him, he became known as 'Turnip Townshend'. Graham Taylor, one- time England football team manager was awarded the accolade 'turnip' by sports writer David Clement in the Sun newspaper following a pathetic display against Sweden in 1992. Sorry Graham, but you weren't the first. See, my young readers, how history enlightens us as to our current behaviour? To this day farmers rotate crops.

We also planted some soft fruit trees, raspberry; blackcurrant and gooseberry just behind the trellis. A crude cold frame consisting of a pile of bricks topped off with an old iron window frame housed cucumber plants. I see now that dad was trying to make a non-monetary contribution, he was providing fresh food. We ate everything we grew, mum would make a vinegar salad of cucumber, tomatoes and onions, nothing was wasted.

The front garden was a much simpler affair, mostly given over to grass with a few plants in the borders and down left-hand side, and we had an attractive rose bed to the fore. A privet hedge was planted around the perimeter to deter people from gawping through the window as they walked past. Of course, we as tenants, had every right to gawp at passers-by. The posh and the richer of our kind deployed net curtains but they had to lift them to observe the outside world, they were called 'twitchers', anyone walking by could usually see the net curtain twitch.

I would never claim that our garden was better than any other, Wilf Rogers' back garden that butted onto ours at the side was prettier, but ours more interesting. Rogers' was a landscaped affair - lawned with a rich variety of flowers adorning the borders, you took it all in at one look. We had diversity and difference, you had to keep looking to register the changes. One remote neighbour stood out in the matter of gardens - a Mr Astbury, situated at the near end of Stretton Road, his front garden was a dream and it won him prizes - deservedly. He was a coal miner at Hilton Main colliery, spent his working hours underground, my how he made up for that with his horticultural skills. Nevertheless, my own dad had surprised me with his prowess in planting and design. I got to help, and I also got to do some double-digging (pssst they call that bastard trenching - don't tell mum).

For a short spell, we kept chickens in a coup at the bottom of the garden. As I understood it they were there for the express purpose of gracing our dining table come Christmas. That meant, of course, that at the appropriate time they were to be slaughtered, killed - ugly words, let's say despatched. Already the shadow of the goose was cast. Big brother was charged with the despatching which he did very ably with the help of a sharp knife. The carcasses were hung up in the outhouse to complete the bleeding and after a few days they would plucked and drawn (the innards removed) that was to be my contribution. As a twelve-year old, I wasn't particularly sensitive about the task, this was just the preliminaries to food preparation. On the first night of their hanging a min-drama unfolded. Mom was in the kitchen preparing the evening meal when all of a very sudden she gave a great shriek and rushed into the lounge.

"They've come back to life"

Who/what has?

"Them bloody chickens"

She'd heard one crow. She flatly refused to go anywhere near the kitchen much less the outhouse. Oh dear, another botched job - the Smiths have form in such matters. Dennis and I went to have a look - and listen. What Mom had heard was the product of a simple reaction of the nervous system of the definitely demised chicken. Its head was severed ....oh dear, that sounds ever so familiar. For the record, it was a fine Christmas dinner.

Trench digging wasn't the only skill we developed and perfected. We became accomplished diggers of holes. Big wide deep holes for the purpose of disposing of unwanted miscellaneous junk - bedsteads, bike frames and scrap iron in general - anything that could neither go in the dustbin nor be burned. Refuse collection in those days was an uncomplicated affair. Every house had one dustbin into which they poured the ashes from the coal fire and general domestic rubbish. There was no room for anything else, although there wasn't so much by way of packaging, we were more into simple wrapping. The dustbin was emptied once a week. Anyone with extraneous rubbish might prevail on the collector's good nature and that in turn would be influenced by the proximity of Christmas and the prospect of a generous tip. Dustbinmen, that's what they were called because that's what they did, empty dustbins, had a policy of knocking on the door of every house on their route just before Christmas. Open the door and a tin containing coins would be aggressively rattled in your face accompanied by the utterance

"Dustbins".

It wasn't really a request, you were expected to donate. Those that didn't, and this included those that weren't at home (genuine or otherwise) would do well to avail themselves of a brush and shovel because during the following weeks much of their refuge would depart the dustbin and deposit itself on their paths. Fortunately, we were spared such a visit since Dad worked for the council.

Anyway, what didn't go in the bin went in the ground -

unless it was burnable in which case it would be saved for bonfire night. We had to dig deep so as not to interfere with the gardening so several feet down it was, the simple rule was that, if you can see over the sides of the hole it wasn't deep enough. In the centuries to come, when they clear Beacon Estate to make way for the new wave of eco-dwellings, archaeologists (probably the same ones that found my pot), will unearth these "strange and interesting objects". In keeping with the thought that today's junk is tomorrow's antique. our scrap iron may well be worth a fortune. Could be their equivalent of the Staffordshire Hoard.

An alternative to burning and burying was provided by the rag-and-bone man, a following immortalised in the tv programme Steptoe & Son. The term rag-and-bone comes from the early 19th century and was a description of the men who stalked the streets of towns and cities, scavenging amongst the debris for anything that might have a value - rags and bones were saleable, they literally collected rags and bones - you don't want to know what happened to the bones. There was no waste disposal then, rubbish simply got dumped anywhere considered convenient - like the street. The 20th century version had long given up on bones, but the name stuck. Now they would take rags, bottles and scrap-iron. There was a market for all three. They came usually on horse and cart and they would call out "rags, bottles or bones" or "any old iron". They were a welcome sight to many, it was great way to get rid of unwanted junk - these guys would pay, only coppers but it all helped. For some inexplicable reason, it was kids who were often sent to take stuff to the rag-and-bone man, kids didn't get cash they would rewarded with either a balloon on a stick or a goldfish. The rag and bone man would carry goldfish in a huge ex-sweet jar. To get one, simply take some old junk and a jam jar filled with water. Asking a second-hand car dealer what he would give you for your old car often still, brings the retort - "You can have either a balloon on a stick

197

or a goldfish" - his way of saying your old banger is a load junk. We don't have rag-and-bone men now - instead we have men in low loaders with horns out of which emanates an unholy wail. They aren't popular, many have been fined for being a public nuisance. All the same, if you have an unwanted domestic appliance, just leave it at the kerbside - it will disappear as if by magic. The government of the day, around 1953, did campaign for everyone to dig out all scrap iron, there being a great shortage of raw materials, and this was collected by the local authorities. I believe it yielded a substantial tonnage.

Gardening wasn't the only thing I learned from the old man. We lads all had to help with the redecoration of 94 Essington Road, whenever it was deemed necessary. Ceilings were whitewashed with a simple concoction made from a ball of whitening, crushed and mixed with water. The ball was hard and chalk-like, mixing it to the right texture was an art - too thin (watery) and it would take several coats to cover, too thick and application would be arduous - and wasteful. In the beginning walls were colour washed using distemper which was colouring mixed with ground whitening and water. Later we used paint from Walpamur, a paint that was thinned with water to the required consistency. Water based paint was the brainchild of Major A W Huntington, a Boer War veteran, who had joined Wall Paper Manufactures Ltd in 1899 as a partner. The process was perfected in 1906 and launched throughout the UK. The company was sold to Reed International in 1965. In 1970 the new owners feared that the name Walpamur was too readily associated with water paint and that this would hinder the promotion of their new product, emulsion paint so they changed the name to Crown Decorative Products ergo we still have Crown paints.

Colour washing was cheaper than wall paper, but we did eventually go for paper covering. The offer of a wide variety of multi-coloured patterns proved too seductive. The art of wallpapering has a chequered history. Both England and France led the way in manufacture in the 16th century. The earliest sample found in England was on the back of a proclamation from London dated 1509. Following the civil war, the puritan government of Oliver Cromwell deemed the practice as unseemly and frivolous and manufacture was (prudently) halted - they tended to burn dissenters in those days. Come the restoration of Charles 2nd to the throne and wallpapering re-emerged and became so popular that a Wallpaper Tax was introduced in 1712 and wasn't repealed until 1836. Politicians - they'll tax anything!

Wall papering was no easy job; all rolls of paper came with a half-inch border that had to be carefully trimmed off before use. There were those that didn't bother and simply overlaid the paper, but this showed up as regular ridges and spoiled the effect. There was often matching border paper that could be used to make designs on the main paper. The glue that held this to the wall was a simple mix of flour and water (or drawing pins - favoured by the weird one) and as far as I can recall it mattered not whether flour was plain of self-raising. Just like Mom's gravy, it had to be mixed thoroughly to eliminate lumps. The woodwork in the house got a coating of gloss paint - source unknown.

A useful skill I picked up from Dad was cobbling. Even new shoes would wear out eventually but taking them to the cobblers wasn't on the menu - too expensive. Instead Dad would buy a piece of leather, usually about a foot square, and some tacks. He would trace round the shoe, cut the leather with a (very) sharp knife and tack it onto the sole and/or heel of offending shoe. A special type of file called a rasp was used to smooth the rough edges and shoe polish would be liberally applied to blend the repair in with the shoe. The downside of this do-it-yourself policy is that you had to wait until there was money to buy leather. Holes in shoes were simply covered with a piece of cardboard or even newspaper in the meantime, and we Smiths endured more than our fair share of such running repairs.

Chapter 12

JOYS (?) OF CAMPING

Living permanently at or near survival mode meant we enjoyed few luxuries. Indeed, what we might have called a luxury would have been a given for most others. There were no family holidays, I was twenty-one before I had my first real holiday away from home. I don't count the week I went camping with my friend Graham Powers and two others. We went to Brewood - about ten/fifteen miles away, boy we knew how to travel then. We pitched tent in a farmer's field and roughed it for about five days. A gaggle of geese sometimes attempted to block our departure from the tent, but they weren't smart enough to stop us using the back door i.e. crawl under the flap. I did wonder if they were related to you know which goose - could have been, geese have a lifespan circa twenty-five years, maybe they were planning revenge.

At the far end of the field a couple of middle aged men had pitched tent. They appeared an odd couple of questionable intent, but Graham and I were fit and able teenagers, that seemed to act as a deterrent and after a few polite sorties, they kept their distance. Somehow a girl got involved in our great adventure in the outdoors, can't recall how. Her name was June Brewster, Graham and I both fancied her, I wrote her a note, she showed it to him and they both had a laugh. She chose Graham, I guess I was lucky, anyone who can make such an error of judgement is no one I should keep close (I jest of course). My camping experience taught me an invaluable lesson - never to do it again. Sleeping (or trying to) in the cramped and claustrophobic environment of a tent; the prospect of wild life meandering about the person whilst one slept; eating barely edible food cooked on a totally inadequate primus stove; washing (even ignoring the neck and ears) in the equivalent of a mug of water and trying to get dressed without being able to stand up - I think that'll do for starters. On top of that, you must build your own home when you arrive. Never been camping since and I don't intend to amend that statistic.

Mom's brother James, Uncle Jim to us, did take us on day trips to the seaside - Rhyl in North Wales - I went once, it was magical. He also took us to visit relatives in Worcester. They either owned a fruit farm or had a large orchard because I well remember coming home with bags (literally brown paper bags) of fruit, notably damsons, a member of the plum family and sadly a fruit that has fallen out of favour in modern times. Uncle Jim was unmarried, so he felt free to indulge his nieces and nephews though not all at the same time. We did get a day out on the occasion of the Willenhall carnival which was held every year and culminated in something of a show in Willenhall Memorial Park which lay close to Uncle Billy's shop and the ill-fated railway station. The park was planned and laid out as a memorial to the men of Willenhall who had lost their lives in World War 1 and the carnival was how the civic authorities sought to raise the necessary finance. There was a gymkhana and all the usual sideshows associated with fairgrounds provided by the legendary Pat Collins Fun Fairs Ltd.

The Collins family have been providing fairground entertainment since 1875. Lying between St Giles church and Shaw's foundry (another lock maker) on the main road running from Walsall, there was a site known locally as the 'fairground' The Collins' turned out there regularly on Summer bank holidays. They must have loved the area because they moved to Walsall in 1882 and lived in Bloxwich. Pat Collins was MP for Walsall for a couple of years (1922/24) and Mayor of Walsall in 1938. The family business is still active today, providing traditional and familiar fairground fun. Seems simple pleasures are ageless. On these occasions, we were hosted by Dad's younger brother Frank who happened to live near the park. Sometimes wondered if he knew how lucky he was having ready access to a park. The first public park in England was opened in Derby in 1840. The land was donated by a local manufacturer, Joseph Strutt. He did so in order that the artisans could have the benefits of a park - but only on two days of the week. I have a suspicion that these were Saturdays and Sundays - on the other days the 'artisans' would be busy in Mr Strutt's, and others, factories.

Even these modest days out cost parents' money, and as there were so many of us it's easy to see the potential for the expense to soar above reason. We simply became accustomed to enjoying the sights without tasting many of the delights but hey, it was a day out - it was fun, and we enjoyed it our way. Even today I can enjoy an experience without the need to spend lavishly so that I can say I had been there or done that - either that or I'm an old meanie. There was no pocket-money, we didn't know the idea existed. If we wanted money it had to be earned and it's surprising how inventive, how creative even kids can get in pursuit of lucre. One of my early efforts involved helping Dad with some extra duties he'd been charged with. As I've mentioned previously, the Beacon Estate was built in mining territory, subsidence was a problem but fortunately, only in a minor way (unintended pun there). Certain roads on the estate were prone to sinking and when that happened warning signs had to be posted for road users. These warning signs were paraffin lamps with red reflectors so that when they were lit they cast a red light to signify danger. They had to go out every night as it got dark and were simply placed on the ground around the threatened site. My job was to fill them up with paraffin and help carry them to the site, Dad placed them in position. The next morning, before school, I would fetch them back home to be readied for the next night. An amazing fact is that few if any of these lamps ever went missing, some got damaged by drivers not paying attention but overall, those that went out at night came back in the morning. I dare not contemplate the consequences of what would happen nowadays. I think that I can say with some certainty that few, if any, lamps would survive.

*****

The next little enterprise lasted much longer. Every house in the neighbourhood was coal fired, everyone burned coal. Some had it delivered and some had it fetched. My elder brother and I did the fetching, along with other lads in the area, oh and a sister got in on the act - see, we even started the equal opportunities movement. We were cheaper than the delivery men - it was that simple. No idea what deliverymen charged but we got amounts from three-pence per collection up to two-bob (shillings – 10p in new money), that could be half-a-hundred weight to a hundred, even two hundredweight, the latter would be two collections so two payments. From an early start that was Saturday morning taken care of. We each had our regulars and sometimes there'd be extras someone's usual kid failed to turn up. Our customers gave us their order and the cash with which to pay, they were very trusting. Off we went to Appleby's coal yard on the Lichfield Road, the only supplier that encouraged our services. It was a simple but effective process; call at the office (the back door of the house) give the order and pay the money. We were given a little chitty to hand to the man who would weigh out the coal and load it into a truck or wheelbarrow

Always the devil is in the detail. Appleby's provided the trucks, a miscellany of contrivances made up from any spare timber that had come their way. They were hammered together in all shapes and sizes and if they shared a pair of like wheels that was a bonus. They were hard enough to navigate empty, drop in a hundredweight of coal and one got some idea as to what it was like to be a pit pony. Think of that supermarket trolley, the one with the wonky wheel, the one you always pick; imagine it full of your shopping, think of the weight and that wheel, now multiply that by a factor of one hundred and you have one of our trucks. There was the odd wheelbarrow but mostly they had buckled wheels and permanent squeaks. Trust me on this, after you've pushed a squeaking wheelbarrow a mile or more it does play on the nerves. Put some oil on it you say? We didn't have oil! Asking for it at the coal-yard would have got you an answer, but definitely not oil. Having secured the best truck available one had then to tangle with the portly figure of Art, that was the name of man who was to weigh and load. He viewed all of us lads with equal disdain, we were nought but a nuisance. He snatched the chitty out of proffering hands and reacted as if he'd been asked to scale the north face of the Eiger - which he could never have managed, whatever he was built for it wasn't climbing - even stairs I shouldn't wonder. He was a five-feet six-inch apple - very round apple. Around the yard there were piles of the various coals available and there was one set of scales. Art was not happy if he had to move the scales from nutty slack to best coal across the yard. Like it was our fault there was only one set or that there was distance between the piles. When it came to the weighing Art was an artist, (natural pun that), we are talking about industrial type scales, not the pound of sugar ones seen in grocer's shops, but he balanced a hundredweight of coal to the ounce I swear. On one side, he laid the hundredweight weight and proceeded to shovel coal into the large scoop on the other side. He would ferret amongst the lumps of coal to find one that he could remove to reach equilibrium - no margin allowed. Then he would tell one to get the truck in "the right bloody place" and deposit the contents of the scoop and wish one bon voyage - or words to that effect.

We pushed, pulled and dragged those wretched trucks to their destination. Almost every delivery involved negotiating Essington Road which had a gradient, albeit modest, that according to a variant of Sods Law (an axiom that has it that if anything can go wrong it will) meant that the laden truck had to go uphill whilst the return journey, when the truck was empty, would be downhill. Ever wondered what the difference is between Sods Law and Murphy's Law? Nothing - they're essentially the same, we British refer to Sods but the Americans prefer Murphy's. We had to unload of course and typically we'd get paid two shillings (10p in new money) - that's £2.51 by today's value, but on a good day and a generous customer we would hear the magic phrase "keep the change". Then it was back to the coal yard and Art for an action replay where one might meet a lad who thinks he has a claim on your truck because "I always have that one". "Get thee gone" one would reply - " all barrows have wonky wheels, you'll soon get the hang of that one". Occasionally there'd be a little fracas, but I never lost a favoured truck. On a good Saturday (earnings wise) the three of us could expect to shift half a ton of coal each.

There was irony in the fact that we were fetching coal, a commodity we couldn't afford, except on high days and holidays, as the saying goes. We did get coal - Barry and I got it the hard way, we dug out our own. At the back of the houses in Stretton Road were fields, and in those fields, there were old slag heaps from local mines and in that slag, there was coal. The slag heaps consisted of heavy grey clay, digging into it was challenging work, it was always wet and cloying. There was no magic formula, sometimes you could dig for ages with little to show but the coal was there and when we struck a little vein we would fill our own hand made truck (a soapbox and four pram wheels) and drag it home. We dug deep, too deep for safety but we were ignorant of the risk of trenches collapsing and we had to have coal. I shudder now at how close we must have come on many occasions to being buried had the trench collapsed under the weight of clay we had piled up at the side - it was our good fortune that that never happened. There were other coal-pickers, but we were the most diligent and we kept our home well supplied for months.

There were also coal nickers - sneak thieves that raided the coal stores on the estate. We were visited by such villains one dark winter's night. We had a dog at the time, Teddy, no idea where he came from, it was his job to guard the coal. One night we heard him barking, knew something was afoot and Mum and I rushed to the outhouse where our precious supply of coal was kept. Teddy was silent now, but we paid him no attention because we were just in time to see some wretch legging it down the back garden. He was near the dividing fence when I picked up one half of a building brick and hurled it in his direction. It fell short, lucky for him, had it hit him serious harm would have been done, even before we caught up with him and explained the error of his ways. We returned to the coal store to check the damage. No coal had been taken, Teddy had wrung the alarm in time. But at a price, Teddy was dead. At first, we thought the intruder was responsible, but it turned out that Teddy had strangled himself with his own tether. Next day I buried Teddy in the back garden.

I increased my income when I accepted an offer from Charlie Pearce to pump the water out of his cellar every Sunday morning. The shop had a small cellar where the draught beer was kept. The cool damp environment was apparently good for the ale. Unfortunately, water seeped in a steady and unstoppable fashion and if left unchecked the cellar would flood, and the beer be lost. A hand pump had been installed and at regular intervals it was prudent to pump the water out. Following a good rainy spell, I could stand up to my knees in drainage and it would take a couple of hours to pump it all out. I was paid the princely sum of one shilling and nine pence for my labours (17.5p in the 'new' money) - that's £2.13 by today's value.

Fetching coal and pumping out the Pearce's cellar provided my regular income so to speak. There were also opportunities to top it up occasionally with some one-off work. Like the time, I helped Dad build a pool in the back garden of some rich folk in Crab Lane - Crab Lane leads into Sneyd Lane coming from the Lichfield Road end. The owner, Jack Vaughan, had a small engineering business in Willenhall. Jack and his wife looked after us handsomely, we wanted for nothing in terms of refreshments (wonderful sandwiches) and they paid well. I was only a labourer but nonetheless, I reckon we did an excellent job on that pool. Then there was the time I sold firewood from the back of a horse and cart. One of Dad's sisters lived in Great Wyrley way and one Saturday afternoon her son, my cousin, called most unexpectedly to ask if I would help him sell his bundles of firewood round the estate. We traversed the whole of New Invention and Essington on a horse and cart, it was a wonderful experience, took hours but I made a few 'bob'. Curious as it may sound I never did a paper round, but then there wasn't a newsagent in New Invention until 1956 by which time I had a 'proper' job. Newspapers were brought home by Dad, in Willenhall on his way to and from work.

Things took an interesting turn when Dad let me help on a work-related exercise. He was always on the lookout to do extra work to supplement his wages, usually this simply amounted to overtime. On, for him, a good Saturday he would be asked to work to clear the market place after trading - good because there was always the chance of some goodies being left behind by a careless trader. I particularly remember him coming home one Saturday evening with a case of tinned spaghetti - 48 tins to be exact. I think we all got rather fed (another great pun) up with spaghetti and were mightily relieved when the last tin was consumed. In winter, it meant driving a gritting lorry around the main roads. The lorries were old and unheated, it must have been unbearably cold. Worse still was the poor soul who stood on the back of the lorry, on the grit, exposed to the elements - his job was to shovel the grit into a simple spreader hooked to the rear of the lorry. This mechanical contraption had a rotating wheel that sprayed the grit in all directions. Bad luck you if you happened to get caught behind during spraying. Dad was now a full-time driver with the local council and would drive anything anywhere anytime - that would be low loaders, dustcarts and even gully emptiers (drain cleaners) they're the ones with a left-hand drive that can be overtaken by a snail and the ones that you always manage to find in front of you when in a hurry - no good gesturing, the driver won't see you, he's looking out the window on the other side.

Still in pursuit of extra earnings, Dad had volunteered to assist in the dismantling of ring after the weekly wresting extravaganza at Willenhall baths. It couldn't have been more convenient; the baths lay right behind the town hall and adjacent to the council yard where vehicles were parked overnight.

The wrestling bill was very popular at the time and it wouldn't be long before television (ITV) saw its potential and launched afternoon sessions every Saturday. The baths proved to be a very versatile building, apart from its original purpose of providing swimming facilities to the people, especially school children, of the town, it also put on the wrestling programmes and regular twice weekly dance sessions. The icing on the dance cake was twofold - there was the annual St. Patricks night (dancing was optional - drinking was compulsory) and the Mayor's Ball. All of this was made possible by simply laying down an artificial floor over the swimming pool. Remembering this inevitably reminds me that I never learned to swim because on one school visit to the baths some of the other kids got me into trouble (well – it wouldn't be me, would it?) - I was barred as a consequence.

Back to the wrestling; there was no real need for us to be there until the bouts had finished but we were allowed to attend from the start, so I always got in free. What great nights they were, watching grown men knocking the stuffing out of each other in front of a baying audience, many of whom took the whole affair very seriously. The perennial question was always the same - was it fixed? Of course, it was. Perhaps choreographed would be a fairer description. Eight five- minute rounds of kicking, forearm smashing (punching not allowed) and throwing each other around the ring would exhaust the best athletes were it to be for real - and the damage that would have been sustained would have the AE department missing its targets by a country mile. Odd expression that - 'a country mile' - a mile's a mile, isn't it? There's a quaint tale about the origin and difference. The suggestion is that a mile in the country is harder to travel than one in urban areas, so it's tougher – hence the expression. Some have it that it's longer, but I can find no actual measure.

The skill and fitness levels of the wrestlers were impressive. The objective was simple and clear - entertain the punters - and they did. There were many in the audience who flatly refused to accept that it was anything other than genuine. They would scream, shout advice and opinions and the women were far and away the most vociferous. There were names like Count Bartellii; Masambula (allegedly an African witch doctor); Kendo Nagasaki; Giant Haystacks; Judo Al Hayes; Jackie Pallo; Mick McManus; Les Kellett - and hundreds more, many of whom went on to become household names virtue of television and they gave a certain Kent Walton (real name Kenneth Walton Beckett) a career as a wrestling commentator that lasted some thirty-three years from 1955 to 1988. In the 1970's the Saturday afternoon spot attracted audiences of more than twelve-million. That's Saturday afternoon, match-day at football stadia around the country and shopping day. Peak time audiences for the best programmes (Saturday and Sunday evening) then was circa twenty-million viewers, that illustrates the pulling power that televised wrestling had. It was Greg Dyke that decided enough was enough and ended wrestling's life on television and it never recovered. Kent Walton died on the 24th August 2003.

All the wrestlers were provided by Wryton Promotions (part of Joint Promotions) from Manchester. They would arrive late afternoon, the bill would start about 7.30pm and with four bouts the proceedings usually ended around 10.30pm. I did get to see all the wrestlers leave together in a fleet of limousines and I promise you, they were sort of best friends. Fixed/scripted - of course, but they were very good at it, especially when compared with the American version. American wrestlers still perform like clowns in a circus, so over the top it's embarrassing to watch.

When they finished, we began; the ring had to be dismantled and stored, seats stacked and stored, floor swept. The place had to be made ready for the Saturday dance - the highlight of the week for many of the locals. I got a few bob (shillings) for helping and it was often supplemented by tips from some of the other guys on duty. To round the night off, Dad would most often treat me to at least a bag of chips from the chippie across the road from the baths and then it was off to catch the last bus home. I did that for many months and there was an unexpected bonus; a few of the lads at school were envious of my being able to go and watch wrestling and insisted on a full report Monday morning. And there's more, I found that I could imitate many of the holds and throws quite well.

*****

Acquaintance with the baths was further nourished when Dad was asked (or did he volunteer?) to manage the gent's cloakroom at the Saturday night soiree. Oh, you poor dears that frequent the modern nightclub, is it not that you must keep your possessions about your person, or at least in as safe a place as you can find? How envious you must be of your forebears that could deposit coats and unwelcome accessories to the safe keeping of an attendant hired specifically for the purpose, there was a bit of a naughty though - there were separate cloakrooms for ladies and for gentlemen, oh the shame. However, I should report that, with the considerable benefit of experience and hindsight, not all attendees would qualify as ladies or gentlemen - some were barely human.

Maybe because he got bored or maybe because it was a job for more than one person, (the latter is most likely), Dad enlisted (later turned into conscripted) an elder brother and me to help out, err long and it was just the two of us - Dad gave it up, at least the weekly bash, he still turned out for the 'specials'. The venue was a mecca for local dance enthusiasts and, indeed for many from the bordering towns of Walsall and Wolverhampton. Saturday night especially was attended by hundreds. The work was simple enough - guys came and deposited their topcoats to which we attached a ticket - they were given the counterpart ticket bearing the same number. Come closing time and they returned with their tickets, we found the matching coat and handed it over. Easy you think: but imagine being faced by a mob of young men all anxious, no - desperate, to get out there and mix it with the girls, having to wait to unload their all-of-a-sudden nuisance coats. Advice as to how we might speed up the process flowed freely, peppered with expletives for emphasis. That was them coming in - just think what it was like come leaving time.

Half-way through the evening there would be an interval so that the band could have a rest. Yes, I said band - that's real live flesh and blood musicians, not a DJ playing recorded material so loud that no one can decipher the incomprehensible high- octane chatter that passes for a commentary. The baths did not serve alcohol. Young men out on 'the pull' need alcohol - lots of it, tis their Dutch courage.

This seeming quaint expression has an interesting history. Opinions differ but some trace it back to the thirty years-war in Europe (1618-1648). It is said that English soldiers took a liking to Dutch gin, finding it warming in cold weather, and calming of the nerves (I've heard that one before). That was the only thing they liked about the Dutch, seems the English didn't have much time for what they considered to be a stolid people and the term 'Dutch' became something of a put down. This is best summed up in the expression 'going Dutch' - invite someone out for dinner and tell them they'll be paying for their own. In 1934 the Dutch government got so fed up with the derogatory use of the term Dutch that they dropped it in favour of Netherlands whenever possible. And here's a couple of bonus points - gin is a derivative of Geneva, that's Geneva Switzerland from where the drink originates, and - Dutch is an anglicised version of Deutsche – German.

Patience boys, I know you're thirsty. So, it was that many of the young men repaired to the New Inns, a pub conveniently situated within yards of the baths. There were others that saw the interval as an opportunity to show a girl the outside of the side and rear of the baths. When I asked one chap why? he said that it was to count the bricks in the wall. This I did not understand for it was dark, how could one possibly see well enough to accomplish such a task? Oh, and were girls really interested? Apparently yes - because they always went. I spent much of the time between the incoming rush and the outgoing crush reading distance learning catalogues of numerous professional courses available. I so desperately needed help in focusing on what I wanted to do but alas I found none.

Interval over, normal service resumed - well hardly, the break, the beer and the brick counting seemed to have had an adverse effect on some. I recall a previous experience of beer when it made everyone happy, very happy, but here it had a different affect, so many became unpleasant and aggressive, maybe there was a dispute as to the number of bricks. Scuffles would break out then fights, the combatants would be ejected. The band, the management and the cloakroom boys just wanted it all to end so that we could go home. End it did and then it was pandemonium, everyone wanted their coat now, right now. Two pair of hands cannot comply with such a demand from hundreds. There were oaths and threats.

"Hurry up mate, I'm on a promise".

I didn't understand that message (a lift home perhaps) but the tone suggested it would not be prudent to enquire. Of course, you always get them, the ones who have lost their tickets. They would launch into a description fit only for the Times crossword. Have to wait until the rest have gone I'm afraid. Then comes the abuse, one would be likened to certain parts of the anatomy (I know we only did frogs, but I still didn't recognise any of those parts - need to refer to Cherry Wilkins on Monday) then they would obliquely query the marital status of one's parents.

This was the era of the Teddy Boy when a lot of lads dressed up in mock Edwardian style. They tended to band together and often threatened mischief to anyone who differed. One such specimen pushed his way to the front of the barrier that separated Barry and me from the mob to inform me that he was coming over to sort me out. I thanked him for the thought but suggested the timing wasn't quite right. No, I didn't - I told him that if he put one foot on that barrier I'd thump the living daylights out of him - given that the barrier was chest high and he was pinched for room to manoeuvre I felt I was on a winner. He was three or four years older than me and bigger, but I was cock of the school, never been beaten in a fight - I was also perhaps incredibly naive and stupid yet I meant every word. I think he could see that because he backed down - phew. About four years later I saw this guy again, he'd moved in with a family across the road. Seemed he'd got the daughter pregnant and they had to get married (as was the custom then). Not sure whether it

214

was parenthood or married life, but the steam seemed to have gone out of him - he was quite affable.

I remember that we got help one night from a guy serving in the RAF and based at Cosford. I knew he was RAF because he was in uniform. He was small guy, he forced his way to the front lifted himself over the barrier and said simply.

"you lads need some help" and he helped, and everyone calmed down.

I think his name was John - John, wherever you are, thanks again. Sometimes the nights were so bad we had to leave by the side door in case any unfriendly souls were waiting at the front to do us harm. By then it would be 12.30/1.00am and we had a three to four mile walk home. Later we did get to use bikes – got stopped once by the police, we had no lights – when they learned from whence we came they let us go on our way – still light-less, the money was hard earned.

St Patrick's day 17th March - how the Irish love to party. We got to do the cloakroom for one or two of these nights. They were noisy, boisterous and an incredible amount of alcohol was consumed. It appears that drinking is a rite of passage to the Irish. But here's the best, they gave us not a hint of trouble, drink made them incredibly happy and sociable. We would never dream of going walk-a-bouts on a Saturday night, just not wise nor safe but on St Patrick's it was not only safe it was almost compulsory. The patrons formed groups and sang Irish folk songs with such gusto and passion, anyone loitering close by would be urged to join in and they never tired of offering a drink. Interesting, drink made the Saturday crowd mean and aggressive - it just made the Irish on St Patrick's night happy, just like the men in Froysell Street at the VE party.

There was a balcony around the baths approached by stairs at each corner. I well remember one Irishman, on being invited to join a crowd on the ground floor, looked at the distance he'd have to walk.

"Tis too far, oi'l not find yer".

They urged him some more, so he climbed on to the balcony and jumped, the distance would be about eight feet.

"Now, wot wer ye sayin?" he enquired.

The little crown roared with laughter at his madness and sang and drank even more. One of these fervently patriotic Irishmen cornered me and said how sorry he felt for the English.

We have St Paddy the Welsh have St Taffy and the Scots have St Jock - wot 'av ye got?"

"St George" says I.

"Dat's wot oi mean - you English, formal to the last - e's always St Paddy to us".

He had a point, we don't have a colloquial name for St George. To the Irish, and I suspect the Welsh and Scots such names were a term of endearment. We English didn't make much fuss of St George's day then and we wouldn't now, if it were left to some of the wishy-washy lefty pc public servants, always afraid of offending the minorities. must be noted that the minorities generally couldn't give a hoot. Point of interest - St Patrick was an English slave taken to Ireland circa 500 AD. Like many of the English then he was a Christian and it was he that converted the pagan Irish to Christianity. Did you know that for centuries after his death no one was given the name of Patrick? It was a mark of respect for the revered old man. What they did was to prefix the name with Fitz which meant ' son of' - Fitzpatrick - son of Patrick. Spread to other names too like Fitzgerald and Fitzwilliam. Anyway, to keep the books balanced - St David of Wales was a Welshman; St Andrew of Scotland was one of the 12 apostles and our own St George was, according to legend, a Roman soldier with connections to Greece.

No doubt about it, St Patrick's night was a good night out. Not so the mayor's ball. I'm afraid it was rather dull and very formal. Ball gowns and evening dress suits were the order of the night. They danced like martinets, all stiff and proper. The whole affair seemed very pretentious. We weren't allowed to wander amongst the gathered dignitaries, we weren't properly dressed you see and it was a civic occasion and we weren't 'civic' enough I suppose. Those nights dragged because there weren't so many attendees as on the other occasions and there was no repartee with the patrons. We got paid the same so that was okay. I love the tale of the cub reporter who, trying to impress his friends was heard to say

"I covered one of the Mayor's balls you know" his friend came back, quick as a flash

"Who covered the other one?"

One of the best jobs I had, came about in the summer of 1954. It was harvest time and I, and many others, as we did every year, looked for casual work as a potato picker at Johnson's farm. During the school holidays that would be seven days per week for a short while but in term time that meant Sunday's only because, apart from school, I had my coal round to look after on Saturday although that largely dried up during the summer months. Potato picking was back-breaking work, you had to follow the tractor as it unearthed the spuds and collect them into portable containers which were emptied into sacks located at the end of the rows. Once out of the ground they had to be gathered in, so you had to work quickly. Work would start between eight and nine o'clock in the morning and go on until tea time, at least for us kids, longer for the adults. We endured it because it paid.

*****

School had ended for the year, there was the long summer break to contemplate. Maybe get some spud picking work during the week. Unfortunately, when I got to the farm I found out that a lot of other folks had had the same idea and there were no vacancies. Then I heard a rumour that someone was recruiting spud pickers to clear a field in Sneyd Lane. There were no farms out there, it was largely a built-up road, but I went anyway. Just too late again, got to the field and sure enough they were ploughing up spuds, but the man doing the recruiting said, sorry you're too late, got enough pickers now. There were two of us that got that news - me and another lad about the same age.

" Hang on a minute lads" the man says, "you look a pretty fit pair. How would you like to do some odd jobs over at the house?"

Yes sir, indeed we would, work was work so long as it was legal, decent and honest - and paid.

We didn't know it at the time, but we had just been hired by a Mr J B Jones. Jones had a small chain of paint and decorating shops around that part of Staffordshire, the local one being on the corner of Lichfield Street in Willenhall. This was long, long before the cavernous hangars that are the modern B & Q. He lived in Sneyd Lane and it so happened that he owned a field and rather than let this lie idle he had had potatoes planted. Clearly, he was a man who spotted an opportunity, he was already a rich man, the spuds were just a little bonus. Across the road to the house we went - house! - when we moved into 94 Essington Road I'd been overwhelmed with the size and space, what now was I to make of the magnificent edifice I beheld? The property alone equalled the combined size of ours, the Morgan's, the Harrisons and the PC on the end. It stood in at least an acre of land, it even contained a small detached bungalow, hidden from the road, in which I believe the mother-in-law lived. It was magnificent.   We were to clean the car, generally tidy up the garden and do pretty much anything we were asked to do.

I can't recall the marque of the car, but it was a large, top of the range black saloon - three makes come to mind, Riley; Wolsey and Armstrong Siddeley. It boasted a walnut dashboard and leather upholstery. We treated that car reverently, like it was a new-born baby and we made it shine. The Jones' had a proper gardener, so our efforts were confined to fetching and carrying, especially stuff to the compost heap. We could get lost in that garden and sometimes did. We didn't get to see much of the inside of the house, but we were close enough to see that it was awesome in its layout and furnishings, nothing but the best. Mrs Jones had a helper of sorts, we called her the maid, but she was obviously much more than that. She was young, late twenty's, slim and attractive - and she was great to us lads. She always made sure we had drinks and sandwiches (not butties). The Jones' belied the common notion that rich people treated the poor badly, we were never put upon and were always spoken to in a kindly and encouraging manner and we were paid religiously every Friday. I didn't envy the Jones' - I admired them. They had worked for their rewards, on what grounds can anyone be denied the fruits of their labours? That job ended when the new school term started.

Ever enterprising in terms of ways to earn money, empty bottles were a great source. Long before plastic was introduced (just to annoy the environmentalists) liquids were presented in glass bottles. Of special interest to me (and others) were beer and fizzy pop bottles because they carried a deposit, included in the price paid by the buyer.

The simple and obvious idea was to encourage return of the bottles so that they could be re-used. Three pence (old money) was the levy and if one could rustle up a few the money soon mounted. They had to be returned to the vendor or at least one that sold the brand because that was the only way the shop-keeper could recoup the deposit. We've become a little smug in recent years, thinking that, amongst other things, the modern world invented re-cycling. Utter tosh - we were doing it way back in the 1950's especially us kids and we made a few 'bob' too, it would be a rare bottle that escaped us and found its way to landfill. The more enterprising kids took to knocking on doors asking if they had any empty bottles. There was no sense of entitlement then, money had to be earned and many and varied were the ways this was accomplished. The lucky few were subsidised by parents but even amongst them enterprise flourished.

Chapter 13

AD – AFTER THE DEATH: BC – BEFORE CHRIST: BTV – BEFORE TELEVISION

In the pre-television age, there was every incentive to play outside and we did. In the summer and milder months, full use was made of the fields long abandoned by farmers but not yet snaffled by developers. My preference was the fields that lay behind Stretton Road and included the clay mounds where we did our coal picking. There were patches of dense shrubs and the fields were bordered by ditches and trees. The bushes made for great den building. Dens were rustic and rough and were supposedly known only to the builder and favoured others. They were our hidey holes and were supposed to keep us dry when it rained, alas we were not the most competent roofers, likely we'd have been dryer had we stayed outside. The trees were there to be climbed of course. The dare was to see who could climb the highest, I shudder now at some of the risks we took. I could shin up a tree like a native, so could some of my friends but they weren't so hot getting down, twisted ankles were common. Not yours truly I'm pleased to say - and the reason? Why the good old forward role, when I got to the lowest branch I would simply jump, land and role - nary scratch. I do recall old fatso getting a wee bit out of his depth in the climbing department, seemed that being the biggest meant that he had to be the best. But, like I've said, going up was the easier part - he got stranded on the lowest branch on his way down. The gap between branch and ground seemed huge, his nerve was in hot retreat. Naturally the rest of us came to his aid. We found a soft-landing pad and urged him to jump, he took some persuading but when we suggested it was time we went and that we'd have to leave him hanging there, he was galvanised into action. Oh, how he complained about the wet and the mud and the trouble he'd be in when he got home and why didn't we find a dry patch? The answer's in the question - because it would have been dry.

On the other side of Sneyd Lane and down red lane, so called because it was made from red coloured waste, lay another popular play area. It was known to us kids as 'camel's hump' for the very un-original reason that it was a hump shaped mound in a rather barren piece of land. I think the major attraction of this site was that it was off the beaten track - well away from prying adults. Alas it's no longer with us, the area yielded to the obsession for motorways and is now smothered by the M6 - the Walsall to Stafford section was completed in 1968.

Games we played aplenty. One odd affair consisted of cutting a short (two feet) twig of branch off any old tree and carving a pointed end. Next, we collected acorns from the numerous Oaks that grew in the hedgerows. We removed the cup from the acorn, stuck it on the point of the stick and then - why, we whacked it on a heel to see how far we could project the acorn. Trying to hit the top of the water tower was the ultimate goal. This crude device was also useful for, shall we say, attracting the attention of someone - anyone for whom there was little affection. Depending on the range our little missiles carried a sting. For those that one positively disliked there was the catapult. Nothing shop bought mind, just about every tree could provide the essential 'Y' shaped branch - just cut off what was needed. A strong piece of elastic secured on the forks and a pouch in the middle and there you have it - a perfect missile launcher. The stronger the elastic, the greater the range. I can attest that it's no easy matter trying to outrun the 'bullet'.

Playing hide and seek was great fun. The places one could hide: down holes, in ditches, up trees. When threatened with temporary boredom we'd often have a few minutes playing tick (called tag in other parts of the country). This innocent pastime is great for developing fast feet, sudden changes of direction and bursts of speed. All very handy if one is going to be a professional footballer or when attempting to out-manoeuvre an angry parent. Kite flying was a favourite pastime. Kites were invented in China in the 5th century and had a sane and sensible purpose. They were used to send urgent messages and to measure distances - angles and all that geometry that kids grew to hate at school. As taught we blamed Euclid and his fellow Greek, Pythagoras, never knew the Chinese were at it as well and at the same time.

Our use of this primitive flying machine was entirely frivolous. None of your modern shop bought kites, ours were all home-made. Two reasonably straight sticks garden canes were ideal (if you could sneak 'em past the old man), formed into a cross (no religious intent), string tied to each corner completed the framework. Next, an old newspaper (the News of the World – it was a broadsheet affair then - reached unheard of heights, in stark contrast to the depths that brought about its demise), folded over the frame and pasted down with a mixture of flour and water (sneaking the flour from Mom was harder than nicking the canes). We made a tail for balance using more of the newspaper twisted into kindle style pieces and tied at six-inch intervals. Finally, a piece of string would be secured at the top and bottom making a loose bow shape and the ball of string that was going to be used to control the kite, was tethered to the bow at a point opposite where the canes crossed. We did not launch NASA style, no ten, nine, eight.... just two kids running like crazy trying to get the kite into the air currents and when we did, why those kites flew like birds. There was one unpleasant downside to our kite flying. The fields we used as launch bases were still in use as grazing for the dairy herd that provided our milk. We all know what cows do in fields - apart from chewing their cud - they defecate. Launching required that one kept one's eyes on the kite - as it rose skywards, eyes followed. Eyes staring skywards do not take in what lies groundward. Splodging in a cow pat was, alas an occupational hazard and not popular with parents, especially if shoes were not removed before crossing the threshold. Nowadays, our juvenile pastime has got all serious, there's even a British Kite Flying Association (BKFA). Wherever you see a kite flying now, you'll find an adult (male) in attendance.

During the summer months when there was no coal to be fetched because nobody was lighting fires and the money could be used for more leisurely pursuits, and there not always being company to be had because friends went away to the seaside, I indulged in a bit of train-gazing. Not train-spotting, I never noted down engine numbers and stuff like that, anoraks hadn't been invented. I just loved to watch the magnificent steam engines roll in and out of the station - sometimes Willenhall other times one of the two stations in Wolverhampton - un-originally called High Level and Low Level. For me the appeal is the sheer size of these beasts and that you can see the beating heart so to speak, all the moving parts were on the outside. I get modern trains, but they haven't got the magic of steam.

We played team games too, cricket and football to be precise. They were the only ones we could assimilate. Couldn't do rugby because we couldn't replicate the 'H', and nobody had oval balls - what a brilliant Carry On pun, I'd offer it to the producer but sadly the films, and most of the casts, are no longer with us. A wicket could be an old oil drum dumped in the fields - it approximated in size to the real thing, or we would chalk stumps on a convenient wall. We rarely had a real cricket ball, just as well given our frenetic bowling and flimsy bats. Most often it was tennis balls, they didn't hurt so much, and they could still be wacked a distance. Our typical cricket bat was a piece of a plank hacked to shape, a proper cricket ball would splinter the bat on contact, to say nothing of the numbing of the hand. Football needed only goalposts and that's where jackets came in, just dump them a reasonable distance apart.

They got stood on a lot in goalmouth skirmishes making them sometimes tatty and often muddy. "I fell over Mum" was the lame excuse offered which was followed by a sermon on the cost of clothes, not being made of money and wait till your dad gets home. Balls were always a problem, just like at New Invention school, we played with just about anything that was round - anything that is but a real football. We were faithful to the seasons - cricket in spring and summer, football in autumn and winter. Again, just as at school, them that had the balls (those Carry-On puns keep coming) ruled the game, their decision was final - or else they'd pick up their ball and go home.

When the farmer disposed of the dairy herd the fields were acquired by the local council. They were to be used as play grounds for the growing population of kids as the housing estate expanded. Didn't seem to matter that we'd been using them for that purpose ever since we arrived. To mark the civic intervention, goal posts were installed, and pitches properly marked out. Now we could have a proper game with real goal posts and pitch markings. The latter soon faded and there was many a dispute as to whether the ball was in or out of play - we were learning dissent. Rather surprisingly, this elevation in status also yielded, as if by magic, real footballs. It had more to do with the fulfilment of a Santa Claus wish list for some of the lads. Oh, how different they were to the balls currently in use – a rubber bladder encased in a leather outer and inflated until it was hard. When it was wet the leather absorbed the water and boy where these balls hard to dispatch. Many a knee was jarred in the process and heading – well it has since been established that heading those old 'casey's' as they were known, when wet, could cause brain damage.

*****

We were growing adolescents, testosterone was coursing through our nervous systems, we played football at a frantic pace - it was always all or nothing. It was during one such game that I came face to face with a certain yobbo, he of the Pugga episode. We were playing on opposite sides, I was goalkeeper, he a forward. There'd been a few skirmishes, we didn't get on, but for a while the game took precedence. The other side had a corner, my favourite yob was jostling in the goal area, over comes the ball, master yobbo and I went for it together, I got it as we both landed in a heap on the ground. He didn't like losing out, claimed a foul and I rubbished the idea. Suddenly the game was forgotten, he was going to sort me out. This, I think, was what he was really after - an excuse to pick a fight. He squared up, fists clenched and ready to go. There was no ducking out, I took one step back and said, "ready when you are - just you and me". Thugs like el yobbo rarely travel alone - always had his cohorts to hand and they were there that day - playing for his side. They hadn't hesitated in aiding and abetting in the Pugga affair and I doubted they'd think even once about getting involved now. Saying what I did put him on the spot -"just you and me". I pushed him further, now my fists were ready "okay big man, remember this, I'm not Pugga". We stood staring at each other for a few seconds and then he muttered something about getting on with the game. I wasn't one to start fights but I've often wished that he'd not backed down that day.

Not that I was entirely alone, there were others who had no liking for the bullying lout, I also had friends who I like to think would have rallied, had the need arose. I had made friends with Graham Powers and his brother Malcolm. Graham and I spent a lot of time escapading together. Apart from a mutual love of cricket and football we often went looking for birds' nests. It was the practice of some to remove eggs to add to collections. In fact, it was only the outer shell that was kept, by piercing opposite ends of the egg the insides could be blown out - no one wanted to keep a bad egg. We didn't collect eggs, not really interested, our pleasure was in finding the nests just to prove that we could.

Granted there was some pleasure in noting the assorted sizes and colours. Nesting involved much climbing and clambering, sometimes very precariously.

A more genteel pursuit was picking blackberries which grew in abundance in the hedgerows. The land not being cultivated and there being no major roads in proximity, meant that these tasty marvels were virtually pollution-free. Occasionally, very occasionally - ok, rarely - we managed to take some blackberries home. "Is that all you've managed to pick?" Nope - it's all that survived. Occasionally we would go foraging for pignuts, or to give them their proper names (there are two varieties) 'Conopodium Majus' and 'Bunium Bulbocustanum' - sounds so much better than pignuts. They're members of the parsley family (Umbelliferon) - I cock a snook at those that say Latin is a dead language and question my gardening lessons. Anyhow, pignuts grow in woodland, often amongst bluebells and their root bulbs are unfortunately similar. Unfortunate because if you eat the wrong one (bluebell) you'll get to be rather poorly - they're poison. Pignuts have a similar flavour to chestnuts and can be cooked or eaten raw - we always went for the easy option.

I recall one occasion when a friend and I were half-heartedly scouring a piece of waste land looking for pignuts. I say half-heartedly because had we been paying attention we would have spotted the wildlife in the adjoining hedgerow. We weren't - and we didn't. So, when one of us (it was him) casually lobbed a half brick found lying in the gutter, into the hedge the consequences came as a very, very scary shock. Said brick landed in a wasps' nest and they were not well pleased at having their hard work pulverised. The wasps decided to take issue with the culprits (it was him) and, seeing as how wasps are so little and we were so big, they came mob-handed as the expression goes. Records will confirm that Sir Roger Bannister broke the four-minute mile on the 6th May 1954. Records will not show that two scruffy boys from New Invention, Willenhall may have broken the record two years earlier, along with the 100 and 200-yard sprints (meters were things we put money in to get gas and electricity). We escaped unscathed and decided to pursue safer sources of free food.

The 'five-a-day' mantra is old hat. We were getting ours for 'free' in those happy times. I say free, I mean scrumping - which isn't stealing remember. Towards the top of Sneyd Lane were the large back gardens of properties that butted onto the fields we roamed, and in these gardens, were fruit trees - apples, pears and plums. There were enough apples on the typical tree to stock a greengrocer for weeks - months even. Come autumn much of the crop could be seen rotting on the ground. They wouldn't miss a few and surely, we were performing a valuable service in helping avoid waste? The owners begged to differ, so we always planned to call when they were out, and we'd not be seen - and caught. That's the thing with plans - they don't always work.

As Robbie Burns wrote in 1785 in a poem called 'Tae a Moose' (To a Mouse)

'The best laid plans of mice and men

Gang aft agley'

Legend has it that Burns disturbed a family of mice whilst ploughing a field so, despite their plan to make a safe home, along comes the plough and the plan goes wrong.

John Steinbeck adapted the line as a title to his world-famous novel, 'Of Mice and Men' written in 1937 (recently 'banned' by our Education Secretary because it isn't British). Steinbeck re-wrote the line as follows:

'Best laid plans of mice and men

Often go awry'

So - there we were, high in the branches of an apple tree, quoting Burns and reading Steinbeck, when charging down the garden comes a very irate and large man. Time to go, down the tree I swung and then hared off towards the garden fence.

"Got you now" he yelled triumphantly, thinking that we wouldn't get over the fence.

"Had enough of this. I'm calling then police."

We cleared that fence like it was an Olympic hurdle - boy was that guy mad. I didn't doubt but that he'd call the police. We were much more respectful of the police then and the prospect of meeting an officer in his official capacity and trying to explain the difference between scrumping and stealing just didn't appeal. I did have what is called 'previous' in such matters.

*****

Whilst the Beacon Estate development was in progress, the building sites were popular playgrounds. Wondering in and out of the shells of houses through open doors and windows was great fun. I was with some other lads exploring one afternoon when an idiot member knocked over a tank of black pitch used on the roofs. The disgorged black sticky mass splashed up the wall, the architraves and, of course, the floor. We all beat a hasty retreat, but we'd been spotted - and reported to the site foreman the next day. He wasn't very keen on kids, less so on boys and even less so on what he called 'Bloody vandals.' To the village constable he did go; one PC Chater. PC Chater called on the homes of all those identified - me included. Must admit that I was terrified as to the consequences. Policemen dealt with bad guys, they took them to Police Stations and made them confess and as if that wasn't scary enough, there was Mum and Dad to contend with afterwards.

There was no Police Station just a long and stern lecture by PC Chater in front of Mum who agreed with every word he said. Turned out that the clumsy noggin who'd committed the offence plaintively wailed.

"It wasn't me."

Which was exactly what the rest of us were saying only we were telling the truth. Typical adult response; if you can't find the guilty party, blame the lot. After he'd left Mum warned me that if the builders asked for money to cover the cost of cleaning-up, every penny of my earnings would go there until it was paid. I had visions of my regular toils - pumping in the cellar at the Outdoor and fetching coal - all being done for no reward. The 'noggin' would get a severe telling off if that came to pass. They didn't pursue the matter - I had had a lucky escape (so had the 'noggin'). Getting caught scrumping and being presented to PC Chater again was all the impetus I needed to clear that fence.

*****

Graham Powers was one of only a handful of people of my acquaintance that knew what they were going to do when they left school. Graham was going to be a butcher - and he was and has recently retired after spending his entire working life in the trade. He began as an errand boy for Johnson's High-Class Butcher's (is there a Low-Class version?) located on the bridge at Lane Head. Johnson's slaughtered their own meat from livestock (cows and sheep) they grazed in nearby fields. Sometimes the animals were brought to the slaughterhouse on a Sunday and Graham and I would herd the unsuspecting victims towards their fate. Cows aren't so bad, once they get trotting they'll dutifully follow the leader and all we had to do was act as escorts. Sheep, on the other hand, can be quite a handful. Believe me, they can run - so could we but keeping up was another matter. They galloped like crazy and weren't too bothered where it took them - stuck in ditches, caught up in wire fencing, they'd just barge on until something, or someone, stopped them. Helping them out of a ditch or disentangling them from a wire fence was fun - not! Once in the confines of the slaughterhouse there was a sort of role reversal. Sheep went like lambs to the slaughter (now that is a very poor pun). Cattle could fight and were more than capable of goring a careless slaughter-man. I do recall one cow that went berserk, those in close attendance only escaped injury when it was finally stunned. I kept a safe distance away. There's much talk about how far meat travels before it reaches the consumer, in Johnson's case then, it was less than a mile from the field to the slaughterhouse and then to the butcher's block in the shop.

Graham's granddad - Grandfather Lemm - lived in an old terraced house on Lichfield Road. At the rear of the property was a small yard and at the far end of the yard was a pigsty, and in the pigsty, they did keep a pig. In rural parts of England keeping a pig was widespread practice. It provided the owner with a source of fresh meat, the means by which they could barter with pig-less neighbours, and a walking disposal unit for food waste. Peelings from root crops and trimmings from greens were mixed with leftovers from the dining table and pig meal to create what was universally called 'pig swill'. It was said that pigs would eat anything - I saw nothing to discredit this claim. The term pig swill was borrowed to describe any meal deemed unfit for human consumption. Many a man, returning late (very late) from the pub Sunday dinnertime would find his dinner spoiled, some rounded on the Mrs and declared the meal as 'pig swill'. They usually got to wear it if the wife's aim was good, otherwise it would add to the interior decor. Drink is, of course, known to make some people brave but, in this scenario, reckless - even foolish - would be more appropriate. Doubtless many would agree when sober as they scraped roasties, cabbage and gravy from their shirt and trousers.

The rationale behind pig keeping is that nothing went to waste, literally every part of the pig was edible, from the feet to the ears, to someone. I recall, during a lesson at school, a teacher made this proud boast that every part of the pig was useful - no waste. In the class was a precocious thirteen-year old girl who had a very high opinion of herself and especially fond of being right. She retorted that not everything was used "what about the grunt" she said, smugly. Back came the teacher with a perfect rejoinder "they saved that for you". Oh, how the rest of the class laughed, little missy went scarlet and fumed. Imagine the furore if that happened today: girl would go home and tell parents; parents would complain to school; the incident would be all over social media - 'teacher calls pupil a pig'. The media would storm the school gates. The teacher would be disciplined, snivelling apologies made. Oh, and there might just be a wee bit of compensation going. You've heard the mantra much loved by 'ambulance chasing' solicitors - 'where there's blame there's a claim'. Never mind a five-a-day diet, a generous helping of moral fibre would stiffen the backbone.

Chapter 14

BEST WAY TO SPEND THREE-PENCE (OLD MONEY)

Between school and sundry outdoor activities kids were rarely bored, but one couldn't be outside all the time, weather and other demands saw to that. I belong to that contrary gang who assert that Sunday is the first day of the week. Yes, I'm familiar with the book of Exodus: 34: 21 - 'six days you shall labour but on the seventh you shall rest....' but most people didn't work six days and I like the idea of the working week (Monday to Friday) being book-ended with non-working days. Makes minor difference now every day is a working day. I suppose it's convenient that the weekly shop can be done on Sunday albeit within restricted hours. Back in the 1950's you could buy a bible, a can of peas but not fresh vegetables on a Sunday - curious logic at work there. All this changed with the passing of the Sunday Trading Act 1994 - why, we've even 'progressed' to twenty-four-hour shopping and I'll wager that someone somewhere pops into Tesco's at 2 0'clock in the morning- just to see if they're open

Our Sundays could be dour, we were shipped off to Sunday school mid-morning. The very nerve - didn't we have enough school Monday to Friday? We had to attend the chapel on Lichfield Road. Cost us three (old) pence (0.03p new money) per head, this was, allegedly, to be used to help the less fortunate in foreign parts. I did suggest an alternative - the unfortunates could come to Sunday school and not pay three pence because we didn't need help. Alas, the proposal was not well received. We got to sit around whilst Sunday school teachers told us stories from the bible, overall, they didn't make a lot of sense - they happened a long, long time ago in countries I'd never heard of and anyway, how did anyone know they were true? Another bad move - seems that if it's in the bible it's true. That's religion for you – any religion.

"That's why, when people go to court, they swear on the bible" offered our assertive teacher.

I wasn't done yet.

"But isn't swearing wrong?"

"You'll understand when you grow up" says she condescendingly.

"So why I don't I come back then?" I asked hopefully.

She gave up on me then. Lessons lasted for about an hour, just as well because the heating was turned off - they saved that for the grown-ups and their services. We scurried back home in good time for Sunday dinner. Rationing was easing by now and in 1954 meat was finally-de-rationed and some inexpensive roasts of beef, such as brisket, could be had. A roast beef dinner with roasted potatoes, vegetables and Yorkshire puddings with lashings of gravy more than compensated for a wasted morning.

*****

The first day of the week then, was of mixed blessings and so, I suppose was the last, but Saturday was more rewarding. There was the arduous work of the morning, although this tailed off a little during the summer months. Cometh the afternoon cometh the highlight of the week. The 'three-penny crush' at the Dale cinema in Willenhall. In times past this cinema was actually the home of a family of Maltsters (to do with making booze). It was a matinee performance for kids and three old pence was the price of admission. For that princely sum, we had starters, a short film about anything and nothing - didn't matter, it was a film and then we had the main course - a cowboy film usually. Gene Autry (the singing cowboy), Hopalong Cassidy and everyone's favourite - Roy Rogers with his wife, Dale Evans and Trigger the horse. We cheered him on as he chased the bad guys, we shouted warnings when he couldn't see what we could see - an ambush. We added power to every punch he threw - in fact we saved him more often that he realised. There were Indians in the films sometimes, not always the bad guys, but they always lost. There was an occasional dose of science fiction in the form of Flash Gordon, I remember this as being serialised, made sure us kids would turn up next week. It starred Buster Crabbe, my big sister was sweet on him - oh yes, she was. The special effects were 'special' right enough, you could see the wires holding up the space ships and the acting was better ham than was available in the butchers. Didn't bother us then, it was all novel and exciting.

The Dale would be packed to the ceiling with raucous kids, mainly boys, order had to be maintained. The manager had a long cane, several feet, that would easily reach from the aisle to the centre of a row of seats. Miscreants could expect a menacing poke and, if they didn't do as they were bid, he'd throw them out. The fear of being thrown out and missing Roy Rogers was a more than effective way of keeping us in line. When he wasn't wielding his long cane, the manager could be seen smoking his pipe - we called it a u-bend pipe because that's what it looked like. It was a smaller version of the one attributed to Sherlock Holmes. That suggestion is a bit of license - Holmes didn't smoke a pipe in any of Conan-Doyle stories and neither did he wear a deer stalker.

Saturday afternoon was a time for indulgence, having done time at school, spent much of the weekend earning a few coppers it was now time to put that money to good use. Time to stimulate the gustatory sensory mode - eat! Great sticky buns that would just about fit into a side pocket and a miscellany of sweets and chocolate washed down with a bottle fizzy pop. The common preference was for Tizer, with vimto in second place, lemonade and orangeade were also popular. Sweet rationing ended in 1953 and now Smiths, the tobacconists and confectioners at the bottom of Essington Road was seemingly flooded with the most tempting goodies - pear drops, aniseed balls, fruit spangles, Pontefract cakes, mars bars, Cadbury's dairy milk chocolate, Fry's mint-cream centre chocolate, Sharp's toffee - it was like a day trip to the Wonka factory.

Our introduction to the wild west had a profound effect on the games we played. War games had become 'old hat'. It was all cowboys and Indians now, but there was a problem getting anyone to play Indians - they always lost because cowboys were the good guys. Hollywood was re-writing history – continues to do so to this day. Naturally we practised being quick on the draw – as quick as Roy Rogers, this usually ended in arguments as to who shot who first. That said we did some brilliant dying scenes, staggering for ages after being hit by more bullets than any gun of the day was capable of firing. Ah, if only Spielberg had been around, he'd have spotted the talent on show. We were every bit as good as some of the characters in the average American cop film. Sooner or later there'll be a shoot-out and cops and villains will exchange fire to the equivalent of the contents of the Woolwich Arsenal, miraculously no one will get hit, and many of those that do some amazing how - survive.

We were kids and completely taken in by the hokum that was propagated by these and other western films. Much of this had to do with a genre of writing by authors such as Ned Buntline (real name - Edward Zane Carroll Judson) who wrote and had published 'dime' novels glorifying the character of 'Buffalo' Bill Cody and others. These writings were comparable with the 'penny dreadfuls' on sale in London in the late 19th century and shared a similar mandate - to glorify the more lurid aspects of life in certain parts (the wild west and London respectively), oh and to sell them of course.

*****

Every other Saturday or thereabouts it was haircut time. In the very beginning, this was done at home by Mum and you can forget the tired old jokes about 'basin cuts' because she didn't bother with one, a basin. Hair was combed in a manner reminiscent of the school nit nurse and anything that hung below the collar at the back, eyes at the front and ears on either side was cut off, there was no finesse. On reflection, I reckon our hair must have looked like low-grade topiary and there was much fun made of us in testimony. That was boys only, of course, girls were allowed to grow hair long and all they had to forfeit was the straggly bits at the end. I blame the army - for I believe it was it that gave rise to the adopted hair style of the day for men - the infamous short back and sides. The services generally held the view that head coverings should conceal all hair - none should be seen outside its perimeter. Sergeant Majors of the time rejoiced in reminding any soldier that dared to defy that demand.

"What's under your hat is yours - what's outside your hat is mine - and I want mine so get your bloody hair cut you scruffy soldier"

Being able to earn a little money meant that at last we could go to a proper barber and get a proper haircut. For us that meant a visit to Harry Cooper's on Lichfield Road, the only barber in town as far as we were concerned. Harry would have been as a God to the army for he only cut one style - yes, short back and sides. I still remember the chill after my first visit as areas around my head were exposed to the elements. Now it so happened that we were moving ever so slowly into a period of social change - not that I would have known what that meant at the time. The particular change I have in mind was the growing influence of film actors. One such chappie by the name of Tony Curtis presented a new hairstyle. I never saw it because, apparently, he made soppy romance films - you wouldn't catch Roy Rogers doing yukkie stuff like that.

The style in question involved growing hair long at the back and then combing it horizontally from each side and cutting a parting down the middle. It was called a 'DA' - never found out why but some of my more uncouth peers had it that DA described a vulgar part of a duck's anatomy - dreadful upbringing. The story goes that it was barber Joe Cirello from Philadelphia, USA who invented the style in the 1940's - well it does take us a while to catch up. For the decent minded amongst us it was also known as the duck's tail. Most of my schoolmates were keen to have the cut. I resisted for a while but eventually succumbed and tentatively I asked Harry if he could do the style, he was a bit tetchy about that saying,

"Of course, I can - I'm a ruddy barber aint I?"

Barber he was, able to cut the style he was not. Not only disappointing but also a waste of precious cash. Still, there was one little bonus; I had once been ragged unmercifully by my classmates, for my unruly hairstyle. To those that advocate to always tell the truth, try telling kids who know nothing better that you can't afford a haircut - understanding they will not be, I promise. Anyway, on this occasion I had unexpected sympathy and support. A pretty girl by the name Noreen Lightfoot spoke against the mocking mob and told me that I had nice hair, it just needed tidying up. Noreen was one of those sweet gentle souls who always went out of her way to be friendly. She obviously came from a more affluent background than I, but she never flaunted it. Noreen, if you're listening, I've always treasured that act of kindness, hope you got the life you deserved.

Back to the haircut; word got around the school that there was a new barber in Lane Head who was young and knew how to cut all the latest styles - whatever that meant. Gordon Marsden was his name and his salon was just a few hundred yards past Lane Head bridge, about half a mile from the school. Gordon was everything they said he was and more, young cheerful and not the least condescending to us kids. He saw us for what we were, valuable customers. There was a bonus too, he always kept a supply of comics to be read whilst waiting. I went to Gordon's for several years. I noticed that, on occasions, after finishing with a customer there would a whispered exchange and Gordon would open a draw and discreetly hand I know not what to the customer and they nodded knowingly to each other. I honestly had no idea what was going on, but I did spot that it never happened with us kids. One afternoon a guy on a motor bike pulled up outside the salon, he kept the engine running. Then a young lad, about eight or nine, came in, went over to Gordon and muttered something in his ear. Gordon looked, positively outraged and strode to the door, flung it open and yelled in loud voice.

"If you're big enough to use 'em, you're big enough to come in and buy 'em".

Next thing we heard was the bike roaring off down the road. If anyone reading this has any idea what he was trying to buy, do let me know, I've puzzled about this for years. I have a suspicion that that young tousle head from the sex education class would have had a good guess.

Chapter 15

IF TRAVEL BROADENS THE MIND – THEN READING BROADENS THE INTELLECT

Many of my generation are disposed to sneering at today's kids because of the time they don't spend playing outdoors.

"We didn't have television or computer games, we had to make our own fun".

Wrong at several levels, I have not a shadow of doubt but had these wonderful inventions been around we would have embraced them just as the present generation does. The smug assertion is also flawed because the weather and dark winter nights often confined us to our own four walls - as they do today.

I well remember playing marbles on the bed by myself. I made it interesting by playing my right hand against the left. As with football, this seemed so obvious and natural to me, we had two hands and two feet, made no sense that we had to choose between them.

It was during such periods that I started reading as a means of occupying and entertaining myself. If I have any criticism of modern kids it is that they appear to have lost or not acquired, the desire for, and love of books. Reading is the only activity that allows us to use our imagination to see, and hear, the characters that the author created, to visualise the scenery and setting as painted by the words. The wonderful thing about this is that no one can interfere and impose their view, it's all down to our imagination. Radio has a similar effect, but television requires only that you watch and see what someone else has created for you, your imagination is redundant.

In the very beginning, there were only the newspapers that dad brought home from work – that would be the Daily Mirror and the local rag, the Express and Star. At the weekend, it was the News of the World. I read all of these from front page to back. I had no idea as to the genre of the paper - it was simply reading material. Later I became aware as to the propensity of the News of the World towards a lurid and salacious style of reporting, later still I realised that it gave its readers what they wanted. Even back then, in the 1950's, there was an apparent fascination with film actors though nothing to match the voracious appetite of today. The word 'celebrity' wasn't used in its modern context, probably because there was no demand for that vacuous breed. I recall an item in one edition of the News of the World telling of an article that would be appearing in the next issue. It was to be a feature about the life of Diana Dors, an actress of the day. Why, I thought, would anyone be interested in a story about someone who spent their working life pretending to be somebody else? I wrote to the News of the World to ask that very question - they didn't answer. I was about twelve then and today I'm still not impressed by such articles. I am genuinely unimpressed with the celebrity culture. Celebrities are like the icing on a cake, it looks attractive, but the real substance is the cake underneath, so it is that the so-called 'ordinary' folk are the most important. Without the cake, the icing has no point or purpose, without the ordinary people, celebrities are equally pointless. We can manage without them, they can't manage without us.

I also read the Express and Star printed in nearby Wolverhampton. I've taken the paper pretty much all my life since. As one who has travelled around the UK and bought local papers in other areas I think that I can say with some authority that the Express and Star is amongst the very best.

It was founded in 1889 and remains one of the few independent newspapers in the country. It didn't, still doesn't, have the drivel favoured by some of the nationals. It is still published six days per week, not on a Sunday. Every Saturday there was a special extra edition - the Sporting Star, or the 'Pink' as it was affectionately known. Pink because it was printed on pink paper and it contained all the sporting results of the day. Football was the dominant game and it was reported at every level that was played in the region. No team, no league was too small. The Pink was launched in 1919 and continued until the end of the 2008/2009 football season. Its demise was brought about by increasing incursion of television that saw the end of the exclusivity of matches only being played on Saturdays. Now, matches are played according to the demands of a greater paymaster than the supporters and are regularly transferred to Sunday kick-offs. Growing media coverage also saw results and match reports being provided on the spot, as they happened. Alas the Pink was redundant, it was pensioned off before the start of the 2009/2010 season.

*****

Sometime around 1953 I think it was, I contracted chicken pox. That wasn't all bad, true there was the infernal itching and so many spots I looked like the inside of a pomegranate and there was the daily dousing with calamine lotion, the pungent pong from which there was no escape. But the blessings my dear friends, compensated in abundance. There was no school for five weeks - five lovely long weeks. Chicken pox was (probably still is) highly contagious, had I gone to school, which of course, I desperately wanted to do, I could have infected the whole lot of 'em. To the kids, I'd be a hero, parents and staff would opine differently methinks. For the very same reason, I had to be isolated from brothers and sisters. Had I passed it on to them mom might not have been well pleased. So, I was bedded down in the front room all on my lonesome. Mom checked on me frequently but the rabble that was my siblings kept a more than safe (and envious) distance.

Confined to bed there was little to do to pass the time. No television and the only radio in the house was in the living room, thus I resorted to reading and more reading. Newspapers were summarily despatched. And then I found an unlikely source of new material - women's magazines. Mom read Red Star; Silver Star; Red Letter; Oracle; Woman's Own and several others - she didn't buy all of them, most were donated by neighbours. It's what they did then, there was no recycling and one small dustbin. Keep passing them on and they become someone else's disposal problem. To a twelve/thirteen-year-old they represented reading material. I had no concept of magazines just for women, of genderism. If there were male equivalents I never saw any.

These magazines were packed full of stories and I was getting to love stories. There was modest advertising and a few pictures, black and white of course. They were to be read, unlike their modern kin that are often little more than picture galleries - in full colour naturally. Stories, as I knew them, are absent from the pages. What we have now is the, often garish, confessional tales of readers' real-life experiences, told for cash. These features share a common theme, the tale-tellers (they are sometimes ghost written) are invariably innocent victims of some dastardly bounder who has done them wrong - they even venture into martyrdom. Lest I get misunderstood, many of the stories are of profound personal tragedies, it's the self-serving tone I balk against. Anyway, tis my opinion that today's offerings fall well short of the standard of their forebears - I like to read magazines, not just look at them. The cliché about a picture being worth a thousand words falls well short.

There's an interesting personal legacy to this experience of reading mom's magazines. It is that, to this day, I am comfortable reading publications designed for women only - as I am for men. Later life's events were to confirm this state. Good though I found them to be, these magazines were quickly devoured by someone confined to bed for five whole weeks. More! I wanted more. I found another source in dad. Turns out he was reading crime novels, westerns (that's cowboys and Indians) and a new brand on the market - war stories. I remember Hank Janson's crime books, they were American based. I read them because they were there but in a more discerning frame of mind, I think I would have dismissed them for the literary drivel they were. In truth, I have never come to terms with the resigned cynicism of the characters created by American writers of this genre. I don't enjoy Richard Chandler's Philip Marlow novels, they're set in the 1930's - the period of the great depression and that's what I get out of them - depression. How do I have such an opinion? Simple - I read some. How else can I form my own opinion? Far too often people allow their minds to be made up by some third party - a critic or a friend. People, do your own research, make up your own minds.

The appeal of the western books was obvious, they fitted well with the films offered at the Saturday three-penny crush. There was a miscellany of authors none of whose names I can recall but there was a common theme - bad guys, good guys, odds against good guys but good guys always won in the end. Like many of our much-loved films of the day, they completely distorted the American 'wild' west. White men were depicted as virtuous explorers frustrated by the uncivilised Indians (the indigenous population). I say again, do your own research, come to your own conclusions. Books on the recent war were in abundance. I read voraciously about the German concentration camps and the Japanese labour camps. By sheer number of books read I got a broad perspective on these indictments of man's inhumanity to man.

Now, dear reader, you may have formed the impression that

choice of reading material was, shall we say, a bit odd. Well, first off, I read what was available, but second - and more importantly - it got me hooked on books. Following a full recovery and return to normality (school - yuk), I enrolled at the library in Willenhall. Joy of joys, the library let me borrow books for free, three books at a time as I recall. There began a long, long period of reading books of choice, the choice being that of a young adolescent boy. I believe I read all the Biggles novels. Biggles was the nickname of James Bigglesworth, a character created by Captain W E Johns. Biggles was a first world war fighter plane ace. Johns himself, was a pilot in that war, he served on the Western front, flying a De Havilland plane. Alongside Biggles, I consumed the Just William series, the work of Richmal Crompton (it was a time before I realised that Richmal was a woman). Her full name was Richmal Crompton Lamburn. Crompton was her mother's maiden name. The Just William books were originally intended for an adult audience, but the escapades of a well-meaning typical lad just couldn't fail to appeal to his legion of kinsmen in real life. Richmal Crompton was a remarkable woman; she contracted poliomyelitis, losing a leg in consequence; she had a mastectomy to repel a cancer scare and still volunteered for the fire-service during the second world war. She was also an active suffragette - no wonder women won the vote with such redoubtable characters. Both Biggles and William Brown fell victim to the pc brigade, at one period they were considered to be too middle class and unrepresentative of modern youth. Garbage, utter garbage - these stories have thrilled and entertained boys across the social spectrum for decades. Strange to relate but, as a child, I didn't read Enid Blyton. Went a long way to redress that shortcoming by reading them to my kids and grandchildren. I'm mentioning that here because she too fell a foul of the PC militia. Tis my carefully considered opinion that that band of 'intellectuals' do more harm than good, despite their oft good intentions.

Over the years that I had access to the library my reading range spread, and I would try almost anything. One thing held true (still does today) if a book doesn't engage me I stop reading it. I am saddened by the fact that reading books has fallen out of favour with many of the young. Given the range of alternative distractions I suppose that's inevitable. If it's travel that broadens the mind, then it is reading the broadens the intellect. Reading introduces the reader to new words, and the varied use of familiar ones. I was once given a sound piece of advice; it was to have a dictionary to hand when reading and then, when you come across a word you don't understand, you can look up its meaning and help your understanding and enjoyment of the book and, at the same time, add to your vocabulary. I have never stopped applying that advice. The bigger the vocabulary, the better you will be at expressing yourself. It's an unfortunate fact that a great deal of dispute between people is a lack of understanding largely caused by an inability to say what is meant in the manner intended. Winston Churchill once said that he could forgive people most failings but had difficulty with the lack of ability to express themselves in their mother tongue. Lest you get the idea that this man born to privilege, was in any way being superior, think again. As a youngster, he was a bit of a duffer at school. His love of the English language was his inspiration for not only those great second world war speeches, but also for his prolific output of writings that were to follow. In 1953, he was awarded the Nobel prize for Literature. The citation read as follows.

'For his mastery of history and biographical description as well as for his brilliant oratory in defending human values'.

He may have been difficult to teach but he was a brilliant learner.   I
I wonder if Churchill ever got to read comics - probably not, his parents were terribly strict, no allowance for frivolity. Anyway, that's where I scored over him because comics I read aplenty.

There was the Dandy - first published in December 1937, the last edition was published on its 75th anniversary, December 2012 but it survives online. Remember the tales of Desperate Dan and his famous cow pies, and Korky the cat? Then there was the Beano, first edition 30th July 1938 and still running. Remember Dennis the menace, the Bash Street kids, Roger the Dodger (could have taught him a thing or three) and Lord Snooty and his pals (frowned upon by a class obsessed lobby). Film Fun (January 1920 to September 1962) and Radio Fun (October 1938 to February 1961) both carried story board style cartoon tales about popular entertainers of the period. For the more mature boy (those that could read proper words) there was Hotspur and Rover, these were full of tales of adventure like Alf Tupper - tough of the track. We had the Knockout (1939) and tales of Billy Bunter who was extremely fat and ate voraciously, wouldn't be tolerated now by the thought police. Mom's brother, uncle Jim bought us the Comet, which had a short life span (1950 to 1958) and resurrected the character of Billy Bunter. And there was the Eagle, lead story was Dan Dare - Pilot of the Future., a sort of Captain Kirk and the Starship Enterprise of the day That was the staple diet - the starters.

The main course was the proliferation of cowboy comics that literally flooded the market. Amongst them was Roy Rogers (of course); Gene Autrey; Hopalong Cassidy and Lash Larue - sorry Indiana Jones but Lash Larue was using the bullwhip long before you were born. And lest you think us boys were obsessed with cowboys (we were), there was also Batman and Captain Marvel (and Captain Marvel Junior); Tarzan and Superman. Fact - Captain Marvel was the first super-hero, he paved the way for Superman.

There were far too many of these comics for any one kid to buy so it was common practice to swap. I remember one neighbour - Billy Francis - who always seemed to have an abundance of comics. He also had a generous sister, Billy told of how she bought him a car just as soon as he was legally able to drive. It was a Ford Consul and Billy proudly boasted that he went everywhere in the car. Anyway, I reckon she also funded his comic collection, always great to swap with Billy who, contra to what people might have thought, was not spoiled by his sister's largesse. Another source of swap was slightly more unusual - it was with a man who worked with Dad - Kenny Walters. Kenny was a big lad, he'd be classed as obese now, he was single and lived with his mom. He would call round occasionally to see Dad, I suspect he was lonely for some adult male company. Kenny was an easy-going guy and could tell a good tale of the goings on at the council depot. For an apparently un-educated man doing menial work, he was no bad speaker. Certainly, I've heard qualified professionals that would pale in his company. Kenny liked boy's comics and always came with a bundle as a gift - rarely swapped.

*****

We're here in the early 1950's. Television is a luxury item enjoyed by the privileged few. Most of the population relied on radio for light relief and in-house entertainment. The BBC had a monopoly - no commercial stations. The British Broadcasting Corporation (BBC) was set up in 1922 under Sir John Reith. It is the oldest national broadcasting organisation in the world. Funded by license fee and free from commercial advertising I am constantly astonished and dismayed at those who would have it become commercialised. The good old 'Beeb' broadcast on three wavelengths back then - Home Service covered news and the serious stuff; Light Programme, the clue is in the title, it offered light relief and the Third Programme, the third offered serious music - now known as classical. Television was launched in 1934 but to a very small minority of receivers. It would be twenty years before most of the population got to watch TV. The trigger point was the current Queen's coronation in 1953 and the launch of commercial television in 1954. Coincidentally it was also around this period that the BBC became known as 'Auntie'. Generally assumed to have been coined by a journalist (unknown) it is said to reflect the staider style of the BBC when compared with the brash commercial channels. Nowadays the term has become one of endearment.

Meanwhile we had the good old radio. I have fond memories of Dick Barton - Special Agent, a fifteen-minute serial that had us kids (boys) hooked. The theme music was an exciting piece called 'The Devil's Gallop' and was specially composed by one Charles Williams. Aided and abetted by his trusty sidekicks, Jock and Snowy, Dick Barton ran from October 1946 to March 1951 when it was replaced by The Archers which runs to this day. We mourned the loss of Dick Barton. The Archers didn't cut it for energetic adolescents. But in 1953 the BBC redeemed itself with the launch of Journey into Space. Forget Captain Kirk and the Starship Enterprise; Luke Skywalker and Star Wars - they were preceded by Jet Morgan, Doc, Mitch and Lemmy who battled aliens on a weekly basis. No self-respecting kid missed an episode.

Mention police dramas and most folk of a certain age go back to dear old Dixon of Dock Green, but he wasn't the first. That position belongs to radio's PC 49 - tales of a police constable with a most unlikely name - Archibald Berkley-Willourby. PC 49 pounded the beat of the Light Programme from 1947 to 1953. I recall listening to Orson Wells as Harry Lime in the Third Man, a radio adaptation of a 1949 film. Wells' distinctive tones gave off an eerie feel to the programme. What may be regarded as the first 'soap opera' in the UK, although the phrase hadn't crossed the Atlantic then, was Mrs Dales' Diary which ran from 5 January 1948 to 25 April 1969. This was about the daily life of a doctor's wife. Doctor Jim Dale had a very formal way of addressing his mother-in-law - he always called her 'mother-in-law'. 'Soap Opera' is the name that was given to radio or television programmes broadcast in the USA and sponsored by soap powder manufacturers. The first such offering was a radio broadcast in 1930 from Chicago, USA and called Painted Dreams.

Comedy programmes were great favourites. Jewel and Warris (Jimmy Jewel and Ben Warris), radio's version of Morecombe and Wise; Life with the Lyons (Bebe Daniels and Ben Lyon); the incomparable Al Read; The Clitheroe Kid (the diminutive Jimmy Clitheroe); The Navy Lark; ITMA - It's That Man Again (Tommy Handley) and probably the most amazing of all - Educating Archie (ventriloquist Peter Brough and his dummy 'Archie'). Surely only us British could come up with the notion of a ventriloquist appearing on radio - and making it work. Those in the know said that Brough wasn't a very good ventriloquist - would he need to be?

Music was of the light variety, the Third Programme catered for the serious stuff, and the 'pop' music genre hadn't matured into what we hear today. There was Children's Favourites with Uncle Mac; Family Favourites for servicemen serving in foreign parts; Music While You Work and the Billy Cotton Band Show, a raucous round of musical merrymaking. Singers were of the ballad style and I must say that I found most of them bland. That, however, is preferable to the modern equivalent. So many 'singers' now drag the words out of a seemingly tortured larynx and as lyrics reluctantly escape, facial expressions are akin to those of having teeth extracted without anaesthetic.

I still love the radio. Radio Four is my choice for its rich diversity of programmes. I'm glad, and relieved, that pop music has its own dedicated stations. I find the standard of music average to poor and the banal meanderings of some presenters patronising, even insulting. That people get paid huge salaries just to play music made by others is one of the weird wonders of our culture. I recall one famous disc jockey (DJ) telling a tale of a meeting whilst on holiday. Seems he met up with a fellow holiday maker who asked him what he did for a living.

"I'm a DJ".

His acquaintance look puzzle.

"What's a DJ?" he asked.

It was in the telling that a DJ plays records on the radio that this DJ realised the shallowness of his work. The great asset of the radio is that it feeds the listeners imagination. We are free to interpret the audio input in any way we choose. We create our own scenery; our own idea of what characters and broadcasters look like. Television takes that away because it does it all - audio and visual - leaving little or nothing to the imagination. The radio can be listened to on the move, in fact it's recognised as a safety factor in driving, helping drivers to stay alert.

Chapter 16

FESTIVE DAYS – SMITH STYLE

Birthdays came thick and fast at 94 Essington Road. Mum always made sure that we had card from her and Dad. Grandparents always remembered and there were usually a few coppers for the birthday boy/girl to spend on themselves. Mum couldn't go to presents, money was too tight and there were so many of us. Didn't spoil the day because there was an unspoken rule that on someone's birthday the rest of the clan had to be nice. We would, of course, save any nasties for the following day or days.

We didn't do annual holidays either, the cost would have been frightening to ludicrous. Bank holidays were kept in accordance with the prevailing tradition. The term 'bank holiday' is a colloquialism for what is a public holiday. The more familiar term 'bank holiday' followed the passing of the Bank Holidays Act 1871 which was the work of Sir John Lubbock MP - and banker - now it becomes clear. Banks would close on the nominated days and presumably it was felt that without access to money, no one else could work either, so they didn't. Here's an interesting titbit of information - in England, Wales and Northern Ireland, Good Friday and Christmas Day are not bank holidays (as they are in Scotland). The reason - they were common law holidays as most significant in the Christian calendar and to even think about working would have been blasphemous. Christmas Day and Good Friday have always been public holidays, so it is that all bank holidays are public holidays but not all public holidays are bank holidays. But what do we care? A holiday is a holiday.

Easter was, and remains, the first public holiday of the year. We weren't churchgoers and not particularly religious, but religion still held great sway over the establishment and influenced the conduct of the population. On Good Friday, we had fish, maybe a boiled dinner with steamed cod, or a serving from the local chippie. Good Friday fish is a catholic thing apparently for no great reason, as far as we were concerned it was food - and good food at that. I guess Mum, like most folk were simply maintaining a tradition. Of special significance, of course, was hot cross buns. They were only available at Easter time - Good Friday in particular. They were especially enjoyed because of the novelty. Nowadays, they're available all the year round and have become just another bun in a world full of buns. Mum got our buns from the local Co-op. They were delivered fresh from the bakery in Walsall and would still be warm when we got them home. Butter was acquired for the occasion - best butter for this was an annual treat. A fresh hot cross bun spread with best butter is one of life's simple luxuries.

In the beginning, the chocolate egg season that was Easter eggs passed us by but as things eased financially Mum would make a special expedition to the great metropolis - Wolverhampton and to the store of one F W Woolworth & Co Ltd renowned for their low prices and, it should be acknowledged, low grade merchandise. Woolies were the proud purveyors of an inferior brand of chocolate Easter egg - hollow but wrapped in silver paper. The chocolate fell short of Cadbury standards in the taste department, but they were Easter eggs and they were ours. The silver paper wrapped around the eggs would be carefully removed so as not to tear. It was then smoothed and placed in one of the many annuals we had at Christmas time. Why? Because it was too pretty to screw up and throw away.

Another annual event to which was paid great homage was bonfire night. We Smiths turned it into a great family party that was renewed every year for many a year. Sadly, it has now been superseded by a vulgar American export - Halloween. How shallow, how superficial that greater prominence now be given to a trashy commercial game than to one of the most significant events in English history. In the early 17th century King James was vacillating in matters of religion. Catholics wanted the country to turn to Rome. Exasperated by James' dithering a certain Robert Catesby plotted, with others (including one Guy Fawkes) to blow up the House of Lords on the 5th of November 1605. Curious how we identify this affair with Guy Fawkes – he was just one of a group of plotters – Catesby was the ring leader. Anyway, there are those today who harbour similar aspirations I suspect. The grand plan was to replace James as monarch with his 9-year-old daughter, Elizabeth whom Catesby and his crew felt sure they could direct to Rome and Catholicism.

The plot was leaked, and soldiers of the king rushed to the House of Lords where they found Guy Fawkes, guarding the gunpowder. For that he was assured notorious immortality - and executed most painfully - he and seven other conspirators were hung, drawn and quartered. It has passed into history as the Gunpowder Treason Plot, but it also has a less familiar name - the Jesuit Plot. Seems that the principal Jesuit of England, Father Henry Garnet was said to have known of the plot and did not report it to the authorities. That made him complicit and he too was executed. Thing. is - it was likely that he heard by way of a religious confession, which was, of course sacrosanct.

In fairness, the tawdry Halloween celebrations we endure nowadays are not a true reflection of what began as a powerful religious occasion. 'All Hallows Evening' is marked in many countries on the 31st October annually - the name evolved into Halloween over time. It is an ancient Celtic festival and can be traced back more than 2000 years in Ireland where it was known as the feast of Samhain. Its purpose was to remember the dead and, because in ancient times death was feared, if not more then, certainly differently to now, the plan was to mock and make fun of death (trick or treat is in there somewhere). Ironically, the growth of Halloween in North America came about largely following the mass immigration of the Scots and Irish in the 19th century. Looks like we've imported that which we first exported - a true case of getting your own back.

Preparations for bonfire night started early - October to be exact. Money had to be acquired for fireworks and there was a fire to build. Money was collected by any means possible, mostly from savings out of earnings. A reluctant practice since some cherished consumption had to be foregone - a sticky bun here, a packet of spangles there. A customary practice was to tout for 'a penny for the guy'. A crude (very) effigy of Guy Fawkes made from an old sack stuffed with straw, a ball of straw for a head, two long sticks for legs, two shorter ones for arms - all limbs padded with more straw. The classier ones had hats. This misshapen scarecrow could hardly be carried about - he would surely have fallen apart. Given his revered status our Guy Fawkes' travelled by coach if you please. By coach I mean soap box cart. A soap box cart was exactly what it said on the box - a wooden box used to transport soap and removed from one of the local shops. Said box was nailed to a short plank of wood courtesy of any local building site when the night-watchman was dozing. Wheels were basically anything that was round and would go, round. Pram wheels where favourites as families ditched perambulators as soon as the offspring got too big to fit - or Mom got tired of pushing. The 'royal' procession then toured the neighbourhood knocking on doors and accosting anyone not smart enough to cross the road when they saw us coming. 'Penny for the guy' was the only cry ever uttered - mostly we were given advice as to re-locating but there were some decent folk who remembered the times they had following the same caper. With the monies raised we would rush to the shops the very next day to buy fireworks. Not just any fireworks - none of your pretty fountains and colourful fizzers and definitely no sparklers - they were too girlie. There two special favourites

- must haves. One was a jumping jack that snapped and cracked as it bounced around on ignition. The other - the all-time number one - Standard Fireworks special one penny banger - exploded like a mini-stick of dynamite. The Standard Fireworks company was once the proud purveyor of British fireworks. Founded in 1891 by James Greenhaigh and located in Huddersfield. Now it's a part of a Chinese company - Black Cat Fireworks.

Neither jumping jacks nor bangers were popular at the bonfire - scared the kids, frightened any pets and annoyed the adults. Pity - annoying adults was a rare opportunity for revenge for making us get up and go to school, come home for tea when we were winning at marbles or something and nagged and yelled at for no good reason - ever. On the other hand, that left more of these explosive delights for 'private pleasure'. Imagine walking past a queue at a bus stop on a cold October/November evening - then, suddenly there's a series of loud snap, crackle and pops (and I'm not talking Rice Crispies) as someone casually drops a jumping jack after lighting the fuse. I'm here to tell you honestly that never ever did I hear anyone express appreciation for the sudden exercise that surely saved them from freezing to death as they stood motionless in the cold.

That, however, was nought when compared with the effect that the penny banger had when it went off - grown men would jump out of their long johns, women out of their bloomers. Here again I must confess to completely reckless behaviour. These bangers were powerful in their way and the instructions for use were crystal clear - 'light the blue touch paper and stand well back' - to the faint hearted that meant 'run'. Yours truly and his kind were not hot on reading instructions - too much like being given orders and boy did we have enough of that. The practice was to light the fuse and carry the burning banger and drop it casually where it would have the desired effect - behind a crowd or outside a front door - especially the front door of anyone who had annoyed one. The most devastating bang could be had by hiding the little bomb under a biscuit tin. You may imagine the effect of putting a jumping jack in a tin as it literally bounced off the sides. These were the days before pre-packed biscuits, they were delivered in seven- pound tins and weighed to order at the grocers. Smith's crisps were delivered in the same sort of tins, but they were already bagged. In the confined space of an empty tin measuring one foot by one foot by one foot the Standard one penny banger was like dynamite. Let one off in the street and doors would be flung open and abuse hurled. Some nasty types were in the practice of pushing these little monsters through letter boxes. That was always felt a step too far for me - sort of made it personal and cruel. Over the years, I must have carried hundreds of these bangers, fuse burning and held to the last possible moment before throwing wherever and nary an accident befell me, still got all my fingers. A charmed life to be sure for others were not so fortunate.

Bonfire night itself was always a family affair. We had one of the biggest fires in the area. It was made up of anything that would burn - old furniture, mattresses, newspapers (there was no re-cycling), cartons and wooden cases - literally anything supplemented by scavenging from neighbours too civilised to have a fire of their own. Old car tyres were favourites, they burned so well and so long. We supplemented this motley collection of debris with fallen branches from the trees in the nearby fields that were our playground. Huge branches were dragged through the streets of the estate to meet their fate. We built the fire up days before the big event and prayed for no rain, but we bought a gallon or two paraffin just in case. Then around seven o'clock came the moment - a dash of paraffin, a lighted torch carried from the kitchen and - whoosh! up she went. A good supply of reserve fuel was kept back to keep the blaze alive for longer. After a while there would be red hot embers gathering at the base of the fire - onto those embers we chucked potatoes to bake in the most primitive of ways. They'd stay there till they turned black, scorched on the outside equalled cooked on the inside apparently - not always so but it was bonfire night and they were good. Mum hated fireworks but nothing in the world would have prevented her from joining in the fun - albeit from the safety of indoors. She made a magnificent contribution - she cooked a huge pan of gray peas and diced bacon - a great Black Country favourite. A bowl, served hot, was the perfect insulator against the chill of a November evening. For some there were unfortunate side effects - wind, not for nothing were gray peas referred to as 'gray farters'.

Gray peas are, in fact, brown and are used by pigeon fanciers to attract their birds (pigeons - not the un-feathered variety). A tin of gray peas shaken and rattled outdoors soon has the pigeons homing in. Peas are funny that way - dried peas, used to make mushy peas, are green but they're called 'blue peas'. By the way, blue peas will grow lovely fresh peas if planted - Dad did this often to save the cost seeds.

So many folks had bonfires in those more carefree days. I don't recall any serious incidents and I never heard of the Fire Service being called out, not in our immediate area anyway. We did pay attention to basic precautions like keeping the paraffin can and fireworks well away from the fire. The fireworks especially, it would have been a disaster had they gone off all together, even though they were mostly the pretty-pretty ones. I say mostly because there were exceptions like one called 'aeroplane' - the one that flew straight at me and hit me on the chest, and just bounced off - no damage. The night air would be filled with acrid smoke that would linger long into the following day - clear vision there was not. Pollution levels would have had the Green Party spluttering in outrage. If the harbingers of doom are to be believed, then our bonfire nights may have made a significant contribution towards global warming. Of more immediate importance, was the fact that housewives (daren't call them that now - they are Homemakers) couldn't hang out the laundry - unless they were looking for the smoky-grimy affect. Our task the following day was to tidy up the ashes and bits of anything that didn't or wouldn't burn. Guess what happened to that little lot? Why - we dug a hole and buried it - over the years we dug so many holes we started to inadvertently excavate the remnants of past burials. No problem - they just had a re-burial with the new stuff.

Alas all of that is but a ghost of the past. Bonfire night, along with so many other things, has been sanitised and subjected to something called 'risk aversion'. Where's the fun in doing anything out of which has been extracted the risk? That's what makes it exciting. Seems like every human activity now is subjected to the stultifying effect of Health and Safety. I guess that that's how us kids discharged the explosive testosterone levels of adolescence, taking stupid risks and, it has to be said, sometimes getting hurt in consequence. Question is, is it better nowadays when the risk has been assessed and any danger compensated for? Where's the thrill? Bonfires behind deep barriers, organised firework displays. Sure, there's some pleasure in watching but there was so much more in being a part of the action. We've turned into a nation of voyeurs. Teenage boys are deprived of a vital means of coping with the rushes of adrenalin that come with their transformation from boyhood to manhood.

Chapter 17

BEST DAY OF THE YEAR – CHRISTMAS DAY

We celebrate Christmas on the 25th December, said to be the date of the birth of Jesus - only no one really believes that that was the date he was born, and it gets better - there is no consensus as to the actual date. The most plausible reason for the 25th is that this coincided with the dates of the Roman Saturnalia feast and of other pagan festivals such as Kalends and Deus Sol Invictus (birthday of the unconquerable sun). This latter was the only one that occurred on the 25th December. In AD 350 Pope Julius, Bishop of Rome decreed that the 25th of December would henceforth be celebrated as the birth date of Jesus. The church proved its guile by simply allowing the existing pagan celebrations and then ever so slowly and subtlety, hijacking them and turning them into one Christian event marked as the birth of Christ. There's more - sources have it that Jesus wasn't called 'Jesus'. Jesus is the English translation of the Greek 'Lesous' or the Hebrew 'Yeshua' or 'Joshua' - you just can't trust anything.

One man who was most certainly born on the 25th December (1642) was Sir Isaac Newton philosopher, physicist and mathematician - he transformed the world and is acknowledged as one of the greatest scientists ever. He didn't discover gravity - it was already known about; Newton's contribution was to do the maths so that the greater benefits of the knowledge could be exploited. So, there we have it, one man who wasn't born on the 25th December and another who was - amazing which one we remember most.

I confess to loving Christmas - always have. I love the

buntings, the garlands and the balloons. I love Christmas dinner, Christmas pudding, Christmas cake and mince pies. I love Christmas cards the carols and carol services, yet I'm no church goer because I can't accept the church's concept of God - in fact, I don't do gods of any kind although I understand the need and function. I love the giving and receiving of presents and the manic shopping.

The cumulative effect of all these different threads of Christmas is to create, for just a brief time – a day, maybe even a few days when most people genuinely make an effort to be kind and good to most others. Doesn't last, in fact for some it doesn't survive the day, so strained are they by the effort that they mentally explode and for them, and those around them Christmas is blighted. But for the majority Christmas is truly a time of peace and goodwill to all men (and women) as differences are set aside and truces declared, fresh starts avowed.

Christmas at 94 Essington Road was never affluent but we rejoiced in the basics. Mum made Christmas cake and puddings, the latter spending many hours boiling in the boiler. Inside each pudding, she would put a sixpenny piece - it was a long-standing tradition. In earlier times mums, would put in a silver three-penny piece, or three-penny bit also known as a 'joey'. These little coins first appeared in 1547 during the reign of King Edward V1 and continued in production until the mid-20th century although there were lengthy periods when the coins went out of favour and were not minted. They became unpopular because of the size - difficult to handle and were superseded by a twelve-sided brass version during the reign of King George V. If you were lucky enough to get the piece of pudding containing the coin, it was as if you'd struck gold - and likely chipped a tooth or two in the process.

We made our own decorations. Crepe paper was twirled to create a series of waves and strung across the living room ceiling, from corner to corner. Paper chains made from coloured paper cut into strips and pasted into a circle, each one looped through the next, like a proper chain. Our Christmas tree was a modest little fellow but had seen good service. A few old decorations and some candles (to be lit on the evening of the big day) completed the ensemble. In the early days, there wasn't much in the way of presents. There simply wasn't enough money. Mum would start buying small gifts around November time mostly from a local 'tallyman working for a company called Home Products. The tallyman was a debt collector collecting payments for goods bought on hire purchase, or the 'never-never' as it was less affectionately known. This sort of trade flourished in the poorer parts of the country, the tallyman was still operating up to the 1960's. The name tallyman goes way back to times before most people could read and write. A record of transactions (usually money owed) was simply carved onto a wooden stick. Amounts decided the depth of the cut. Typically, contributions would be carved on one side and final settlements on the other, doubtless there were variations. It was an ingenious device. Hire purchase has been largely replaced by personal loans, overdrafts and credit cards and the tallyman consigned to history.

The sort of presents we could look forward to, included board games such as ludo, snakes and ladders and drafts. There were also comic book annuals, these were bumper Christmas editions of the favourite weekly comics like Dandy, Beano, Knockout, Film Fun and Radio Fun. Presents were not gift wrapped, that would have been money wasted. Each of us had our own little pile and as we came downstairs on Christmas morning Mum would direct us to ours. Aunts and uncles chipped in with the boring essentials - socks and handkerchiefs. Handkerchiefs were the forerunner of the tissue but unlike the modern alternative, they were not thrown away after use. Instead they were laundered and re-used - over and over. Sensible people, hygienic people would replace their handkerchief frequently, depending on use. Boys of a certain age could be trusted to keep the hanky (the shortened name) in their pockets for days, weeks - months even. You do not want to know of the contents or condition of such hankies, they would have violated Health and Safety at every level.

It was widespread practice for kids to hang up a stocking (preferably one without a hole) so as to accommodate certain small items. Ours would contain one apple, one orange and a handful of mixed nuts. There might also be a new coin, or coins, minted with the coming new year's date - maybe up to two shillings on a good Christmas. The crowning glory on the food front would be a selection box of the most popular chocolate bars put together by either Cadburys or Mars. We had more chocolate at Christmas than we could possibly have dreamt of. This sock of goodies would last the duration of the school holidays - two weeks. To our most appreciative eyes we were well blessed. We had no notion of what other kids were getting and it wouldn't have mattered anyway because we had riches beyond compare.

In these days of plenty it's curiously sad that kids, in fact no one, gets a thrill out of an apple, an orange and a handful of nuts handed out just once a year. Apples, oranges, nuts - all available throughout the year and in such variety and abundance they've become common place. Such simple things yet they gave us so much pleasure. I'm prepared to wager that we were happier then, than our counterparts are today in that regard. Familiarity does indeed breed contempt - this old saying goes back a while. First appeared in Chaucer's - Tale of Melibee - written circa 1386.

Undoubtedly my favourite present was the comic annuals. They were thick volumes, packed with all the familiar cartoon characters we knew from the weekly edition and there were full length stories and quizzes and games one could play alone. They typically cost the sum of seven shillings and sixpence - that's 37.5 new pence. A miserly sum for hours of entertainment and the best part was that, because we each had a different one, we would swap and read each other's. I look at today's offerings with dismay. Thin to the point of malnutrition they consist of endless glossy pictures of pop stars or so called 'celebrities' that ooze out of the TV screen. Most of them have about as much charisma as a block of lard.

As I grew up Mum added to the pressie list, jig-saw puzzles and it being Christmas, they would be the biggest - 1000 pieces. I got to love jig-saws, enjoying watching the picture slowly revealed, literally piece by piece. In later life, I realised what a great character- building quality they had instilled in me - patience and the ability to organise, build slowly and certainly with a clear vision of the outcome. I must hastily rush in here to say that I'm not claiming to be a good advertisement for those qualities, only that I can see them inherently in jig-saw assembly. I made jig-saws a metaphor for life.

We were warned not to guzzle chocolate or any Christmas goodies before dinner. Tempted as we were by and large we dutifully observed the order - we were always on our best behaviour at Christmas. None of us wanted to risk not getting any pressies. Had nothing to do with Santa Claus - don't think we'd heard of him - anyway, we knew that it was Mum who got the presents. That said, and for the benefit of kids everywhere, let me be clear - there is a Santa Clause - a Father Christmas. He started out as St Nikolas (or Nicholas) -a 4th century Greek Christian Bishop who was known to be generous to the poor. He was born in Patara (now Turkey. St Nicholas' Day was celebrated on the 6th December. He had a name change following the Reformation when venerating the saints was frowned upon, so he became Santa Claus and the celebrations continued. The name Father Christmas goes back to 16th century England and the reign of Henry V111. It was the name given to a rather avuncular benevolent character who gave gifts to children at Christmas time. Since England no longer observed St Nicholas' Day celebrations were shunted to the 25th December, a date in keeping with ancient pagan customs and Father Christmas took over. In the beginning, it is likely that St Nicholas; Santa Claus - wore a green outfit. At some uncertain time during the 19th century red was introduced. A popular myth had it that it turned red during the 1930' s courtesy of a Coca Cola advertising campaign. No truth in the yarn at all. Now, here's a good bit - St Nicholas is the patron saint of banking; pawn-broking; pirating; butchery; sailing; thievery; orphans; royalty and New York City.

Our Christmas dinners were basic and traditional in so far as resources would allow. In the beginning, we had chicken or more accurately, chickens. One measly chicken wouldn't go far amongst fifteen greedy mouths. Sometimes there would be a leg of pork, and what a leg it would be - huge, but meat generally was inexpensive then as beef supplies from Argentina flowed into the UK (didn't last because South America economies were stagnating in the 1950's and trade became difficult) anyway pork has always been the a relatively inexpensive meat. In later years, we joined the rest of the world and had turkey. We didn't buy our chickens at the butchers. We reared our own. Come Christmas they would be killed, hung, drawn, plucked and cooked. Dennis was the slaughter man - I removed the innards. I was quite blasé about it then - ask me to do it now and I'll send you to KFC.

The episode of the headless chicken mentioned earlier was forever thereafter used to tease Mum. Here's a thing - in 1945 one Lloyd Olsen, a farmer from Fruita, Colorado, USA attempted to kill a chicken for dinner. He botched the job and although he severed the head he left most of the brain stem unharmed, so chicken didn't die - it did run around frantically for a while though (remind you of anything – goose perhaps?). No doubt a substitute was called from the chicken subs bench and dinner was saved. Thereafter the headless wonder earned Olsen lots of money as a side-show freak. Maybe that was the origin of the expression 'running around like a headless chicken'. Thing was, Mum hated birds - hated that is, having them near to her and wouldn't touch one for a ransom.

Christmas dinner was a magnificent affair by our normal standards. Very traditional, plenty of good meat, roast potatoes, stuffing. two types of vegetables and a rich gravy made from the meat stock. This was followed by Mum's very own Christmas pudding, containing not only the silver three-penny piece but also laced with brandy and served with lashings of custard. There being so many of us we ate at two sittings, but it was worth the wait. Dinner would be around 1 o'clock and some four hours or so later we indulged a lavish tea, Mum would prepare a favourite of hers, pickled salad with onions, cucumber and tomatoes perfectly preserved in vinegar. There would be a miscellany of sandwiches and a rich homemade trifle or jelly and blancmange. The crowning glory would be the Christmas cake, again made at home and from which I got the taste for good fruit cake and it didn't come better than Mum's - her mince pies weren't bad either. I suppose it's fair to say that we gorged on Christmas day.

*****

In later years, as we were all growing up and working and earning Christmas became, in its way, an even more magical time. The cards we had! There were literally hundreds as those of us at work came home laden with cards and small gifts from colleagues. The cards were strung along the wall and soon there was no wall to see. We could have been a real-time advert for Clintons. The financial contribution the workers were making enabled Mum to buy more and better presents for the younger ones, still at school. I think we did lash out a bit on factory made decorations. We also added a fine breakfast to start the proceedings. Only the best gammon (acquired by yours truly) to be served with fried eggs was available to one and all - cooked by the not-so-fair hands of big brother Barry and me. We'd be knocking out umpteen breakfasts whilst the kids were unwrapping (forgot to mention - we went a bit posh and wrapped presents). That would be about 9 o'clock and dinner would still be on the table some four hours later. Now it would be turkey - like everyone else, but still an un-fussed traditional Christmas dinner. Later, at tea time, out came the salad, the trifles, the mince pies and the cake - always the cake. Amazingly, some of us could still manage a cold turkey sandwich at supper time - even more amazing I suppose, is that there was any left.

One special Christmas I do recall. My elder brother was serving in the army and had been posted to Hong Kong. As this was a long distance posting he didn't get leave every six months like those stationed in Germany. He was coming home for Christmas after a stint of eighteen months in the rented colony (Hong Kong was handed back to the Chinese in 1997) so a special effort was made all round. Following his arrival Barry went out for a drink with other family members, me not being a drinker didn't go. He came home that night a little the worse for wear but swearing that he'd had a great time. Drunk he might have been but not so much as to hide his shock at the price of a bottle of brandy - £5 I believe was what it had cost. He clutched this bottle of brandy close to his chest like it was a baby as he unsteadily climbed the stairs. At the top of the stairs he turned to once again express his opinion on the outrageous cost of his beloved brandy. Being unsteady on his feet and being at the top of the stairs could only end one way - he fell down. Down he rolled, step by step and, as I rushed to him, I felt certain harm would have been done. Now there's the thing with drunks and falling, their muscles are already relaxed and they're beyond being able to tense up - net result - no broken bones, in fact no nothing. My un-sober brother climbed triumphantly to his feet and held out the bottle of brandy - still in one piece and that had been his only concern. He managed a slurred reference to £5 a bottle got up and made his way back up the stairs - successfully this time - and bed.

*****

It was around the mid to late 1950's that Mum gave a broad hint to a desire for more of a social life. The first expression was New Year parties. We observed the tradition of first footings, but we didn't play party games - we were all too self-conscious. She'd lay on the usual favourites - jelly, blancmange, trifles, cakes and sandwiches and invite family, relatives and friends. Friends were usual one or two neighbours and the boyfriend or girlfriend of those that of my siblings who had been bold (or reckless) enough to venture into that strange world of the attraction of the opposite sex. That was not me - not yet anyway. How we manage to become besotted with one another at such an early age is a perplexing mystery. Relatives included just about every aunt and uncle we had and mostly they all came. They brought their off-springs with them and being of like ages there were clashes and some fisticuffs - we shall gloss over these episodes because several of them are still living. Not so Dad's two brother - Frank and Harry. Uncle Frank was a frequent visitor party, or no party and he would hold forth on any subject known to man. Changed his job like most men change their socks (once a week I was once told - phew). Any donkey within earshot would have been at risk of losing a hind leg. Whenever he started a new job it wouldn't be long before he knew exactly what was wrong with the business and how to put it right - if only they'd listen to him. Uncle Franks favourite word was 'bloody' - it was bloody this and bloody that. This, my friends were a time when bad language was frowned upon and bloody was bad language. Hard to reconcile with the propensity towards profanities so commonplace now. Uncle Harry was altogether different, he feigned wisdom and was in the habit of whispering little nuggets in a confidential sort of tone. He'd slide over all casual like and cock his head to one side a little and say something like 'I'm going to tell you something now'. Can't remember a single one of his pearls of wisdom. In sharp contrast Mum's brother and sister, Uncle Jim and Aunt Ida would sit quiet and reserved, speaking only when spoken to.

There was little by way of alcohol at these little soirees - too expensive but that tide was turned when Dad had a big win of the football pools. They were called 'pools' because all participants paid to join each week and the money was pooled to provide the prizes - or dividends as they were known. In the days before the lottery many vested their dreams of affluence and plenty on a weekly punt on the football pools. The objective was simple - predict the result of at least eight football matches as draws and if your prediction matched the results you were in the money. Depending on how many others had also got the results right, a fortune was to be had. There were two main providers of this accepted form of gambling - Littlewoods and Vernons. Littlewoods was set up by John Moores in 1923 and later expanded into mail order and retailing. By 1982 it was the largest private limited company in Europe. The decline in interest in football pools was exacerbated by the launch of the National Lottery on the 19th November 1994. I find the National Lottery fascinating for one reason only - it can persuade people to buy into the dream of £multi-million winnings despite the odds being 14,000,000 to 1. Ask these same people to put the same amount of money on a horse with the same odds and they'd want you certified.

*****

Before completing his coupon, Dad would tune into Radio

Luxemburg, this was the only accessible commercial station at the time. He listened to a programme made by a man known as Horace Bachelor who claimed that he had devised a secret plan that would ensure that anyone buying it would eventually win on the pools. He called this plan his infra-draw method. I have no idea what the plan was or how it was supposed to work but since he broadcast every week and that must have cost money, I reason that he must have sold a lot of plans. When Dad was filling in his coupon he would surround himself with newspapers that droned on about form and apply the 'magic' formula. There was however, one nagging thought and I had to put it to Dad. It was this - if Horace Bachelor really had a secret winning formula - why didn't he just use it himself and take the winnings he promised everyone else? He'd never have to work again because he could surely just go on winning and winning. Apparently, I didn't understand. I still stand by my scepticism, but Dad had the last laugh because one week he won £365 - that's circa £7,500 in today's value. One of his prized purchases was a home bar, these had become popular at the time and would likely be called 'bling' nowadays. Having a bar meant of course, that one had to have booze and, so it was that henceforth family parties would have alcohol provided. These parties soon had a regular source of inspiration - the coming of age of us Smiths. Reaching 21 years of age was a milestone - boys became men and girls, well they just got older.

Much of what I've written in this chapter may appear dull - bland even. I have intentionally not 'jazzed' it up or given it a coat of gloss. It's ordinary and it is so because that's what we were - ordinary - everyday ordinary people living ordinary lives doing ordinary things and there were (are still) millions like us. But here's the thing - it's the ordinary folk that make the world go around because they do the work that keeps it turning and not the vacuous 'celebrities' spewed out by the media. They are but decorations on the cake but we ordinary folk, we are the cake. Without us those in the limelight are nothing. I say this because the mood has for long been that celebrities are special people - but being well known doesn't, of itself, make one special. We're all special in our way. We all have an equal right to be here. I have had the great privilege to work with and for many exceptional ordinary people.

Our Christmases were, I later learned, Spartan by some standards. There were no 'big' presents like bicycles but what we did have we treasured and from that we got the magic of Christmas. Many years late my wife remarked that what must have prevailed at 94 Essington Road in those bygone days was close to the true spirit of Christmas and the irony was that many of those financially better off than us were trying to buy what we created in our hearts for free.

Chapter 18

DISCHARGED FROM COMPULSORY EDUCATION – WHAT'S A JOB?

I completed my compulsory education in the summer of 1955. Leaving school then was just a matter of fact, no fanfares, no parties - at least so far as we Smiths were concerned. I confess to not being an admirer of another American import - the rather grotesque proms. Grotesque because of the vulgar extravagance that is heaped on school leavers in a seeming bid to upstage everyone else. Have a party if you must but it ought not to be a circus. I digress: we were expected to get a job and go straight to work. Here we had a profound advantage over today's youth, there were jobs aplenty. So many of the working population had been lost to the war that there was permanent need for labour of all kinds. Kids leaving school were directed to the Youth Employment Service. Cynically, kids (like us) coming from secondary schools were considered as good factory fodder. The notion that some of us might have higher aspirations had already been decided - four years back by the eleven-plus examination. Once there we would be expected to field such searching questions as 'what do you want to do?' or 'what job are you looking for?'. The answer to both was the same - no idea and by the way, what's a job? That they seriously expected kids of fifteen, fresh out of secondary school to be enlightened in such matters was incredible, given that no one had ever talked to us about such worldly matters.

I was spared any further visits to this place of enlightenment by our next-door neighbour, telling Mum that there was a job going where he worked - 'suit your Brian down to the ground'. The job was as a trainee pattern maker in a company engaged in brass castings of small items of brassware - namely horse-brass and cabinet locks. I would later question our neighbour's judgement in thinking this was just right for me but for now it paid £2.50 per week which in today's terms would be £58.58 (ironically about the same amount paid out as jobseekers' allowance to those out of work). Making comparisons like this are misleading. Because of the increase in numbers many assume that they're better off now than in say 1955. They're not - all that this means is that whatever cost £2.50 in 1955 now costs £58.58.

It was at this point that I had an interesting experience, the full significance of which completely eluded me for many years thereafter. I recall reflecting on my schooldays at Short Heath Secondary Modern. The focus of my thoughts was on the teachers or teaching to be exact. Amazingly for one who had endured challenging times at school as a pupil (students went to universities - pupils went to schools), I found the idea of teaching attractive. I can offer no rational explanation for this turn of mind. I wrote to Mr Statham, my old headmaster and told him of my thoughts. He replied that it would take a lot of demanding work and that I would have return to school to study for what was then GCE's (General Certificate of Education). I couldn't go back to school, Mum needed me to earn my keep and contribute to the household budget. The idea of becoming a teacher seemingly died there and then. I say seemingly because many years later I was to qualify to teach in Further and Higher Education.

So, I went for an interview and got the job. The company was called Dunton & Marston Ltd, situated on Fibbersley Road in Fibbersley, Willenhall - just over the canal bridge. It was a small business, around twenty personnel altogether. There were three of us in the pattern-making shop. Calling it pattern-making was misleading - we didn't make any patterns, these were brought to us by customers. Our task was to prepare them for the guys in the foundry - the casters. We made bases out of plaster-of-paris which was painted with a sealant. The sealant was a sort of industrial home brew, it was made with spelter which was placed in a heavy-duty pot and covered with metholated spirits and a lighted match thrown in - almost as good as a penny banger except that it gave a 'whoosh' not a bang. Guess who got to do the mix. The pattern to be cast was then soldered onto a brass ridge and mounted on the plaster base. The casters would set our plaster base on a bed of special sand in an iron frame. A second frame was placed on top and filled with sand, the casters would then pound the sand with a wooden mallet until a sharp, firm outline of the pattern was set in the sand. My how they pounded those frames - wonder who they thought of as they rained the blows. Next, molten brass was poured into the frame and left to cool before releasing the frame and its contents - the castings. There was real skill at work here, the molten brass had to be at just the right temperature and these guys were so good they could guess exactly when this point had been reached. Pouring hot liquid brass at exactly the right speed was another skill - too fast and it would back wash and the cast spoiled - too slow and the liquid would cool prematurely leaving a flawed casting.

The casters had their own individual furnace set below ground level into which they lowered pots containing brass ingots for smelting. For some castings, scrap metal brass was used. One of the casters kept a special shovel which looked brand new. That's because it never saw service as a shovel - it was a 'frying pan'. I saw raw bacon laid out on this shovel to which was added one or two eggs, cracked for frying. Into the furnace the shovel went and within two minutes out it came with crispy fried bacon and two well done eggs. Breakfast was served. Some of the other casters had a hot lunch brought to them by their wives but mostly it was sandwiches and because they were paid on output, breaks were short. Recalling the shovel frying pan reminds me of a tale told by demolition expert Blaster Bates. He was blowing up some tree stumps at a crematorium, it got to lunchtime. He was about to tuck into a tasty pork pie when one of the guys from the crematorium asked him if he'd like his pie heated up. It was a freezing day, a hot lunch had appeal, so Blaster agreed. He thought they had a cooker or something like; not a chance - the pie was heated up in the same place as.... Blaster blanched. They told him it would be okay but - 'just watch out for fingernails'. I guess Blaster took sandwiches thereafter. Some of the casters got into a little group and played cards. They weren't heavy gamblers by any means, the stake was in pennies (old ones). A deck of playing cards has an interesting history. The four suits are said to represent the economy of the Middle Ages. Hearts was the church: spades the military; clubs, agriculture and diamonds the merchants. Playing cards originated in China in the 9th century. They spread to Europe during the 14th century. The cards with which we are so familiar (the four suits) are a French concept. See - we didn't invent everything. There's more – the queens in a French deck represent women from history and mythology. The queen of hearts is Judith, the queen of diamonds is Rachel – both characters from the bible. The queen of clubs is Argine which is an anagram for Regina – Latin for queen, and finally the queen of spades is the Greek goddess Athena. Queens in an English deck are said to represent Elizabeth 1st.

The tools of my trade were basically a soldering iron and a collection of files each designed for a specific purpose - from a smooth file to a rasp (a very rough file). Joy of joys there was also a bastard file, of such a construction it didn't fit neatly into any classification of files, so it became an outsider, illegitimate - a bastard. Don't think I'll tell Mum about that. You will recall that I reported on my lack of manual skills in the woodworking department whilst at school; well nothing had happened to improve them in the world of patter-making world post school. Now I really did wonder just how my dear old neighbour figured this job and I were made for each other. A divorce was only a matter of time. It wasn't that I was bad at the work - I just had no aptitude for it. There were three of us the pattern shop, Alf Wildman and Geoff Marston (son of one of founders) and me. Apart from preparing the patterns for casting we also had to make running repairs to those already in use. The casters had their skills but being gentle with patterns wasn't always one of them. Patterns would become dislodged from the ridge and had to be soldered back in place - that was one of my jobs. Patterns were held in place by a little attachment known as a 'git'. If this was too thick the casting, when it was made, would be difficult to break off. If it was too thin, the molten brass would not flow through properly and the casting would be useless. I managed to commit both felonies – gave a new meaning to through thick and thin. Sometimes I had to rebuild a whole ridge of patters. So, that no one would find out just how 'good' I was not, I would do the job discreetly and hurl any damaged ones over the fence into the canal. If they ever dredge that canal they'll find a few quid's worth of brass lying on the bottom and since Dunton & Marston no longer exists and the building have been raised, there'll be not a hint as to where that brass came from.

Alf went home for lunch and Geoff disappeared into the office, so I got the place to myself for an hour. Naturally I mooched - found some pornographic magazines. Reveille! Anyone remember Reveille? It had pictures of ladies in swimsuits and various stages of undress. By now I was ahem ahem, taking a slight interest in what was described as the opposite sex - not girls but the opposite sex. A very subtle shift. By today's standards Reveille would be on a par with tabloids such as the Sun and the Daily Star but far too highbrow for the Sport. We were deprived of salacious material back then - along with Reveille there was Tit-bits (a name that would surely incur the fury of the PC militia today) and a couple I did see once at school - Spic and Span. These latter two were very naughty - not another word. Reveille was launched on the 25th May 1940 by the Ex-

Services' Allied Association - it was an early tabloid newspaper, bought by the Mirror Group in 1947. The last edition was printed on the 17th August 1979 and the following month it merged with Tit-bits. Tit-bits was founded by George Newnes on the 22nd October 1881 and is still published as Titbits International. Early in 1973 a big decision was made concerning Tit-bits - it was to drop the hyphen so that Tit-bits became Titbits - wow. Reminds me of the time Abbey National spent a King's ransom on re-branding and the outcome of the deliberations of the geniuses in marketing? To drop the word 'National' leaving the bank standing as simply Abbey. Hardly mattered in the end because the bank was swallowed by the Spanish outfit - Santander.

I got to earn extra money by cleaning out the furnaces for some of the casters. They paid me out of their own pockets, so it wasn't added to my wages. I did the work on Saturday mornings and grim work it was - the dirt and dust were thick and being below ground level, only made cleaning them out harder. These were pre-Health & Safety days so no protective masks or anything. Reckon I did my lungs some mischief. But overall, it was a good place to work - the guys were all friendly in their way. There was however, one moment of industrial strife. One of the guys went to the lavatory at the bottom of the yard and was dismayed to find that there was no toilet paper. So, he went to the office to get some only to be told there wouldn't be any more supplied - by order of the management. Seems that some of the guys had been in the practice of taking to the lavatory with a copy of a horse racing paper that published riders and runners of all the daily horse race meetings around the UK. Hitherto Dunton & Marston had equipped the lavatory with Izal toilet rolls. To the uninitiated Izal toilet paper is not the soft sensitive stuff unravelled for TV adverts by a cute Labrador puppy. Izal had a smooth side and a rough side - work it out for yourselves please. So - the scene is set -man in lavatory with copy of paper studying form, makes his choice and writes his bet out on - yes that's it - Izal toilet paper. This had probably been going on for years but unfortunately, the office manager apparently one day, fancied a punt on the gee gees himself. So, he went across the road to what passed as the bookies to place his bet. The bookie told him that he'd a few guys from the factory in that morning and showed the manager the betting slips - all made out on Izal toilet paper, hence the ban. Just after the ban had been imposed one of the men was spotted walking out the factory gates, the manager called after him "where do you think you're going?" The answer was a gem. "Going home to have a s..t" - perspicuity over eloquence. Toilet rolls were re-instated the next day.

One of my first tasks most days was to call on old Mr Dunton (the co-founder of the business) to enquire after his well-being. The two founding directors had retired for different reasons, Dunton on the grounds of ill health and Marston so that his son could step into the roll whilst he was young - that would be in his 40's - they called that young? The irony was that it was poor old Marston who departed for that great brass foundry in the sky first. Being in rude good health, everyone was shocked by his passing, the popular money had been on Dunton. They did, of course, overlook the blindingly obvious; Dunton was under regular medical supervision and medicated to the gills. He was almost indestructible as one pill or another neutralised any threat. Marston had no such cover and when he had a heart attack the way was clear for it to prove fatal.

*****

The unwritten rule at the time was that kids handed their wage packets over to parents and were given an allowance to meet travel and social costs. This state of affairs would prevail until one reached the age of majority - 21 years then – 18 now. On that day, the kid became an adult and their wages were their own. Now it was parents who got the handout - by way of board money - money paid over to cover the costs of providing food and shelter. In our case, it was Mum who controlled the purse strings. I handed over my wage packet - unopened. I got £1.10s.0d back (£1.50). I got to keep the ten-shilling note Geoff Marston gave me the first (and only) Christmas I was there - ten bob! That was 20% of my weekly wage.

*****

With the extra money, I earned from cleaning furnaces I saved up a deposit for my first bike. I would save on bus fare and have greater freedom all round. My first bike - my pride and joy, was a Norman Invader and I bought it on HP from Dainty's in the Market Place, Willenhall. Parents had to sign as guarantors and I was left in no doubt as to my fate should I miss a payment. The bike would be re-possessed and me - well I probably wouldn't have been able to ride it anyway after the threatened changes in my bone structure had been executed. Norman bikes were British, made in an enterprise set up in 1920 by two brothers - Charles and Fred Norman. Norman Cycles was taken over by Tube Investments who preferred the name Raleigh. The Norman brand disappeared in the early 1960's.

My attempts at learning to ride a bike gave rise to another of those curious idiosyncrasies that marks me out occasionally. There was no instruction to be had on the subject - one just 'learned' to ride a bike. I started with the notion that balance was the secret, the ability to remain upright whilst the bike was stationery. When no one was about I spent, ages practising on Dennis's bike which he kept parked in the hall. It was gleaming red BSA which critics insisted stood for 'Best Shoved Along'. It stood/stands for Birmingham Small Arms. BSA was founded in 1861 in the gun quarter of Birmingham. The name gives its preoccupation away, but the group soon moved into manufacturing bicycles and motor-cycles. At one point, it was the largest manufacturer of bicycles in the world.

Anyway, I would sit astride the saddle, both feet on the pedals and strive to keep the bike upright without touching the wall. When certain family members found out I was mocked unmercifully. It was finally explained to me that balance was maintained by keeping the bike in motion. What I was trying to do was more like a circus trick. Now laugh they might but I got a great big unexpected bonus from my balancing act. It was that I had a much better sense of balance than most of the other kids and when I finally got to ride I could corner and manoeuvre a bike better than most and I had the confidence to go for speed. Of course, I had some near misses and nasty falls but apart from a few scratches and bruises I came to no lasting harm. However, there was one incident that almost ended my good fortune - and my life. I was speeding along Beacon Road when a cat darted across the road right in front of me. I couldn't miss it; I hit it at speed and went over the handle bars in a perfect arc - back pocket over fly buttons. I hit the ground like I usually hit the ground when falling and went automatically into a forward role. I came to rest sitting in the middle of the road. Passers-by gasped in shock, I thought they must have feared I had hurt myself when I landed, well they had had a pleasant surprise - no? No! It wasn't my gymnastics that had caused them to gasp. I followed the horrified looks and there, just about eighteen inches from me was the front grill of a motor car. I never saw it, never heard it but I sure came close to feeling it. Charmed - I had a charmed life - so did the cat – it got away before I could remonstrate with it.

*****

Must get this in: elder brother and I were in the habit of 'borrowing' eldest brother's bike when he was out on a date or something. We'd take it for a spin, elder brother was in the saddle when taking a bit of road too fast he lost control and slammed into a concrete lamp post. He was a bit shaken, but the bike seemed okay – the lamp post was unmoved - both of us would have taken a few bruises in exchange for avoiding the wrath of big brother should his bike get damaged. Looks can be so deceiving – it (the bike) wasn't ok, the front forks had been almost straightened on impact. Eldest brother didn't find out immediately, someone at work I think mentioned that the bike didn't 'look' right. He hadn't a clue as to what had happened and resigned himself to getting a new set of forks. A charmed life indeed. From Hayward's corner to New invention was about half a mile and the road sloped downhill. There was a wager that I couldn't get to 30 miles per hour down that stretch of road. Some of us had a tiny milometer fixed to our bikes - mine showed that I did indeed reach a speed of 30mph and I could have gone faster given more road. There were some that said I was mad - reckless perhaps but not mad.

I did manage to fall off my impressive Norman Invader - just once. One of the guys at work was trying to sell an accordion and he persuaded me to take it home and try it out. Unfortunately, the accordion and I were not really made for each other, according to the family that is. It was on the journey to return the instrument that I learned that balancing an accordion on the handlebars is not a smart move. I ended sitting on my backside in the middle of the road - no damage to me or, more importantly, my bike. The accordion? Got what it deserved - a good bouncing along the road and it made a better noise than when I tried playing it - it survived.

One of the products made at Dunton & Marston's was the old styled penny-in-the-slot lavatory locks. I think this was the largest lock they produced and was made from gunmetal - a mixture of (mostly) copper, tin and zinc. I was given the task of cutting the gits off the castings of these locks. Thing was - I cut them off right up to the casing of the lock which meant there was nothing left to polish unless the polisher ate into the lock-case, which he wouldn't do on pain of the sack. The gaffer tore me off a strip for ruining a day's work (they would all have to be cast again). He then said that I should think of all the folk who were desperate for a s**t and wouldn't able to because I had buggered up the locks. Where will they stick their pennies, he demanded to know? I couldn't possibly say. Seems that every industry has its perennial pranks to be played on newcomers. I was once sent to the boss by one of the casters to get sky hooks from which to hang some castings. I fared better with a request for a left-handed screwdriver - asked for a ratchet screwdriver, I knew that these could be switched to turn left or right.

At the ripe age of almost sixteen I sort of broke my surviving-accidents-without-harm duck. In the centre of the pattern shop was a stove kept burning throughout the day to heat up the soldering irons the three of us used continuously. It stood on a heavy-duty steel base, a stove pipe took the fumes up through the roof. Over time we all got quite adept at reaching round the stove to place an iron in the fire. On the occasion in question I did just that - reached round but, stubbed my foot of the steel base and over-balanced. Instinctively I put out a hand to steady myself - right on the hot stove pipe. It was there for maybe a few seconds as I righted myself, but it burned like crazy. My reaction harkens back to schooldays and the cane, the bullying and the mocking endured - I never gave any of my assailants the satisfaction of showing any emotion. Instinctively I made the same response here, I just turned back to my workbench saying nothing and determined to carry on working. But Alf had seen the incident, he said 'bloody hell, that must hurt'. I didn't answer. He took hold of me and marched me to the office where my, by now blistering hand was bandaged. I refused to go home so I was consigned to simply fetching and carrying patterns to and from the foundry using my left hand only - the other one hurt a bit. The fact that I had not made a sound variously shocked and impressed Alf. I wasn't and I'm not now - a wimp. What I did then wasn't smart - it was obstinacy, I was not going to surrender to the pain. Fortunately for me someone with perhaps more common sense intervened.

My stay at Dunton & Marston's lasted one year. I was restless, the work didn't excite me, and I wasn't really that good at it, though I did genuinely try. I began trawling the situations vacant columns in the Express & Star. We were still in a time when jobs were aplenty so there was a lot of scope. Looking back, I think I so desperately needed someone to counsel me as to what I really wanted to do but as it was I simply meandered along until I found a vacancy that appealed and applied. I didn't appreciate it at the time but working at Dunton & Marston would become a unique experience in my life. Save for the company secretary, every employee was male. Henceforth I would forever work in businesses that had a typical ratio of two thirds women to one third men.

*****

Whilst in their employ I did get to play my first proper game of football. Proper that is in that I was registered as a player and we played in proper kit. One of the casters, a guy called Jock (yes, he was Scottish - how original). Jock was trying to form a club called Willenhall United Services and was desperate to bring together eleven lads capable of kicking a football in the right direction. He was enthusiastic and confident that he could train a winning team. He got the team into one of the lower leagues where novice teams start out. Our first match was against the side that had won the league the previous year but hadn't been accepted into the next league up for some reason. They thrashed us 13-0 but here's the best bit - I was Willenhall United Services' star player. I admit the rest were poor. But I remember fondly a wonderful moment when I dribbled the ball some thirty yards before crashing a great shot against the cross-bar. I did manage to get into the referees' naughty book, not for foul or anything like that - when the opposition scored their thirteenth goal I said that thirteen was an unlucky number, they won't score any more. The referee took exception to my flippancy and ticked me off – he said that football was a serious game. Silly man - a game of any kind is just that - a game - light relief from matters that are serious. The referee was wrong, football had always been a game played for fun and pleasure until it was corrupted my money. It's recognised the world over that we Brits gave the world the game as it's known today. Scour the archives however, and you'll find reference to something similar being played in China around the 3rd/5th century BC. The Romans and the Greeks also had kick-about in the 2nd/3rd century AD. The game was played in England and in 1363 King Edward the 3rd gave it the name of football. Much later in 1586 there are records of British sailors playing football with the Inuits of Greenland. The dour Scots banned the game in 1424. A little over four hundred years later, in 1863, the Football Association (FA) was formed. I had just played my first game in what was an ancient sport, it was to be a first of many and I wore quite a variety of jerseys. Here's a nice anecdote about football that puts most modern players to shame. In 1910 a team from London, Corinthians FC was touring Brazil. Local enthusiasts were said to have been so impressed with the sportsmanship of the visitors that they decided to form their own team and give it the same name as a mark of respect. The Brazilian club Corinthians plays to this day.

My growing interest in football was fuelled by my following Wolverhampton Wanders FC (Wolves). These were the heady days when Wolves dominated the old first division. A time when a 'foreign' player meant someone from another part of the country. They were a different breed of men when compared to today's overpaid prima donnas. Footballers are obscenely overpaid for what is essentially a part-time job. Today there is little room allowed for loyalty as players maraud the world of football like mercenaries for hire, ready to swap shirts for the highest bidder. For this I blame Sky TV and latterly BT for lavishing so much money on a hardly impoverished sport. Sadly, and cynically, little if any, of this vast wealth finds its way to the grassroots of the game. Agents too have contributed to the moral corruption of the game, an expensive and surely pointless profession if ever there was one. Happily, none of this tainted the glory days that were the 1950's for Wolves. They trounced the continentals who dared to venture to the Molyneux - what supporter could forget the defeat of Honved (Hungary); Spartak (Moscow - Russia) and Real Madrid (Spain)?

What players they had, Bet Williams (the 'cat') in goal; Billy Wright, the finest centre half ever; Eddie Stuart Eddie Clamp; Ron Flowers; Bill Slater (at the time the last surviving amateur playing in the professional ranks); Johnny Hancocks; Jimmy Mullen; Roy Swinbourne: Peter Broadbent; Dennis Wilshaw (nicknamed Gladys) - players that would walk into any premierships side today. The Honved match was especially significant. Their team contained six of the players that had earlier destroyed England 6-3, at Wembley and 7-1 at the re-match in Hungary. Wolves ran out 3-2 winners and unbeknown to them and anyone watching set a force in motion. At the match was the editor of the French newspaper L'Equipe. He was so impressed with the enthusiasm and celebrations of the crowd that he thought how wonderful it would be if teams throughout Europe could play matches like this in a friendly competition. A few month later in 1955, the European Cup was born.

On the social side of life, I discovered roller skating courtesy of my good friend Graham Powers – the butcher. Graham had an uncle who worked at the roller-drome in Temple Street, Wolverhampton. Uncle Arthur got us in for free. First impressions were not encouraging - seemed to have spent most of the time picking myself up nursing an increasing sore backside and elbows and knees. An early conclusion would have had it that the task was nigh impossible and were it not for the many capable exponents on show I would have endorsed the impossibility and left, never to return.

However, I am amongst other things, an obstinate so and so. I persisted and after a few weeks I managed to navigate the rink without falling over. From that point on I just got more confident, and faster. Management of the rink identified two broad groups of skaters: one, the performers who liked to dance and such like - the other, the speed skaters who just wanted to go fast and faster. The two weren't compatible on the same floor collisions would be inevitable and there would be injuries. So, a special session for speed skaters was introduced each night. For a time, the rink was ours - yes, I joined this mad throng. We hurtled round the rink at breakneck speed, boy was it exhilarating. There were tumbles from time to time but miraculously I witnessed no serious damage. That is, until I had the closest of calls. We were in mid-speed skating session, along with the rest, I was flying. Then, someone watching from the behind the safety barrier carelessly spilled orange squash on the rink. I was the first to hit the wet patch with my lead foot, it was as if someone had yanked the brakes on, my right foot stalled in the sticky mess, my left, already following through attempted to go on its very fast way. The conflict between my two feet ended when I got airborne and literally flew over the barrier and smashed into the swing doors that thankfully did what it said on their tin - they swung. Had they not it would have quicker to count the bones that weren't broken. There are those that say my guardian angel was on duty (again) that night. I passed through the swing doors and landed in a heap in the corridor - no fancy forward -roll this time. The manager rushed to check what the owners might be sued for, he needn't have worried - we weren't litigious then - if we fell we didn't look for someone to blame so we could screw them for money. We blamed ourselves for being careless. Have you noticed how often those that sue say that it's not the money but the principal? I have two things to say - one, remarkable how they always manage to sue an organisation with the ability to pay - never one that couldn't or wouldn't- and two, if it's not for the money, why not give it to charity? They don't of course - pssst - it is really for the money.

The only mark I had because of that escapade was a small gash at the base of the thumb on my right hand. Nevertheless, the manager insisted I be taken to the Royal Hospital in Wolverhampton - he feared shock might set in. It did - when the nurse attempted to put in two stitches I nearly passed out. That was the first time I heard the corny old joke about feeling 'just a little prick'. The consensus was that I'd been lucky, very lucky - how I didn't break my neck when I hit the doors was, apparently, a miracle. Didn't put me off skating and I soon returned to show I hadn't lost my nerve.

I remember being at Graham's house once when somehow, I was persuaded to drink half a pint of vinegar. I have no idea whatsoever how I came to do such a thing but, to a guy who had once drunk a bottle of disinfectant, vinegar was almost a mark of sanity. Oh, and it was much better than half a pint of beer - well almost anything is.

*****

Poor Graham had to get married all a very sudden when he was just seventeen. Seems he did a bit of a naughty and got his girlfriend pregnant. This was an age when such happenings were a social disgrace. Two families brought low by the lustful conduct of their off-springs. This was a time when to be called a 'bastard' meant something - and nothing good. In some parts, they were called shotgun weddings because one of the sad pair didn't want to get married - they had only wanted sex - and one parent or another would explain to the miscreant that his/her (usually his) life would be a constant torment for ever should they fail to do the honourable thing and get married. It was fun to watch how the neighbours gossiped about such a disgraceful state of affairs - they whispered.

"Have you heard, so and so is expecting yes.... her...hmm who'd have thought it.... The father? Oh, it's young ...... or so I've heard, dirty little bugger......anyway, teach her to stick her nose in the air......." They loved it!

Anyway, Graham got married and as far as I know lived as happily ever after as most others - poor sod - I jest. Such weddings would be at the Registry Office, they wouldn't have been allowed a church wedding nor a white wedding dress, that would have offended the natives more than anything. Sex before marriage was sin enough but a forced marriage because of pregnancy was hellfire and damnation. I wasn't invited, I suspect there was the minimum number of guests and the minimum 'celebrations' afterwards. The twist in the tail was that Graham and his wife got to live with her parents - I love irony. Long before their fate befell them Graham took me to meet his then girlfriend. He asked me if I'd heard a Slim Whitman record - 'Rose Marie'. He threw the record to me across the room, I jumped up to catch it afraid that it would land on the floor and break. It didn't, it floated down ever so gently. It was a new 45rpm record made of vinyl. It was the first of its kind I ever saw. Lost contact with Graham around this time, partly because of his enforced marriage but also, I was about to take a change of direction - a new job beckoned.

*****

It was while I was working at Dunton and Marston's that I had my last fist fight. As it was at school, so it was now, I wasn't looking for trouble - it just found me. I was walking home along Essington Road with another lad, coming towards us I saw three young guys whom I believed came from a gypsy encampment berthed on fields once a part of Sadler's farm. There'd been talk of the gypsies causing trouble and though I'd seen nothing of this, I was instantly on alert. They spread themselves across the pavement so passing them was impossible without them breaking their line, which I knew they wouldn't do. The one in the middle was the biggest, a broad, stocky fellow wearing a flat cap. He demanded to see what we had in our pockets, I guessed they were after money. We moved to go around them by stepping into the road, but they cut us off and back to the pavement we went. By now I knew what was coming and I was having none of it, if it was fight they wanted, they'd got one. Flat cap lifted his clenched fist, he got no further, he was eyeing my right hand, I hit him with a perfect left cross and I floored him. He was shocked, his mates were suddenly scared - as was my friend, he thought the big guy would get up and the three of them would give us a hiding. I stood over flat cap and beckoned him to get up. He did, and he did he did something else - he stepped aside so we could pass. I struck the first (and only) blow. It was out of necessity. I see no virtue in waiting to be hit before defending oneself. It's an adage that 'The best defence is a good offense'. This is based on an American maxim coined circa 1775 (source unknown) - ' The maxim is that it is better to attack than to receive one'. Imagine two armed combatants, both have the weapons primed to fire - does it make sense for one to let the other fire first? So, to those that say turn the other cheek, I say – this, all that you do is to present a fresh target. On this occasion this boy wasn't for turning. Now, where have I heard that before?

Around this time my eldest brother, had a very, very unhappy experience. For some time, he'd been going out with a girl by the name of Linda Hyde, it went by the quaint term 'courting'. Linda lived around the corner and one street back. She was raven haired beauty and a lovely personality. Apparently, they got engaged, I say apparently because I don't recall any celebrations. Not sure how long after the engagement but Linda broke it off - said she wanted to end the relationship. My brother was distraught. He asked me, probably because no one else was around at the time, to go with him to collect the ring he'd given Linda. I was bewildered by the emotional outpourings, seems that they both still loved each other but it just wouldn't work out. By now I'd developed a sort of interest in girls but if this is how it turned out, it was going to a very 'passing' interest.

I learned later that it was Linda's parents who objected to the engagement. My brother wasn't considered good enough and they didn't want him marrying into the family. It's common for parents to think that no one is good enough for their son or daughter, but this was different; this was because her sutor was a Smith - we were known as the 'Smiths', it was a derogatory reference. We were many and poor. In later years, I often wish that my brother and Linda had stuck to their guns, they were made for each other - one of Cupid's better efforts. Alas, it was never to be, they went their separate ways, and each married someone else eventually. I do hope that Linda found herself someone worthy.

Chapter 19

JOB NUMBER TWO

I saw an advertisement in Express & Star, F W Woolworth & Co Ltd were looking for a young man as a management trainee at their Victoria Street, Wolverhampton branch. Quite on impulse I applied, got called for an interview and got the job. Wasn't so remarkable. there were more jobs going than people to fill them so, short of being a complete idiot, providing one turned up reasonably sane, sensible and sober jobs were relatively easy to get. The job description required that I begin my quest for management in the warehouse where I would learn of Woolworth's style of merchandising. Woolworths, or Woollies, as it was affectionately known, was at its peak then. Stores in every mayor town and city and, here, in Wolverhampton, there were two, the other larger store was in Dudley Street and many years later moved into the Mander Centre.

The first Woolworths store was opened in Utica, New York on the 22nd February 1878 as a 'five and ten' store - that is to say, everything it sold cost either five or ten cents. The company expanded to become one of the largest retailers in the world. The first UK store was opened in Church Street, Liverpool in 1909. Increased competition amongst other things eventually brought the Woolworth empire to its knees and it finally ceased trading in 1997. Interesting to compare Woollies with Poundland, the latter thriving on the same basic principles that fuelled Woollies success in the early days. A measure of what Woolworths would and would not sell comes from this little anecdote. There was a small manufacturing company called Samuel Parks Ltd based in Willenhall. Parks' made companion sets for hearths. These hark back to the days of coal fires and comprised a small hand brush to sweep the hearth, a little shovel to scoop up the debris, a pair of tongues with which to pick up hot coals to pick up that fell from the fire and a poker used for the obvious - poking the fire. Parks' tried to get orders from Woolworths, the prospect of the hundreds of Woolworth stores stocking these companion sets was mouth-watering. Woolworth's buyers invited them to send a representative with samples. The meeting was cordial and might have been thought to be going well. Then the buyer picked up the sample set of tongues brought in by the representative and dropped them on the floor - nothing happened. He then brought another set, the type Woolworths were already selling, and he did the same thing - dropped them on the floor. They shattered.

The buyer then turned to Parks' man and said "

"Do you know why we buy these, the ones that broke? The people that buy them also drop them, and they break, and the customer comes back and buys another set. If we buy your product and our customers drop them, they won't break, we won't get another sale."

Parks' didn't get an order but perhaps a salutary lesson in marketing. Cynical perhaps but surely a fair reflection on what's now become a throw-away society. Woollies always went for the cheap and cheerful merchandise and, like Poundland today, their customers loved it. There were very many manufacturers who thrived on making goods especially for Woolworths. One that stands out was called Miners (not certain of spelling) anyway, they made make-up for women. In keeping with Woollies style, the products were cheap and cheerful. But, it seems that women were just a little more discerning than had been anticipated – the products were not selling as well as expected. The solution – enhance the product? No – improve the packaging, that was cheaper to do – and they did it – and it worked – sales went up significantly. Judging by appearances worked.

Next door to Woolworths was a retailer of electrical

appliances - Murdoch's. Potentially embarrassing because a few months earlier they re-possessed a TV set that Mum was buying on HP. She couldn't keep up with the repayments and in those dark days there was no recourse to county courts to get an order. Credit providers simply sent a man with a van and took possession themselves. The people at Murdoch's were friendly enough and nobody made a connection between me and the repossession. An advantage of being called Smith I guess.

*****

There were six of us in the warehouse. Three on reception taking in delivery of stocks from a multitude of suppliers, some direct but mostly courtesy of British Rail as it was then. I was one of this three along with a mature lady called Dolly and the Warehouse Manager, Malcolm McGregor. Beyond the goods received area lay the warehouse where all the unpacked goods were stored according to the department charged with their sale. This area was looked after by three ladies., each taking responsibility for several departments. Dolly was looked upon as an 'odd bod' because she didn't indulge in the gossip that was forever rampant in any workplace employing a large number of women. Sorry PC' ers but that's how it was (and still is I'm told but I won't say who told me because they don't deserve a visitation from the feminist heavy mob). She was, however, good at her job and that irked some who weren't so conscientious. Malcolm McGregor, or Mac, as he was generally known, was a great guy to work for. He was fair and firm, all he wanted was for his team to do what they were paid to do. Now I probably had my faults (yes - I can hardly believe it either) but I was never work-shy. The warehouse was below ground level, so delivery of goods meant sending them down a specially adapted ramp which was like a steep slide - one on either side of steps that allowed us to reach ground level in a dignified manner. Have you ever tried climbing a steep ramp? I did - several times for the hell of it.

On a summer's day, some of the large crates of crockery would be unpacked in the open air. One could get lost in the straw used to protect the not-so-valuable china. Once we had a tea chest full of mothballs delivered and the carrier just shunted the heavy tea chest down the ramp, only being so heavy he didn't quite manage to set it down square and it sort of twisted round and came down the stairs instead- and split open at the bottom. If you've ever used moth balls you'll know the pungent pong they emanate, and likely talking about a handful. Imagine if you can, the eye watering pungency of several thousand when they all escape confinement together. There was not a dry eye in the place. Dolly said something about there being moth balls all over the floor, I said I didn't know they had any - completely wasted, she just looked sort of puzzled. This unfortunate event was only surpassed when a carton of twelve bottle of ammonia was sent down the ramp a little too fast - the carton overturned halfway down and opted for a somersault to complete the journey. Naturally all twelve bottles were broken. We operated a no-go zone for a while whilst the vapours drifted off in the air and likely accounted for the demise of a few birds, unfortunate enough to have been flying by.

A warehouse such as ours accumulated a mountain of packaging. It was not wasted. We had a manually operated bailing machine into which all paper and cardboard was piled and by operating a long lever which worked on a ratchet, steadily compressed the paper and cardboard. In its compressed state four threads of binding wire were passed around the bale and then the lever was used to release the pressure and the waste expanded causing the wire to tighten around the bale. These bales were sold to a company call Southern Stock Paper Co Ltd - we were re-cycling long before the seeds of the Green Party had been sown.

During the summer vacation Woolworths took on part-time student labour. We got a bright upstart of a lad of about the same age as me. He was arrogant little so and so. He was studying law and he insisted on telling me just what he was prepared and not prepared to do.

"It's your work after all. you're full time".

We did have words. I was not smart enough to not allow him to wind me up and, so it was that, having tired of his lording it over the rest of us, I gave him an ultimatum.

"Either you work like your paid to do or I will stuff you in the baling machine."

He was not prepared to be spoken to like that and gave his full and frank opinion of yours truly - not altogether complimentary. I took him by his lapels and lifted his feet off the ground and half carried, half dragged him to the empty and waiting baling machine. Mac stepped in and told both of us to grow up and get some work done. Mr High and Mighty got the message but whether it was mine or Mac's I was never quite certain. Saw the back of him at the start of the next academic year. Later in life I represented many people at court (at the judge's discretion – I was not/am not a lawyer), idly wondered if I had ever sat opposite this little upstart - couldn't say because I can't remember his name and I wouldn't have recognised him. I would have liked that, especially as I got the order I wanted in most cases, that would have meant that I beat him on his own ground.

That wasn't the only run in I had whilst working at Woolworths. The assistant manager was guy called Longton and he didn't take to me at all. Middle class, grammar school educated he felt superior to anyone less privileged. For the record, they weren't all like him. He took every opportunity to criticise my work and assured me that any ambitions I had for progressing in the company were mere fancy - apparently, people like me didn't get into management. He also took issue with the way I spoke to the office staff. Seems I wasn't deferential, that's never been my strong point. They were working for a living just like me - they were only human, just like me - yes? seems not because they had complained. I was seventeen by now, I had put up with this garbage at school where it was easier to deal with in some ways. Usually a punch-up settled such issues. I knew instinctively that such blunt action would be frowned upon in the workplace. Unfortunately, one day, Longton pushed too far and I retaliated. Told him to forget he was assistant manager and invited him to meet me outside at the rear of the store. He was half way there when he realised that he could more damage by not forgetting he was assistant manager - he would report to the manager and get me fired. Naturally, I was all defiant, but Mac took me on one side and gave me a lesson in the harsh facts of working life. The sack would mean it would be harder to get another job and it meant no wages and - as Mac kindly put it - your Mum needs what you take home. I was stumped. Then came the hardest part of the lesson - Mac said to go and apologise and save your job. That was so hard to do but Mac was right, I couldn't go home with the news that I'd lost my job.

By now the store grapevine had spread the tale of the incident to every department. As I walked up the stairs to the sales floor and then on to the offices in the floor above, I felt eyes following me every step of the way. I was aching with embarrassment and hurt, I did what I'd always done when feeling threatened and vulnerable. I called on all the resolve that I had and set my face, Longton would get his apology but nothing more - nothing. He sat at his desk, I stood in front of him. He looked at me, very cool, very calm. What had I to say for myself? I simply said - "I'm sorry for my behaviour earlier". If he was expecting more he would be disappointed. But all he said was "good - now get back to work". I know he could have pushed me for more but to his credit (given at the time reluctantly) he didn't. I made the return trip back to the warehouse red-faced. Felt like everyone could see right through me. Mac gave me a pat on the back and said, "well done". That made me feel better. Learned something valuable that day - what it takes to apologise when you're wrong, how humiliating it feels at the start, but how it converts to simple humility on execution, and it is humility that helps restore one's dignity. Longton treated me very differently from then on. I think he knew what it took out of me to make that apology - I earned his respect.

*****

One of the best perquisites of working at Woolworths was the subsidised staff canteen. For the princely sum of 5/11d - that's five shillings and eleven pence (30p) I had a cooked lunch for five days out of the six worked, plus three cups of tea per day. We had every Thursday afternoon off - Thursday was known as 'early closing day'. We worked all day Monday; Tuesday; Wednesday; Friday and Saturday. The cook was a redoubtable Mrs Dempsey who knocked up traditional English cuisine - roast beef and all the usual trimmings for example, and tasty puddings - apple pie with custard being a speciality. Woe betide anyone who didn't clear their plates, Mrs Dempsey took that as a slight on her cooking. She had no cause for concern on my account, clean plate was assured every day. She was assisted by a nervous colleague who seemed terrified of Mrs Dempsey, yet I swear Mrs D fussed over her like a mother hen. Lunch hours were split as the store didn't close. The sales staff shared tables amongst themselves, I was allowed to sit with the store supervisors who sort of looked after me - felt rather strange but nice.

The supervisors were also known as 'floor walkers' (remember Captain Peacock in, 'Are you being Served'?). We call them 'security' now - all uniform and peak caps and allegedly fit. Mrs Roberts, the senior member, and her cohorts were middle-aged women, uniform was blue overall but no peak cap. They dealt with any miscreants as well as, if not better than their present-day counter parts. They had the stern authority and demeanour of Mums whose word was law. I never got to count the number of sales staff but there was a lot of them - all girls and they were supplemented by Saturday girls - students mostly. Only a few do I remember by name now. There was Jean Springthorpe, a truly lovely lass, blonde with bright blue eyes and a smile that made a 100-watt bulb appear dim. Jean was one of the nicest people I've met. Never an unkind word about anybody. Mary Shaw who went out of her way to make me welcome, a lovely friendly girl. She was dating an IRA sympathiser, like to think she did better in the end. Margaret Morris - Margaret was my first attempt at proper dating. I asked he out. Gosh, I made that sound so simple. You can have no idea how long it took me to do that. The times I got so far and then bailed out at the critical moment. By now everyone in the store knew of my plight and I just ran out of excuses and did the deed - and she said 'yes'. We set a date for one Sunday afternoon. Only she didn't turn up - she stood me up. She avoided me the following Monday, but Mary pressured her to apologise - poor Margaret did her best. Turns out she'd had a better offer from an older Polish guy. Funny thing was - she didn't seem altogether happy with that decision. I was far too young and naive to pursue the matter, so I licked my wounded pride and moved on.

This was not as tragic as it sounds. The lovely Jean Springthorpe came up to me one Saturday morning and asked me if I'd like to join a party of the girls at the Palais De Dance - a local dance hall in Temple Street. Mary Shaw was going and urged me to join them saying that it would be good fun. No one could resist Jean, so I agreed. The Palais was an upstairs room, not large but comfortable. It had a five-piece band (no vocalist) and they played a variety of music from modern pop to the standard oldies. This was pre-rock n' roll. It was warm and intimate. Modern day DJ's can't hold a light to live music. Where's the fun in playing records on a night out? We could all do that at home. Never understood DJ'ing. Not really a proper job.

Anyhow, we had a live band at the Palais and I got to love going. It opened twice a week, Wednesday and Saturday, our little party ended up going on both nights. There was no alcohol, so there were no booze-fuelled incidents. All the popular dances of the day were played - the waltz (the favourite); the quick-step and the foxtrot were the staples. Truthfully, I could barely distinguish one from the other, this was my first introduction to dancing of any kind. I sort of shuffled around doing the same sort of thing only slower or quicker as the music dictated. Seemed to me that a primary objective was not to stand on partner's foot, which I managed to do until I got the hang of dragging my feet across the floor. My reasoning was sound, if my feet were flat to the floor it would be impossible for anyone else's to get underneath. Jean had a boyfriend, no surprise there at all - lucky guy - but she insisted on letting me have the (my) first dance. I was clumsy and nervous in equal measure, Jean bless her, made light of it and said the important thing was to have fun - and I reckon she knew how. Mary took up the challenge next and survived with both feet more or less intact. Then I was introduced to some of the regulars, some lovely girls, and from that day on I had a ball - at least twice a week. One girl in particular - Marilyn - took a shine to me and me to her. And then she found out that I was only seventeen - she was nearly twenty - and reckoned I was too young for her. That was a second romance that failed at conception, but I did have the company of my friends from Woolworths and they never allowed me to become a wallflower. Christmas and New Year dances at the Palais were great fun. All the usual stuff plus the Hokey Cokey; the Conga and a poor attempt at the Gay Gordon topped off with Auld Lang Sine of course. They were happy care-free nights at the Palais and for the first time my friends, those lovely Woolworth girls, didn't give a damn about how many there were in our family or how poor we were. I shall forever think that this had much to do with the influence of Jean Springthorpe. If anyone deserved a good life it was Jean and it is my fervent hope that she has had a long and happy one.

*****

Back at the warehouse work was going well. One of my duties was to clean the manager's car every Saturday afternoon. This was also the day he disappeared for one of his infamous liquid lunches. He'd be gone for a couple of hours or more and often returned the worse for drink. On one such occasion I was putting the finishing touches to his car when he got dropped off and staggered towards the door. He saw me and paused and said "Whatshh your name?" I told him. "Have you... have you had a pay rise yet?" No - I replied. "Well you've got one now" and off he stumbled. Mac said to make sure I got it, but I wasn't convinced it was legitimate - intoxicated managers don't give staff pay rises. Mac took it upon himself to make sure I got my raise.

My last task of every day was to sweep the sales floor. I had a broom that was a good yard wide, a lot of floor could be covered in one sweep (that's a rather clever pun). That said the sales floor was not small. I usually started whilst the store was still open, it was then that I realised just how inconsiderate the public can be. The view seems to be that if a store is open till six o'clock it's okay to stroll in at two minutes to six and then spend half an hour deciding what if anything to buy. Rapped a few ankles with the brush I did, accidentally of course.

Whilst the social life was good I was once again getting restless. Something in my unconscious was stirring - there was an inner dissatisfaction that I'm afraid I didn't fully appreciate much less satisfy. I couldn't stay at Woolworths, I had to move on, but I had no clear idea as to what or where. Walsall and District Co-operative Wholesale Society were advertising vacancies for shop staff. Without much forethought, I applied and after an interview I was offered a job - Woolworths and I parted company.

Many years later Woolworths also departed.

Chapter 20

JOB NUMBER THREE

Unbelievably I was posted to the Co-op shop in New Invention, I could walk to work every day. The Co-operative movement is popularly believed to have begun as the brainchild of Robert Owen in Rochdale in 1844. Members became known as the 'Rochdale Pioneers'. the movement was a response to the growing industrialisation and the poverty of the workers. However, that's not quite how the movement started, in fact during the early part of the 19th century hundreds of so called 'co-operatives were formed before Owen launched his version. The concept of mutuality, which was the bedrock of co-operatives, was first recorded in 1498 in Aberdeen. It was called The Shore Porters Society. Owen attempted to replicate his success in Rochdale in Scotland and in the USA - both ventures failed.

Walsall Co-operative Wholesale Society was formed in 1866 and eventually became a part of the West Midlands CWS and this in turn became the Midcounties Co-operative in 2005. The idea of co-operatives is simple: there are no shareholders, only members. Members get to share the profits in ratio to their spending. Sounds good in theory but the fact remains that co-operatives can't compete with the major supermarkets on prices. Back when I joined, those supermarkets weren't even embryos, so the good old co-op did okay. Shops were located in community areas rather than in town centres, they're called convenience stores now - it being convenient to charge higher prices.

*****

Off to work I go. The manager was one Fred Grew and there were five other members of staff - six counting me. Fred Grew was, by default, a bit of a character. He had mannerisms that looked just odd. One was to hold his head right back and rub the side of his nose when he was having a serious conversation or making a delicate point. On the one hand, he was impeccably honest, I saw him several times taking a bit of cheese to have for his lunch and he religiously weighed and paid for it - one old penny. But on the other hand, he would slyly conceal bacon off-cuts by slipping them between proper rashers. He reckoned that that was the only way of getting rid of bacon bits that would otherwise be thrown away. Why not sell it for what it was thought I? Answer - Fred knew that he could get top price doing it his way. Naughty Fred.

The shop was personal service - customers presented lists and the staff scurried around collecting the items from stocked shelves. Self-service was only just creeping in from the USA where it all began. The first self-service grocery store (we call them shops) opened in 1916 in Memphis Tennessee by a man called Clarence Saunders (no relation to Colonel Saunders of KFC fame). In 1917 Saunders successfully applied to the US Patent Office for a patent for his concept of self-service shopping. Like a true entrepreneur, he then licensed his idea to other grocery stores. They all operated under the name of Piggly Wiggly - doesn't really resonate like say, Fortnum & Mason.

Found out why I got the job so easily. My predecessor, a young male (not as good looking as me of course) had just been promoted and they needed someone - a male - to go out and collect orders and payments from customers in outlying areas. I carried the money in open a leather cash bag and by the time I had completed my round there would be a few hundred-quid tucked therein. Like the rent man, there was no thought of being mugged. Not a job for the ladies apparently although they did do some local calls. I had to have transport, didn't have a bike then - can't remember what happened to my Norman Invader. The shop provided a butcher's bike, well it was better than walking.

My 'round' as it was called, started in Essington Road and reached right up into Essington and beyond to a new housing estate, returning via Hobnock Road and Sneyd Lane. An unofficial perk was that I got to call at home for lunch on my way back. I returned to the shop early afternoon. After cashing up I would go out again to cover a smaller round covering Short Heath. I got to enjoy the outdoor life and meeting people at their homes. The orders I had brought in would be put together ready for delivery on Thursday. Reckon I covered between 25 and 30 miles every Monday.

The grocery division 'borrowed' drivers and vans every Thursday from the bakery division to facilitate delivery of the orders. For the drivers, it was extra pay. For me I had the pleasure of calling on some lovely people like the farmer in Hobnock Road. I usually managed to arrive during his lunch break, he and his wife insisted that I sit down and have a mug of tea. Theirs was a lovely traditional farmhouse with a range that dwarfed any I had seen. Black leading that must have taken an age. Then there was the railway worker - always had the kettle on ready for when I called. The scariest one - scary because of my youthful innocence was when I called to deliver an order to an otherwise ordinary house. I knocked the door which was opened by a woman in her early thirties I guess. The only other thing she was 'in' was a flimsy dressing gown which she had 'forgotten' to fasten properly. I was a little over seventeen - I got flustered sort of knew what she wanted but didn't know at one and the same time. I made a hasty retreat and would forever wonder what an opportunity I may have spurned. But here's the rub - I had no real idea what to do. Had I gone into that house I doubt I would have emerged the same - assuming that I did emerge.

Of course, there were the other sort - the miserable, moaning minnies - they complained about anything and everything. Visited a gold medal standard whinger one day, I was on my best behaviour, determined to avoid any conflict because she would complain, and I'd get an earful when I got back to the shop. She ushered me into the front room. It was immaculate and there was the pleasing smell of furniture polish. On the table was a vase of flowers, an attractive arrangement. "Lovely flowers" I remarked and then I sniffed them "and a delicate scent" I added. She looked at me in a way reserved for the village idiot - which I was about to become. "They're plastic" she muttered contemptuously. One of the drivers was a former vacuum cleaner salesman who had fallen on hard times. Working class folk didn't buy vacuum cleaners and I suspected he'd been 'run out of town' from the more affluent areas. He had an eye for the ladies, frequently asking which where the best houses to call on and then he'd offer to make the delivery. My ability to create attractive housewives and nubile daughters was infinite. Whenever he came I knew that I was in for minimum legwork that day. It wasn't that I outsmarted him, rather that he was an eternal optimist.

For the rest of the week, that's Tuesday, Wednesday, Friday and Saturday morning, I worked in the shop. It was an old building by any standards but was somehow functional. A single storey building with an attic style roof space which was large enough to serve as a storeroom. There was a small space at the rear of the shop used by staff for breaks and otherwise as Fred Grew's office. In the corner was small desk affair upon which stood, a candlestick telephone. There was a cellar large enough to accommodate perishables such as cheese - nothing too heavy, the steps were steep and narrow.

Not being self-service, the concept of stack it high - sell it cheap hadn't been coined. Shops went for a more artistic display, showing goods off to best effect. This art was never more manifest than in the window displays. Window shopping had its own special appeal then, it was a joy to see the creative ways in which household goods and certain foodstuffs could be displayed. I got into window displays. One year a competition for the best dressed window was organised. Surprise surprise – I was charged with planning and executing our entry. We didn't win but my effort got a commendation. Every Friday afternoon I would burn waste cardboard and packaging at the rear of the shop. Recycling by the local council hadn't been invented. On one occasion, an unopened tin of something (I know not what) was inadvertently dropped in the burnables. You know what happens to such tins in a fire - they explode. This one did - parts of the tin and its contents flew within inches of my face. If that happened today I could sue for stress and trauma.

*****

The girls at the shop were a friendly enough bunch. By now I had grown into a not bad looking youth, not my opinion - one of them told me so. Barbara Evans - an effervescent lady, who was having an affair with one of the bakery delivery men. It was a sort of open secret. She also had a younger sister, Rita, and Barbara thought that Rita and I would make a good couple, so she set up a date. Rita was gorgeous, little wonder that she had won a beauty competition. We had a couple of dates and then what was becoming the inevitable, she dumped me - but nicely. But hey - at the rear of the shop was the entrance to Henry Squires' - manufacturers and they employed office staff - young girls. Without fully realising what was happening, I was starting to take an interest in girls, apparently it was bound to happen, everybody said so. We might have had the NHS then but there was no medication that would cure this sickness - boys/men making complete idiots of themselves just to get a girl. Obviously, I wasn't going to be like that.

I got a date with one of them - girls that is - nice enough but all she wanted to talk about was Cliff Richard and insisted on being taken to see his films - Expresso Bongo and

Summer Holiday. I'd like to express an opinion but even in these liberal times the publishers have their limits and Mr Richard (or Harry Webb to give him his real name) has become a national treasure. so why isn't he tucked up in a museum somewhere? Now you may be thinking that I am not his greatest fan - spot on. Well, there's only so much of this idolatry one can tolerate, the dear young lady and I went our separate ways - to watch different films of course. I did get to learn an important lesson - girls that work together stay together. When I tried my luck again with another of the Squires' girls I was given short shrift. The moral was - dump our mate and you've had your lot here. No trouble because by now I was getting a little bit fond of one of the girls I worked with - Jackie Shepherd, an attractive dark-haired girl. Remember that I said I wasn't going to make an idiot of myself over a girl? Didn't need to - she did it for me. I must have trailed after her for months and she let me, obviously flattered by the attention but the harsh truth was that she didn't think that I was anywhere good enough for her. Could have made working there awkward but on the one hand I had the support of the senior female staff member - Marjorie Perrins. Marj was a good sort, kept out of the tittle tattle that is gossip and set about teaching me her job which was the management of provisions - bacon, cheese, butter and lard. I also had to my advantage, the ability created at school, to completely hide my feelings. Miss Shepherd never got to know how hurt I had been by her rejection and I eventually got over the experience.

Marj taught me how to bone a side of bacon. That is, remove all the ribs, the shoulder bone and the ham bone which lurked at the other end. We used sharp knives - very sharp, slip with one of those and one would be well advised to count their digits. In those halcyon days, the Co-op bought most of its dairy supplies from Denmark. The bacon was superbly cured and easy to work with - I could remove all the ribs in minutes, out the rib-bones came, as clean as a whistle. One dreadful month the Co-op's buyer must have either fallen on his head or his budget was at breaking point. Instead of the usual supply of Danish bacon we received the Polish equivalent. It was ghastly - uncured, wet and sloppy. Boning that stuff was very dodgy as the knife jerked through the soft meat. Worse, being uncured meant that it was particularly attractive to the flies and they happily made their home in the bacon. I was privileged (not) to be allowed to clean the side of bacon up.

That meant immersing it in the sink in the back office and giving it a thorough wash - only in clean water mind. Thing was, it was now riddled with maggots and I had to stick my hand inside each orifice I could find and remove every last grub. I got my arm in up to the elbow and when I withdrew it, kit was teeming with maggots. Anglers would have been orgasmic at the prospect of free bait. Now, you might think that customers would want nothing to do with such a 'delicacy' as fly-infested bacon. Well - they didn't get to know – by the time I'd finished with it, there was no 'fly' evidence to be seen. But there was one remarkable moment: an old lady customer came into the shop wanting some bacon. Dear old Fred Grew hit her with a sales pitch that would have earned the approval of old Arkwright (Open All Hours). Fred steered well wide of the bacon's shortcomings, which was difficult because shortcomings was all it had. The old lady wanted to know if it was Danish - "No" said Fred, "It's Polish - that's better" He lied so well he might have had a career in politics. Now, the old lady knew a thing or two about bacon, like most folk in the area, she and her now deceased husband had kept a pig. She knew that only the Danes cured bacon properly and she also knew what wet, sloppy bacon was about - that it was neither cured nor matured. Bacon is best served after a period of maturity. "have the flies been at it?" she asked. Fred fell for it "No" he protested. "Then I don't want it, it's no good till the flies have been at it". Her logic was superb - flies attacked meat only after it had hung for a while - that was the nearest this bacon was going to get to maturing. Her generation were canny shoppers, the modern marketing men would have met their Waterloo had they crossed the paths of folk who knew all they needed to know about food.

One other commodity we got from Denmark was butter - Danish Lurpak butter, probably the best butter in the world. It arrived in one hundredweight wooden casks, shaped like beer barrels. Once the restraining hoops were knocked off one end the laths sprang open. In those super-fit days, I could easily hoist a barrel of butter in the air and upturn it onto the serving base in one flowing movement. It would be cut through with cheese wire and cut into required portions using a butter knife. Butter patting was considered so old hat then. I was sent on a course to learn about boning and cutting bacon properly. It was held at the Co-op's central premises located on the corner of Bridge Street and Lichfield Street in Walsall, in a room adjoining the Kenmare Restaurant - the aromas that emanated forth were divine. The Co-op was big in Walsall then and one of its biggest attractions was the Santa Sleigh-ride which operated every Christmas. Sadly, as with so many old customs and practices, this faded into the memory and the Co-op surrendered its prime site in town to a miscellany of shops and such like. The old Kenmare was converted and became the home of Walsall County Court.

*****

Whilst I was serving my time at Woolworths Mum fell pregnant (for the last time) with baby brother Stephen. My how the tongues wagged, and acidic barbs muttered. "She should know better: you'd have thought they had enough kids: they can't provide for the ones they've got: it's a disgrace: ought to be ashamed of themselves." These and others were said, not to us, but always in earshot. When Stephen was born, I sort of adopted him, looked after him, looked out for him. Anyone who had an issue with his being born or had an opinion on Mum would have to deal with me

- I took the slights very personal. I was working at the Co-op in New Invention. so, the gossip was hard to avoid. Financially Mum continued to struggle feeding and clothing a large and growing family, despite the contributions made by those at work.

It made sense for her to switch grocery shopping to the Co-op and to this day I can remember her membership number - 83724 - I wrote it down countless times. I took her order with me on a Saturday morning, leaving for work early so I could put it together and deliver it before the shop opened. Seems incredible now that Fred Grew trusted me not to cheat - putting in stuff and not charging and I'm proud to say that I never did. He always checked the pricing and addition but that was the practice for all orders. The routine was that I took the groceries home on Saturday and paid for them the following Friday being my payday. Mum would give me so much and I made up the shortfall by way of my so called 'board' money. Over time Mum's contribution got less and mine more. It was never spoken about at home. My siblings had no idea. I was on holiday from work once (but still at home) and Mum had the order delivered by the shop's errand boy. Because I wasn't at work I gave her my board money in cash and she said that she'd pay the bill direct. Unfortunately, she didn't, she'd paid other creditors who were pressing and there was nothing left. Fred Grew raised the matter of the unpaid bill a month later. It was hugely embarrassing to know that everyone at the shop knew - except me. I paid it in full the very next payday. I couldn't raise the matter with Mum - I felt for her. Paying most of the grocery bill became the norm. The rest of the family, including Dad, didn't know - wasn't that it was a secret, rather that such matters were never talked about.

*****

It was Christmas, 1958 I think, Marg Perrins was off sick with a slipped disk. She lived just around the corner from me so Fred Grew asked me to call on her at lunch time to ask how she was. I got there just as her husband came home and, it being Christmas, he insisted that I have a tot of whisky to celebrate. Whisky and I had first met when I was a blissfully unaware child - I didn't remember it and it not me. Oh, would that it had stayed that way. I took from him a tiny glass with a very modest offering - so I thought. I have since learned that that glass and measure was exactly how whisky was served. Anyway, I knocked it back in a single swallow - which is, apparently, the very wrong way to drink whisky - sipped and savoured be the way. My reaction to the experience was twofold - first I thought it be the most disgusting stuff I had ever put in my mouth- worse than beer and even more so than the infamous cod-liver oil and malt. I have never been near the stuff since. The other thing that happened was that I started to glow like a furnace. I reluctantly concede that the case for whisky as a form of central heating was made - but I'll take the cold any day.

*****

This was a period when I started to come into my own. My interest in music would likely have astonished dear old Mrs Bailey - the choice perhaps even more so. So, called pop music exploded in the late 1950's and I went with it all the way. Getting a record in the top 20 best sellers was every artists' dream. Sunday night 11pm to midnight - Radio Luxembourg - the Top Twenty show. The top selling records of the past week were played in ascending order, climaxing in the number one. In those halcyon days, a performer had to sell one million copies to get a gold disc from the record company - the ultimate accolade. Now it seems that there are so many awards in the music industry - there might even be one for performers who's never won one - 'And the Crap Music Award for never doing anything worthy of an award in 2016' goes to..............'

I kept pace with the exciting developments through the

pages of New Musical Express and Melody Maker. I knew every hit record and many more besides. Saturday was the day to breeze into Walsall and buy whatever was taking the fancy.

In the beginning, they were 'long playing records' (LP's) but over the years they became 'albums' - much more sophisticated. The very first LP I bought was The Student Prince - a film musical featuring the voice of the incomparable Mario Lanza - said by many to be the finest tenor since Benjamino Gigli. If you think Pavarotti was good, lend an ear to Lanza. He didn't appear in the film because sadly he surrendered to booze (whisky) and was incompetent on set. So, when he was sober, they got him to do the singing and dubbed the film. The next LP I bought was from the Pye Golden Guinea collection; Ravel's Bolero and on the other side Rossini's Thieving Magpie, I enjoy those pieces to this day. On the pop scene, my favourite of the time was an American lass - Connie Francis, she had such a rich and unique sound.

*****

Around this time, I made a sort of quasi return to learning. I enrolled on a distant learning course. This was a good period for these private and commercial institutions of learning. There were no colleges of further education (universities qualified to be called 'higher' not 'further'). Such post- school facilities as there were, were provided by night school classes and available only from selected day schools. The courses were predominantly vocational and intended to- help those in work enhance their skills to the benefit of their employer but at no direct cost. It had already been established by my experience at school (woodwork) and my first job (pattern making) that practical skills were not my forte.

I reflected on what I was good at – words – writing. I was always way ahead of the rest at English. But for what sort of work could that qualify me? Copywriting – that's what – that's what it said in the brochure. Learn to be a copywriter and work in advertising. Really? I enrolled and over a year earned a diploma in advertising. It was a most interesting course – I learned a lot about advertising and marketing. My most memorable moment was producing a TV campaign for ball-point pens. An impressive (if I may say so) cartoon story board with "some clever wording" (my tutor's comments. Alas, successful though the course had been, it did not propel me into neither advertising nor copywriting. A valuable lesson was learned and not one available on this, or any other course to my knowledge. It isn't only what you know. There's a host of other influencing factors like where you were educated, connections – in and out of the profession. Advertising proved to be an exclusive business and, as far as I was concerned, a closed shop. I do remember the local newsagent being impressed with my weekly order – New Musical Express and the Advertisers Weekly – the latter being a trade magazine for those in the business seeking change.

Despite the negative outcome, I enjoyed my experience of distance learning. I liked being able to work alone, as and when it suited. In any event, it was the only way I could have studied anything other than manual skill- based subjects.

Chapter 21

MY BEST FRIEND – VIC EVANS

I met Vic Evans at the Co-op. He came into the shop to do some shopping for his mum every Saturday morning. We both liked sport (football) and the pop music of the day so we had lots to talk about. Vic lived towards the back of Beacon Estate with his parents, one brother and a surviving grandmother. The whole family were kindness itself to me - such a rare experience. We became great friends and spent most of our social time together.

Vic worked at Vaughan's Drop-forgings in Willenhall. Alas another fine business that is no more. He was a draughtsman - a profession that has largely suffered the same fate as the factory. We played football together most Saturday afternoons, to my shame I can't recall the name of the team. Up to then I used to turn up at the local pitches just off Stretton Road and play for any team that was a man short. Registration was no problem - I changed my name as often as the jersey. Had a modest spell at a youth club in Wednesbury where I stunned them at one match by saving two penalties - I was in goal, like I've said, play anywhere for a game. We played in one match at the back of New Cross hospital, memorable for two reasons. One, there were horses grazing nearby and every time the ball went down the right wing, near to where they were they'd gallop towards the guys chasing the ball and I don't think they wanted to join in the game. That was also the match when I pulled a hamstring. I limped off the pitch and had to walk all the way home, about four miles - very painful.

We played the occasional game of cricket at the youth club held in the school on Beacon Estate. I do so remember the first game I played. They were a man short and I was seconded to make up the number. The captain said that he'd put me in last so no pressure. They were close to defeat when I went in, the first two balls I sent clear out of the ground for a pair of sixes - the match was won, and I was guaranteed a place in the team anytime I cared to turn up. Couple of years previously I'd been playing a sort of makeshift game with a crowd of others, nothing formal like stumps or pitch markings. We had an old oil drum for the wickets and a crease mark scoured by the bat - oh yes, we had the essentials, bats and ball (one ball). There was an older guy there who seemed to know a bit about the game. He watched me bowl - fast naturally, and I was very quick, but erratic. He came and spoke with me and advised me to try slow bowling with a bit of spin. That's skill he reckoned, anyone can be fast but to beat a batsman, skilful spin bowling was the thing. I gave it a go and got a hat-trick later in the game. A hat-trick is taking three wickets with three successive balls. Football hijacked the term and accords it to anyone scoring three goals in a match - not the same thing at all. Played in a match at school and had the ignominy of being run out before facing a ball. My most impressive fete at cricket came whilst fielding in the slips. As noted elsewhere I had a blind faith in my ability to avoid harm so I got as close to the batsman as the umpire would allow. The bowler was fast, I was there to take a catch if the ball was just nicked. It wasn't - I heard the solid thwack of bat on ball and I was facing the batsman. Instinctively I ducked, that ball was boundary bound and no mistake, you just didn't want to get your person on the same line as the ball. The ripple of applause that followed confirmed the boundary – I assumed. But as I rose I saw the batsman walking and my team mates were rushing up to me to congratulate me - for what? As I straightened up the reason became clear, the ball fell out of my lap! They all thought it was a brilliant catch, why should I disillusion them? Truth was that, to this day I had no idea what happened - I felt nothing. Fielding close to the batsman is always dodgy and I suppose inevitably my luck ran out when the batsman did snick the ball and I was after it in a flash - I met the bat on its follow through, one

315

broken nose - very painful. A moment I still savour occurred during a game I was put to field in the mid-on position (don't ask - if you have to ask you won't understand). The batsman had demonstrated a propensity for driving through the on-side. Third ball of the over, I could tell from the solid 'thwack' it had been 'middled' – hit perfectly with the middle of the bat. Nobody moved, the batsman watched the ball soaring towards the boundary. It didn't get there, I was ball watching too and at exactly the right moment I took off, I fled through the air, right arm extended. There was the most satisfying 'smack' as the ball hit the palm of my hand, my fingers closed in, I crashed to the ground, hand and ball held aloft. He was out! He was also a great sport because he walked over to me and congratulated me on what he said was the best catch he'd ever seen.

We English like to think that we invented most of the popular sports played around the world. Cricket is no exception. The truth is that there is no clear and firm evidence of exactly where and when the game was invented. There is circumstantial evidence that it was played in French Flanders in the 15th century. There is also oblique reference to it being played in Surrey circa 1550. In my opinion, it is by far the most superior of games demanding intelligence and a knowledge of human psychology. Players study the opposition: bowlers note a batsman's favourite stroke, weak points, his technique: a bowler's style and delivery, noted by batsmen. Each looks to provoke the other to gain advantage. Fielders do not stand randomly in the field of play. They are placed and have a specific task to perform. A bowler will place a fielder in a spot and then tempt the batsman to play a stroke that will deliver the ball into the hands of the fielder. Doesn't always work - the batsman works it out and does something different. These are complex mind games.

As a Co-op employee, I was entitled to use the social club facilities located in Bridge Street, Walsall. There was a snooker room on the first floor - three full size tables. There was also a dartboard to help those waiting for a table to pass the time. Vic and I went there at least once a week to play snooker. First time was also the first time I'd held a snooker cue - I had no idea how to play the game but watching others, it didn't look so hard. A few weeks later when I had the balls sorted out (in my head) we could play what passed for a game. Time often ran out long before we came close to clearing the table. On one occasion an older guy, and a better player by far, offered to play us one at a time. Crafty blighter then got the table for two sessions. During my game with him the cue ball came to rest on the side cushion. Old guy started to explain about keeping at least one foot on the floor and how the rest helped do that. He went to get the rest and when he turned back he was surprised to see me playing the shot left handed. "Where the bloody hell did you learn to do that?" he asked. I shrugged, seemed perfectly natural to me. Next time we saw him he was waiting for a table and suggested a game of darts. "Suppose you can do that left handed an' all" he said sarcastically. Yes, I could and yes, I did.

*****

One of Vic's passions was playing the guitar, he was pretty good in an age when it seemed that every teenage lad wanted to be like the new wave of rock 'n roll singers. Vic was in a band with three other guys. The lead instrumentalist played the mouth organ, electronically adapted to ramp up the volume, he was a very accomplished musician. Another made a passable attempt at the drums and the third member was the vocalist - a title that demanded a very charitable interpretation of the verb 'to sing' - he couldn't, he was dreadful, couldn't work out why they kept him. At one rehearsal/practice there was a small gathering of friends of the band - when the vocalist did his bit the room suddenly emptied, he was completely immune to the message the departures sent. I was invited to join the band. To do what I wondered, my only experience music wise had been that infernal triangle cum coat-hanger. They had the astonishing idea that I should learn to play the organ - that lasted all of two weeks. Seemed the drummer wasn't too enthusiastic about his role, I reckon it was because drummers were always located at the back and he wanted some of the limelight. Whatever, I made a decent fist out of the role and learned to play to a passable standard. Only played at one gig though, the Amery Club just off Cannock Road. It was a local Conservative Club affair and I hit the summit when, sufficiently fuelled with Ansell's best bitter, the gathering launched into an impromptu Conga and I rose to the occasion and gave the band a drum backing that matched the guests' enthusiasm. It was wild - abandoned even and at the end we (I) got rapturous applause. Now, having built me up, allow me to bring me down. Flushed with success and having reached what I believed to the night's finale, I left the platform and went to the loo. Walk with me through this - slowly. They're Conservatives - Tories, loyal to the establishment - the Crown. What do you suppose such a band of brothers and sisters might end their functions with? Why - the national anthem of course and what do you need to start the national anthem? A drum roll - and what do you need to get a drum roll (okay - apart from drums)? A drummer - and where was the drummer? In the loo. I was also in disgrace. I shall say no more.

*****

My earliest memory of the Queens in Queens Square Wolverhampton was as a cinema. I went there once to see 'Gone with The Wind'. I was a restless active teenager, three hours or more of romance was too much for my insensitive constitution. I've grown to have more respect for it since. Soon after, the cinema was converted to a ballroom but retained the name Queens. At six-bob (30p) admission charge it was the elite of its kind in the area. It was the place to be seen if you wanted to meet a classy girl. Naturally Vic and I and some of the band went as often as we could afford. I recall one who shall remain nameless smarming over a lovely looking girl and bragged that he'd be taking her home that night. He tried - but when she told him she lived in New Zealand I think he got the hint - a blunt brush off, that put a dent in his ego.

Just across the square was a branch of the Halifax Building Society and there worked a really lovely girl that Vic fancied. Don't know how but he got a date with her and at the next band practice he asked me to make up a foursome the coming Saturday night. I was chuffed for him but wary of blind dates, that is until he showed me who my date was to be. she was there at the practice with Vic's date. Her name was Rita, a raven-haired beauty. I said okay - well words to that effect. Come Saturday and the Queens and some unwelcome news - Rita couldn't make it but a replacement had been found - Hilary. That's Hilary with the barge-like feet. I did my best, put on a face that told Vic, 'I'm doing this for you and you owe me.' I don't want to be unkind, but Hilary and I weren't made for each other. I knew that from the start, but it took several weeks for her to get the message. She took to calling me at work (never did find out who gave her the number - Vic Evans).

If you're still awake and are possessed of reasonable powers of recall you may recollect my less than complimentary remarks about what is allegedly Ireland's most famous export - Guinness (my money would have been on blarney). I shall here recount how I came to my scathing conclusion regarding this witches' brew. One quite ordinary Saturday night Vic and I were at the Queens. We decided to go get a drink from the bar upstairs. There we encountered a rather large man who was giving the impression (and the odour) that he had drained all the vats at the nearby Bank's Brewery and was embarking on what might have been early break-dancing. The bar was crowded, it would be a struggle to get through, rather large man took pity on us and offered his services

"I...I...Ishh I sshhlll get (hic) yousshh a drinksh".

We declined, rather large man looked a teeny bit hurt; miffed; cross even. There are moments in one's life when to argue seems less than prudent. Half- a-bitter and an orange squash thank you, kind sir.

"Youssh gonna av a prop...prop....proper drink".

He waded through the crowd with a blundering indifference and returned triumphantly bearing two pints glasses full of an ominous thick black substance with foam on top. I smelled it, as you do, and it smelt rank.

. "I'm not drinking this" I hissed to Vic.

"It's Guinness - I don't think he'll be pleased if we don't. He might get nasty and I don't fancy taking him on" was Vic's nervous response.

I looked again at this giant who I swear could have knocked the pigeons off the top of Nelson's column without the aid of as much as a step ladder. My friend had a point. So, against every instinct I had I took a sip - a very tentative sip. By the gods, it was worse than I feared. I stood up and made as if to take off my coat.

"Hold this Vic" I said.

"What are you doing?" He asked.

"I'm gonna take this big bugger on. I'd sooner fight him than drink this sump oil".

In the end, I didn't have to do either, rather large man lost interest in us and went off to attempt to poison some other unsuspecting soul.

The Queens was a treat - an indulgence - and expensive. Cheaper, and no less agreeable, were dances held at the Wolverhampton Civic Hall and the Dorchester in Temple Street, a little lower down from the Rollerdrome. Over time we transferred our social life to Walsall and the Mayfair in Bridge Street and the Town Hall. It was at the Town Hall that we saw the singer Susan Maughan before she became famous (bet nobody remembers her now). Vic and I do because she was standing on the stage one Saturday night, wearing a flared skirt. She was up high on the stage - we were down low on the floor - and we got an eyeful – well Vic did, obviously I looked the other way.

*****

Buses from Walsall terminated at the Mossley Estate, a mile or so out of Bloxwich but we ended our ride home at the latter, so we could call at the chippie. Fish, chips and mushy peas in open wrap, eaten walking along the road late at night seemed the right way of ending a good night out. Wrapped, I might add, in newspaper donated by customers, this was the way then, no fancy hygiene. We got salt, vinegar and newsprint on our chips.

Weekdays I'd go to Vic's with my record player, bought and paid for out of my wages and we'd play as many of the latest records as we had. Sometimes we'd practice - Vic on his guitar - me on the drums. Vic and his family were so kind and friendly to me. I recall one Christmas, I'd decided to buy each member of the family a small gift to show my appreciation. I saw them on Christmas Eve and I was puzzled why they all gathered round me - then Vic gave me a small gift-wrapped package. I opened it and there was a watch - the first watch I ever had. He said it was from all of them. It was one of those eye watering occasions. I never forgot that moment.

I shared an amazing experience with Vic's Dad. Horse racing was a regular feature of Saturday afternoon's sporting programmes. The old man used to place a few two- shilling (10p) bets to give watching the races a bit of excitement. It was harmless fun and sometimes he won and most times he didn't - well, poor bookies don't exist - do they? Come the big races - the Derby and the Grand National and special measures applied. He would choose two horses and put a whole pound on each. It was Grand National day, I was round there as he was choosing his two runners. He'd whittled it down to four and was finding it hard to choose. Eventually he settled on a couple and placed his bet - the gods smiled on him that day because his horses came in first and second. They would have beamed outrageously had he backed the other two for they came in third and fourth. He would have ruined the bookies day that's for sure.

*****

Not so much a day but one of our nights came near to worse than ruin. Vic, the band's vocalist, and I (still don't know what he was doing there) were walking through the Littleton Road Estate, just off Cannock Road, it was dark murky autumn night. Suddenly, a car raced past us and screeched to a halt. Six rather unpleasant youths disgorged and ran towards us. You could tell they weren't after directions. There was a ludicrous reference to some offence but as we - and they - knew, we had never set eyes on each other before, it was plainly spurious and a poor guise upon which to base aggression - in short, they were spoiling for a fight. Our vocalist discovered a talent far superior to his singing (which in all truth would be just about everything), he learned that he could run - very fast - and he did. The omens were not encouraging for Vic and me. Strange to recount but the fact that we didn't run seemed to dent their bravado because they just huffed and puffed making threats and got back in the car and drove off.

"Damn close that Vic old chap" I says.

"Thought we were in for it" he answered.

"Saw you clench your fist, bloody sure you were going hit the one nearest to you and if you had...." his voice trained.

Now, here's the thing, I hadn't realised I'd clenched my fist - but I had - it was still clenched, and Vic was right, I was moments away from hitting the yob, like I say, go down fighting.

That little episode was the impetus for us to take up Judo. Judo translates into 'the gentle way' and draws on the Zen philosophy. It's my thinking that the mind is more powerful than the body, perhaps I could say that the body is a tool of the mind. Probably because it comes from the far east (Japan), judo is often referred to as an ancient art. Truth is that it was founded by Jigorio Kano in 1882 and evolved out of other similar arts. It was brought to England in 1918 by one Gunji Koizumi who opened the first dojo in 1918 in London.

We enrolled at a club in Temple Street Wolverhampton. What is it with Temple Street and me? The Palais; the Rollerdrome; the Dorchester and now the judo club. Hello!! There is a world outside Temple Street. The guys that ran it called it a club but that was a misnomer. What it was, was a disused factory warehouse and us, would-be judoka (practitioners of judo), were the labour force that would convert this industrial slum to a proper dojo (practice area). Miraculously it seemed at the time but from amongst the motley band of volunteers all the required skills emerged, and the building was renovated, the judo club was formed and opened. The man who brought the art to the UK, 84-year Japanese master Koizumi, performed the inaugural throw on opening night followed by a tournament between the members. This was the moment that I shone. I was pitched against a much bigger opponent (judo dismisses differences of size as irrelevant - judoka just adjust). We fenced around for a bit and then I went for it - Morote Seoinage (a shoulder throw), perfect for a taller opponent, and I caught him just right - over he went in a perfect ark and landed in a winded heap on the mat. A clear and outstanding winning ipon (point). That was it though, I got walloped in the next round.

At a practice session, I got confirmation of a characteristic I was said to possess. Vic and I were being put through our paces by a veteran judoka of brown belt grade, that's one below black. Vic spent about ten minutes on the dojo, after being splattered on the mat umpteen times he decided enough was enough. Now it was my turn. It turned out to be a battle of wills, for forty-five minutes he bounced me all over the dojo and still I got up for more. Finally, he called a halt and delivered his verdict. Vic had the better skills but:

"You (me) - bloody hell, don't you know when you've had enough, when you're beaten?"

I didn't, I've never acquired that knowledge. No surrender. But I have learned the virtue of a tactical withdrawal to fight another day - another way even. That same guy pulled my shoulder out of its socket during a later randori (practice). He got a couple of guys to sit on me and he yanked it back into place. I will only say that it was rather painful. The one activity that impressed my instructors was my forward roll. In judo, it is a skill trained into judoka to help break a fall. Many struggled with it - to me it was second nature. During practice one night, one guy just couldn't get the roll right despite the patient directions of the instructor. In mild exasperation, the instructor called me over, took hold, and sent me flying through the air and watched as I curled up in mid-flight and rolled up, off my shoulder and back on my feet in less than a second. His final instruction to the student judoka was:

"Do what he (me) just did"

I don't recall exactly how it came about, probably from a chance meeting at one of the places of dance we visited, but Vic and I got in close with a crowd of student teachers (girls) from the Teacher Training College in St James' Square in Wolverhampton. That illustrious building was raised to accommodate the ring-road at the top of Horsley Fields. One of the girls happened to be a member of the Willenhall Tennis Club. The WCT held the occasional party at the club premises located at the back of the old railway station in Willenhall. We got an invite to some of their gatherings. Much drinking went on and something that passed for dancing - basically just shuffling around the floor, the males leaning on their female partners. It was not a new style of dance - rather an old style too-drunk-to-stand-on-own-two-feet affair.

There we were, about fifteen of us, all sitting round a table, chatting and drinking. One of the girls suddenly exclaimed,

"Damn, I've dropped something on the floor. Brian, would you be a sweetheart and pick it up for me?"

Of course, Brian would. So, down I went, couldn't see a thing, foraged around for a minute or two and got back admitting defeat.

"Not to worry" said pretty girl.

They, the fourteen others, were grinning and smiling. At what I knew not, I assumed I missed something amusing whist underground, searching.

"A toast" somebody cried.

"To a bloody good night out"

Glasses were raised, including mine which was half-full of orange juice. Glasses back on the table and all eyes on me again.

"You feel alright Smith m'lad?"

A curious question surely.

"Yes - why?"

"Why? Why? he asks. Why sir, we the gathered ensemble each with the vintage of choice - that's whisky over there, next to the brandy, then comes the best bitter and - what's yours Kate? Ah yes - gin and tonic...................well you get the picture. Whilst you were tunnelling we know not where we took it upon ourselves to improve your beverage. Er.... we all poured a little of what we had into your glass. You have sir, a deadly cocktail known as a 'mickey finn'. You should by now, by rights, be a bit wobbly on the old pins. You should be drunk - why aren't you drunk? "

Actually, they were wrong to call it a 'Mickey Finn'. Mickey Finn is thought to have been the manager of a bar - the Loan Star Saloon - in Chicago in 1896. It's said that he was in the practice of lacing drinks with drugs that would render drinkers' unconscious so that he could rob them. So, strictly speaking a 'Mickey Finn' is not just alcohol - there has to be drugs as well. For the record. there were no drugs - me and them (drugs) have never been acquainted.

Being teetotal I was expected to be extremely vulnerable to the hard stuff. On that occasion, it had no effect whatsoever. The disappointed spikers of drinks were convinced that I was not 'normal'. One of the party was a girl by the name of Katey. Katey planned to teach in primary school after graduating. She lived in Brownhills. She took a fancy to me and we had a brief encounter. Sadly, she had issues that she only hinted darkly at without actually naming and shaming. There was much dwelling on the past and how it affected her future. I reckoned she was living a twenty-one day - yesterday, today and tomorrow - all at the same time. Much later in life I came to appreciate what the Katey experience had taught me - that it's only now that counts. Now is the only time we can influence - yesterday is beyond reach and tomorrow, well that never happens. Some of 'now' can be spent mending the errors of yesterday but that's about it.

I learned something else too, odd and unexpected I suppose. I'd spent pretty well all my life being pilloried for being of a large family and in poverty. The tormentors were my own kind - the so-called working-class kids. Through the college and the tennis club I rubbed shoulders with the off-springs of the middle classes. They never once adopted a superior air or cast reflections, they treated me as one of the crowd - guess that won't suit the class-obsessed working -class agitators out there.

I went to my first pop concert with Vic and his brother Tony. We went to see Shirley 'foghorn' Bassey at the Civic Hall, Wolverhampton, she sure was/is loud. The best part of that night was the drum solo played by the backing band's drummer during the interval. He called it 'the land of drums', it was fantastic, all done without gadgets - just his skill. Sometime after Vic took a shine to a girl who lived a little further along Essington Road from us. The hours we spent talking about the right way to go about getting a date. We analysed everything in minute detail - Freud would have been proud. Must have worked because eventually they got married but that was after Vic and I sort of drifted apart as he obviously (and rightly) spent his time with her. I didn't get an invite to the wedding, I don't think the parents of his wife-to-be approved of us Smiths and in those days, the bride's family decided the guest list - suppose that was fair since they paid the bill. Wherever you are now Vic I sincerely hope you had a good life. You were my best friend for a few years - never to be forgotten.

Chapter 22

BACK TO SCHOOL

I was around 20 years of age and I was getting restless again. The Co-op didn't seem to have anything more to offer so I went on the lookout for another job. Must have shades on because I finished up as an encyclopaedia salesman for George Newnes Publications Ltd. There is no reasoning that I can offer for such a move for a salesman I was probably not - a cold-call salesman I definitely was not. I spent less than a week trudging around the streets of Ashmore Lake estate in Wednesfield, knocked on a few doors and got the sort of looks that were usually reserved for Jehovah's Witnesses - and they gave their books away. Surprisingly nobody wanted to buy a book that was as good as Encyclopaedia Britannica but more compact and with better colour plates (that's pictures) and had all the information to help kids do their homework and do well at school and pass exams and go on to university and get a good career and have a great life. Heck - if it was that good I should buy one and the world would be at my feet - why waste time selling the magic to others? I didn't believe, how could I convince anyone else?

Pressing problem was that Mum needed money coming in, so it was humble pie time - again. Back to the Co-op - they took pity (they needed staff) but not at New Invention, oh no, they had to have their bit of revenge. They picked a shop in the middle of Bentley Estate which meant that there was no direct bus service. Whichever route I took meant a mile walk to the shop. The manager there, one Harry Rowbotham, took an instant dislike to me - just the start you want. He was straight in asking after repayment of the superannuation payment I had got when leaving but a couple of weeks earlier. These payments represented savings built up whilst in the Co-op employ to help provide a pension on retirement - if you went that long. I didn't so I got my payment sooner, it was about £200. I didn't have the money - spent it on vets' bills. A few months earlier I had bought a dog - a border collie. Just before I left the Co-op the dog contracted distemper, he ended up running around and around in circles and in an increasingly distressed state. I took him to a vet. Nothing could be done, and the dog had to be put down. That's where the money went.

*****

Harry Rowbotham and the Co-op had to accept that it wasn't coming back but he left me in no doubt what he thought. He fancied himself as a bit of a ladies' man and I reckon I represented competition - I was younger (and better looking). The shop was tiny, one of those precinct-built affairs but it was self-service, the first of its kind I'd seen. No counter, just a check out girl at the one and only till. The most amazing thing was that two of the girls (there were four in total) could remember the price of almost everything in that shop. When managers went on holiday the convention was to leave the senior male member of staff in charge - sorry ladies, equality wasn't on the horizon at this time. Harry made a point of telling me that he wasn't going to do me the honour because I hadn't been there long enough, although my service with the Co-op was longer than anyone else's. This was the best opportunity he'd had to show he didn't like me. He put one of the ladies in charge. No problem with her - didn't care for the humiliation. She was a colleague and a friend so there was no problem in supporting her and anyway, she was good at the job. Interesting, when Harry came back to a 'little problem' his protégé (nor the rest of us) could sort out, he looked accusingly at me but realised that as I wasn't in charge he was stumped.

One of the girls there was the sweetest and kindest lass one could wish to meet. I did so wish to meet her. I'm granting her anonymity by giving her a pseudonym, you'll understand why shortly, meanwhile I shall call her Emma. Emma was popular with everyone - staff and customers alike. I don't think she ever had an unkind thought in her pretty little head. Blonde and beautiful - and I was besotted but she only had eyes for another. Emma used to go home for lunch, she lived on the nearby Beechdale Estate. One, otherwise ordinary day she didn't come back to work after lunch. We ran through the usual gamut of probable causes, she'd had an accident (she was a young driver), been taken ill, plain forgot the time. Truth was far worse - truth was tragic. When Emma got home that lunchtime she found her mother with her head in the gas oven - dead. There aren't words adequate for such experiences. Emma was off work for a while of course. When customers started asking after her I said that she had some personal issues to deal with, Harry didn't like that, he insisted we should tell the truth. I objected most strongly, that wasn't our decision to make. Only Emma had the right to decide who and when she told what. Harry was doing what so many still do - looking at it from their perspective - what they would do. That simply is not the point - it wasn't him so what he would have done is irrelevant. He should have deferred until he knew how Emma wanted to deal with her tragedy. She came back to work eventually, still as sweet as ever - we all looked out for her - even Harry.

I don't think he was a bad guy, he simply didn't like me. I never got to find out why, never really tried, I was so used to people taking a dislike just because of who I was. I have no doubt my siblings had similar experiences. Work was second nature to me, I'd long learned that that was how one made one's way in the world. He had no grounds to complain there but the day I turned up with my arm in a sling he did lambast me for being unfit for work. That was the day after I'd had my shoulder put out of joint at the judo club, the sling was a precaution. I so wished I had taken the soft option and had a day off - he would have had something to complain about then, being short-staffed and all.

Most of the customers were women of course (as befits the period). As a ladies' man Harry never passed an opportunity to try and impress with his knowledge of this and that and nothing in particular- oh, and his general manliness. He was, in fact, a chauvinist. But one dear, dear lady outsmarted him on one wonderful occasion. She was considering which brand of dog meat to buy. Harry had a dog and therefore considered himself an authority on the subject. He proceeded to extol the virtues of a brand of canned dog meat called PAL (prolongs active life).

"There's proper pieces of beef in there" he said.

"I could eat it myself"

She laughed at him, that caught him on a raw spot, doubting him.

"I'm not joking. That meat is good enough for human consumption" he emphasised.

She called his bluff.

I'll buy it if you'll eat it " and she was deadly serious

In a corner was our Harry. She bought a tin - I obliged with the tin opener, probably not the most diplomatic move but I was enjoying this, so much so that I even went back for a spoon. Poor Harry had to eat a spoonful of dog meat. Of course, he insisted that it was delicious, why he could eat the whole tin - but he didn't - chicken.

*****

In the late 1950's the cinema was still a major source of entertainment, television was having an impact but young people in particular, didn't see any virtue in staying at home to watch something on the 'box' when they could be out with their friends. By way of reinforcement of the influence of cinema we also had magazines giving 'back' stories to the goings-on in Hollywood – believed by devotees to be the only place in the world where films were made (not true of course). One of these magazines was called 'Picturegoer' and amongst its glossy pages they ran a series of personal advertisements for readers looking for pen-friends. Since the latter half of the 20th century we, particularly the young, have had social media – Facebook and suchlike – as vehicles for engaging with strangers and making new friends. Back 'in the day' we had pen-friends. I placed an advert and I got a steady stream of replies – all from girls (lucky me). I met a couple in the flesh, one a girl from Stoke-on-Trent – Sylvia Palin was her name I think. The other I do remember – Linda Staines from Forest Gate, London. I remember Linda because that was the first time I went to London and the furthest I had travelled from home in my nineteen years.

An abiding memory of that period is that of my eldest brother and I spending the late hours of Saturday night/Sunday morning reading the letters received that week. We had both had a night out – me with friends, he with his fiancée. It was he, worldlier than I, who explained the strange acronyms that were scribbled on the back of the envelopes of many of the letters. SWALK – sealed with a loving kiss: ITALY – I trust and love you: HOLLAND – hope our love lasts and never dies: BURMA – be undressed and ready my angel. I reckon some of the letters were written by frustrated adults, posing as teenagers – some things haven't changed then. Eldest brother and I were quite close in those days, with his greater wisdom I think I averted contact with the nutters who were surely amongst the replies.

*****

By now the desire to do something meaningful with my life was pushing its way through the undergrowth that was my mind. One Sunday morning I got dressed in my 'Sunday best' and I walked to Walsall - about 5 miles away. It wasn't planned, a completely spontaneous and seemingly pointless exercise. Yet, I was very specific in my destination - the Walsall and Staffordshire Technical College in St Paul's Street. Having got there, I stayed a while looking at the building and acknowledged that I was going there - to study. Still not a plan but a knowing - I just knew. The following weekend, Saturday, I caught the bus to Walsall and went to Grice's newsagents on the corner of Ablewell Street. Grice's had a second-hand book store at the rear of the shop. I bought three books one each on English and Mathematics, the third a copy of Charles Dickens' novel Barnaby Rudge. I went home and for several weeks began teaching myself. The touch paper had been lit. In the autumn of 1960 I enrolled as a part-time student studying English and Geography at GCE 'O' level, these were the only subjects available for evening classes. It would take two years to complete the course and pass (hopefully) the exams. The minimum requirement for a decent job was five 'O' levels. At the current rate, it would take six years to get to first base as it were.

*****

I celebrated my 21st birthday in 1961. The age at which a boy became a man; an adult; legally accountable - able to do all the things adults can do (and many they shouldn't but this isn't that kind of book). It was a family tradition that Mum gave all her sons a signet ring on their 2st birthday - I still have mine, it is beyond value. Along with the ring came 'the key of the door'. The child that became an adult overnight as it were, received they key in recognition of their newly acquired status, a key to the door of the family home. This was a sign that they no longer had to submit to curfew and were, in theory at least, entitled to come and go as they pleased. In 1970, the age of maturity was lowered to 18 years to fall in line with pretty much the rest of the world.

Another family tradition was to have a special birthday party to celebrate a 21st. Mine was held at the Essington Church hall. Vague as to numbers that attended but I do know that I paid for a coach to relay guests from 94 Essington Road to the hall. In 1961 not many people had cars - come to think, none of my guests had one, unless they were keeping quite in case they became an involuntary taxi service. It was a good party - lots of boozing (inevitably), plenty to eat, courtesy of family catering and a creditable array of gifts for the birthday boy. The bit I didn't look forward to, was making the expected speech - traditional and compulsory. But hey, all one has to do is to stand up and talk - say thank you to everyone. How hard can that be? Well, when you stand up and look at the expectant faces staring up at you, very hard - it's very hard. It wasn't so much starting to talk - the really hard bit was stopping. It wasn't because I had anything interesting or useful to say - it was simply that I couldn't stop talking - nerves you see.

*****

It was plain to the powers that be that Harry Rowbotham and I weren't ever going to be bosom pals. Not sure whose idea it was but somebody engineered an escape route that ostensibly made it honours even. Harry was getting rid of me, but I wasn't losing face. They promoted me to branch manager, an age-old way of getting rid of trouble makers I gather. I was to take charge of a shop in Blockall, Darlaston. Well done you I hear you cry - not so fast my faithful followers. There was a sting in the tail - Blockall, Darlaston was to be closed. They couldn't offer it to a career type, no upward mobility you see. It was a dead-end job - it was my dead-end job. I had a staff of one - a lovely girl (I shall call her Kate). We got on like a house on fire - that's to say hot. There was a budding romance there and we had all day to explore it, save for the interruption of customers of whom there was still a few. But there was the time before opening in the morning and the time after closing in the evening - oh and the lunch break. Kate did omit to tell me one teensy weeny thing - she had a boyfriend. I found out when I invited her to a tennis club bash and she turned up with 'him' in tow. The following Monday morning she tried to explain that she wanted to dump him, so we could be together but when he turned up on his motor bike at closing time she sure made off in a hurry. Women – honestly!!

*****

The closure of Blockhall; the uncertainty as to my future within the Co-op and my growing discontent in general - all conspired to force me into decision time. Things could drag on as they were and in six years' time, at the age of 27 I'd have five/six GCE 'O' levels. Another three years and, maybe I'd have two/three GCE 'A' levels and then, if the gods smiled on me, three more years and a degree. Seemed straightforward enough although I hadn't a clue what I wanted to do career-wise and there was the not inconsiderable problem of how I would support myself during this epic journey.

Mum and I had a chat. She had always been grateful for the support I'd been able to offer earlier. It was decided that I would go to college full time for a couple of years to gain GCE's. That at least would accelerate my progress. Mum said that she would forgo my contribution to the family budget because of what had gone before. I think too that she wanted to help right the 'wrong' that kept me from grammar school years before. There was no real comment from brothers and sisters - they appeared to simply accept it and I was grateful. Sadly, years later it transpired that the decision was rather less popular than I thought. Seemed that some family members felt I was getting special treatment - favouritism. This was rooted in a time-honoured tradition. When Dad was out of the house, the eldest son was deemed to be the man of the house, someone to whom Mum could go for manly support. Both Dennis and Barry were my elders, both had been called up for National Service and had to leave home for the duration of their service, so they never really got to shoulder that mantle properly. By sheer coincidence I was spared the call-up - didn't have to leave home and consequently built up a continuous and close relationship with Mum. I got to know of some of the fixes she found herself in, all because the shortage of money. I got to do what is fondly known as the 'dirty work' - getting her out of these jams. Much did I learn. In several ways, I paid for that education, in hard cash but it was Mum, and it was the family. On reflection, I guess I can't blame those of my siblings that thought ill of the arrangement. None of my brothers and sisters knew about what had passed between Mum and me, the financial bailouts. Mum had her pride, she didn't want everyone to know. But what I thought of as simply doing right by Mum, must have looked very different to some of my siblings and, of course, in not telling them they never got to know how they benefited. Still, my conscience is clear although I understand their feelings.

Chapter 23

A FULL-TIME STUDENT – FOR A BRIEF TIME

Thus, it was that, in the summer of 1962 I enrolled at the Walsall and Staffordshire Technical College as a full-time student. I had a free student bus pass and a grant of £150 for the year. I also had free board and lodgings courtesy of Mum and Dad. For the record, Dad was involved in the negotiations, first of all he raised no objections and secondly, he deferred to Mum.

"It's up to your Mum" is what he said.

He didn't enthuse one way or another.

The 1960's was a period when part-time work, especially for students, wasn't so hard to come by so I wasn't too depressed by the apparent lack of money. College holidays, like schools, were extensive, plenty of time to make earn some cash.

*****

On a mild September Monday morning 1962, I returned to school. That's exactly what it was like, going back to school. Hadn't given much thought to this side of things - how I'd feel. Now I felt out of place and out of step. Academically I had no fears, I'd been practicing using books written for this level, mentally I found it so hard to adjust. After a few weeks, I realised that the others in the class weren't bothered at all about having an older guy in the midst and when I learned that in some of the other non-vocational classes there were others like me, but studying for pleasure, I settled down and got to work in earnest. The subjects I covered were English Language; English Literature; Geography; Economic History; Commerce; Latin and French. The first three were as they had been at school and I soon got into the swing. A sad reflection on the educational policy of the day was that even at college there was discrimination. In English Literature, we were denied Shakespeare and the great classics, the powers that made such decisions assumed that we wouldn't get to grips with such works - clearly, they hadn't heard of my Shylock.

Our selected works were Arnold Bennett's Clayhanger; Nicholas Monsarrat's The Cruel Sea; Flora Thompson's Larkrise (adapted as a TV series many, many years later - and well sanitised too) and a volume of 20th century poems. I carry forward these little gems from each of the books. Clayhanger is about a family printing firm. In one chapter, the son of the founder is holding a freshly leather bound, book and is enraptured by the feel and the smell of a new book. Not so potent now with paperbacks, but the feel of a new book is still special - try getting that from a kindle.

In his book, Monsarrat describes the sinking of a British escort ship and how some men died badly - fighting for a place on a lifeboat, even at the expense of a shipmate, these were the "why me?" brigade. This is how some people live their lives - self, first last and always. Others, realising the impossibility of their situation, gave substance to the creed that goes something like this. 'Grant me the power to change that which can be changed, the courage to accept that which cannot be changed and the wisdom to know the difference.' These were those that simply floated away in sublime dignity to await their end.

The Cruel Sea was about sailors - men who used ripe and rich language. The edition we were using was an expurgated copy, edited to render it suitable for the tender ears of teenagers. Out went the naughty words that (dis)graced the original. As part of our learning Miss McMillan (lecturer in charge) got us to take it in turns to read aloud to the rest of the students, just as we had done at school, except that here, at college, the book was placed on a lectern at the front of the class. One dark day some naughty soul acquired a copy of the original (likely from the local library) and laid it out on the lectern in readiness for the forthcoming lesson, opened at a particular page. The unfortunate reader instead of reading that so-and-so 'was angry with the officer and cursed him under his breath' read out that ' the rating called the officer a bastard'. There was much sniggering, dear old McMillan didn't turn a hair - she just called a halt to that part of the lesson. Dear reader, you are not shocked of course, in the 21st century the word 'bastard' is common place, as are far more offensive expletives, but back then, in the innocent 1960's such language was used by drunks and uncouths.

Thompson's Larkrise spoke of the drudgery of the period. There's a moment when a labourer is seen staring at squire's mansion by the vicar. When asked what, he was doing, the man replied that that was the sort of house he dreamed of owning one day. Aspirational you might think. Not according to the vicar who chastised him saying that God had put all men in their rightful station and it was against His will to wish it to be different. BBC glossed over that bit.

The poetry was memorable for the contribution of Wilfred Owen on the horrors of World War1. Owen was wounded at the front line but insisted on returning to active service on recovery. He was killed on the 4th November 1918 - one week before armistice day, which was also the day his mother received official notice of his death.

Economic history was a revelation - gone was the monotonous parade of monarchs that had punctuated history lessons at school. In their stead came an expose of the history of England from the onset of the Industrial Revolution, the plight of the workers and the rise of trade unions. Organisations I had hitherto considered as hostile and aggressive were now seen in a more rationale light. Commerce was business studies in disguise and was no real challenge. Latin - a dead language, now that was something else. I railed against it at first but then I began to see its real value - as a foundation of our own language, one capable of such precision of expression. I struggled with French a little because it was taught through its grammar. Not the best way but the tried and trusted (mistakenly) way. We didn't even learn our mother tongue that way - still don't. We literally pick it up as we go along, the schools attempt to teach the grammar later - and fail miserably if the general standard of communication is anything to judge by.

The teaching staff - known as lecturers not teachers were, overall, a good bunch. I remember Mr Wootton - Maths - he led and taught by example. Not for him neatly prepared lessons. He explored the contents of the text books with us and sometimes, like us, found the logic of the author baffling. Mr Spencer taught Commerce. His lectures were punctuated by repetition of the expression 'you see'. We used to take bets on how many 'you see's' he could get into one session. Mr Walker taught English Language and encouraged me to write, he also advanced my appreciation of classical music at selected lunch time soirees during which he would explain a piece of music and talk about the composer. Can't forget poor David Evans who made a valiant effort to teach Geography. He told me that he'd had few job prospects on leaving university with a degree in geography. Either teach or work in drainage and sewage. There were times when I'm certain he felt that he'd made the wrong choice.

It was around mid-October, some four weeks or so since the term began, that a bright -eyed attractive girl snatched my scarf. I was walking down a flight of stairs in the college, I think it might have been the end of the day and we were all homeward bound. Anyway, said girl refused to return her misappropriated booty so we were compelled to negotiate. I got my scarf back; her name (Susan Grimes) and her telephone number, and in return I gave - er..er.. nothing as I recall. She seemed quite happy to have got my attention. Well, she's had plenty of time to rue the day 'cos we eventually got married - still are. What was so different about her was that she didn't spout endless drivel about pop singers, though she liked pop music. Her passion was ghosts and ghouls and all things supernatural. We became what's called an 'item' these days. Often, we'd take our lunch in the arboretum, share a bag of chips or on a wet day, beans on toast at the local Wimpey bar. Sometimes we would meander around the shops and I found out what an amazing shopper she was. This was the age of the juke box and records were made especially for playing on these machines. When records fell out of favour, they would be sold off to local record shops for retail. We went into one such shop and Susan asked the guy if he had a particular record. Yes, he did, would she like to hear it - yes, she would, and she did. Then she asked him to play the other side and he obliged. I think he was confident of a sale. His face was a picture when she simply said "I don't think I'll bother thank you".

I said we should have bought something, but she just asked

"Why? He didn't have anything I wanted".

Faultless logic. She's still that way today. Buys only what she wants, never what someone might be trying to sell.

What was so very special to me is that she treated me with the same kindness and courtesy that she did everyone else - well actually quite a bit more. For the first time in my life I felt properly valued as a person, as an equal, by the opposite sex. Maybe college wasn't going to be so bad after all.

The teaching staff were generally very good. There was

little of the authoritarian control as practised in schools. The head of the department was, however, a different proposition. I fell foul of him on two occasions. A period had been set aside each week for some physical recreation. This amounted to travelling by bus a couple of miles out of town to play football under the supervision of an ex-Walsall professional. Now I liked a game of football, but I was at college to learn, to make up for lost time. This was a waste of time and I asked to be excused. I was refused point blank - no discussion. So, I said I would go but I wouldn't squander my meagre cash resources paying bus fare getting there, if I had to go I would walk. Apparently, others from other classes feeling the same way, heard of my response and adopted it. There was much ado about nothing really. The head of department wrote to their parents saying that their sons had been led astray by an older student. I went to see him again to inform him that I had done nothing of the kind, as he well knew but this was the best part, I told him that he couldn't write to my parents because I was an adult - that seemed to upset him.

I think that he remembered this when, just before the term ended for Christmas I asked for permission to take the last week off, so I could do some part time work and get cash for Christmas. This was the time of the year when the Post Office employed students in the hundreds to help cope with the seasonal rush. Apparently, the Royal Mail expects to handle around 750 million Christmas cards in 2015 and the number is said to be in decline. In 1962, I'm guessing that the number would have been nearer 1,5 billion cards. That would mean a lot of paid work to be had. But he turned me down flat and added a warning, if I failed to attend college during the last week for any reason whatsoever he would have me expelled. I learned later that it was common practice for students to simply offer some typical excuse for not being there, even getting sick notes from their GP's. They were then untouchable. My mistake was playing with a straight bat - telling the truth. As on this occasion, that doesn't always bring its just reward. This mean-spirited man denied me the chance to earn a few quid, so I could better join in the festivities and make a little contribution. Still had one my best Christmases ever because at last I had a girl friend who accepted me for who and what I was.

The following summer (1963) I did get a part-time job with the Royal Mail. For six long weeks, I delivered mail to a new development on the edge of Bloxwich town centre - Lower Farm Estate. Had to get up at 4am and cycle to the sorting office in Walsall. For the next three and a half hours I would be sorting mail into the order of the 'walk' - that's the name they give to a postman's delivery area. Then, with two bulging, and incredibly heavy, mailbags I got a bus out of Walsall to Bloxwich. By tacit agreement, one of the mailbags would be left with a local newsagent, I'd do the first part of the walk and end up where I started (how so like life this could be), pick up the second bag and do the other half. Being a new development meant that this walk was longer than most because many of the properties were not yet occupied and I could walk a hundred yards between deliveries. It was an ok job and fairly uneventful. I remember pushing a fistful of birthday cards through a low-down letter box only for them to grabbed by an aggressive sounding dog. Hate to think what the beast did with them - too late to retract unfortunately. One house had two Alsatian dogs in a secure compound at the side of the house. I had been cautioned to only go up the drive if I could see the dogs in the pound. If they weren't in sight that meant they were loose in the grounds - best not go through the gate. One day I didn't see them, I didn't go in. I took the mail back to be re-delivered on the second delivery done by a man with van. He mopped up the loose ends from the morning walks. I didn't get to see man with a van - man with a van didn't know about the dogs. He came back with what would nowadays be called a 'designer tear' in his trousers. He offered me some very colourful advice, but although I was a newbie I was sure post was not intended to be delivered there.

My new girl friend's father was transport manager for the then Beecham Group - that's Beecham of Beecham's Powder fame. It was one of the great cure-alls of its day. Supposed to be mixed with water but some hardy souls just poured the powder down their throats. Tried that once - it was like swallowing chalk dust. Beecham's had expanded by acquisition and in turn it was acquired by Glaxo Smith Kline. Now the name of Beecham is virtually extinct. Anyway, back then they had a depot at Perry Barr and my father-in-law-to-be-one-day offered me a temporary job in the summer of 1964 whilst I awaited my exam results. I was a general dogsbody in the warehouse, helping out where I could. They even let me drive a fork lift truck. Oh - big mistake. My major activity was sorting and stacking the empty bottles brought back by the delivery drivers. On a single pallet could be stacked 24 x 12 cases of empty bottle - that's 288 bottles. Given the choice would you (a) move these case by case by hand or (b) stack 'em on a pallet and use a forklift truck to shift the lot in one move? Of course, you would and so did I. Imagine if you can, the sound they make when 288 glass bottles are sent crashing to the floor. One hell of a bang about sums it up. Apparently, the first thing to do when the fork lift is in position and ready to lift the load, is to tilt the pallet towards the driver otherwise contents of pallet are likely to fall off. Well, I proved that hypothesis. The number of empties return that week took a sudden dive.

I estimate that I cycled 24 miles per day (12 there, 12 back) in the weeks I worked there. It was worth it - had a great time, and my dear Susan worked in the offices, that might have had something to do with job satisfaction.

*****

At the end of my first year at college I was awarded the Head Postmaster's prize for the highest average marks in the college 85%. See - even I can creep when I want to. My prize was a copy of the New Testament - no I haven't read it - yet. In my two years at college I took and past fourteen external examinations, including the Royal Society of Arts (RSA) level 3 paper in English Language. I sat exams in a variety of subjects for the RSA board, all in preparation for the GCE examinations. I sat six passed five - didn't pass French. The irony of it was that I waltzed through the oral exam which was said to be the hardest part because one had to converse with the examiner. I guess five wasn't such a great haul measured by the number kids walk away from school with today, but the system then would never have facilitated sitting umpteen exams, for a start I can't recall any school or college that was resourced to teach such a wide range of subjects as exist today.

Decision time, the results were out, it was time to make the next move. I wanted to go on and do 'A' levels, I even dreamed of university, but I didn't feel I could prevail on Mum any longer, she needed more money to be coming in, not an extra burden. So, I gave thought to the different jobs for which I could apply. I might have only five 'O' levels, but this was a time when school leavers from secondary schools left with no accreditation. My five elevated me into competition for jobs with grammar school kids who had decided not to stay on for 'A' levels. I should be honest and admit that I was quite proud of the fact that I could apply for white collar work - and work with a future, a career. Truth was that I had no idea what I really wanted to do, a fact that caused me much agonising at the time. I have never really wanted to do any one thing for the rest of my life. Looking back over my shoulder I'm rather glad that I've had such a mixed and varied work experience - like to think I've had at least two careers already and I've a mind for a third.

Eventually I got an interview with an insurance company

and would likely have taken their offer had not my father-in-law-to-be-but-he-didn't-know it-yet suggested banking. I have no idea why but then I saw a sign outside a local bank with this sign outside:

'Hours of business 10am to 3pm.'

Perhaps that had something to do with it, anyway, I reckoned I could manage hours of work like that, so I applied. The bank was Midland Bank, long since taken over by that monolithic Chinese takeaway of a bank HSBC. I got through the interviews and was offered a job. Have to say that an awful lot of people were variously impressed and surprised. Banking in the 1960's was worlds apart from what we know and hate today. It was a respected profession and bank staff were the snobs of the commercial world. My Mum was particularly proud, Dad said little - as usual but I like to think he was at least pleased.

Here endeth what I have called 'my early life'. More than a new chapter, a new beginning beckoned. I had no idea what to expect and typical of people facing like situations, I was both apprehensive and excited. Bank's recruited from grammar schools and universities and, as I was to discover, private schools. Career bankers were not garnered from secondary modern schools, but then, I applied as a college student possessing of the essential GCE's. I do believe I may have started a new genre.

It is an understatement to say that family; friends and acquaintances were surprised that one of us – the 'Smiths' should have landed such a prestigious job. Going to work wearing what hitherto, was regarded as 'Sunday best' was a considerable culture shock. I was to quickly learn that the whole experience was a shock at so many levels. My time in the bank is the subject of the next volume of my autobiography. Suffice to say here that it bore no resemblance to what had gone before.

Chapter 24

MOM

The social aspirations of the world were modest back then. Many looked forward to a weekend meeting and greeting in the local pubs or the working men's club. Bank holidays were usually spent sprucing up the gardens and visiting (or being visited by) relatives. Most managed a week at the seaside during the 'industrial fortnight'. This was the two weeks every year that factories shut down and workers took their annual holiday. Apart from the legal obligation to employees, this was also the time when machinery in the foundries got its annual overall. Mostly the foregoing didn't include us though we did manage the gardening bit. I was twenty-one when I had my first holiday away from home.

Neither parent was a regular drinker, they liked it well enough but couldn't afford the luxury. Whilst it may appear that we were deprived, this was a time when you had what you could afford and if you couldn't afford it you went without - a clear and simple rationale. Nonetheless, it must have been particularly hard on Mum who rarely got out of the house save for shopping. Many the times she despaired of her life - the constant struggle to make the proverbial ends meet - they never did. Dodging the rent man and the tally-man, often with no money to feed the meters so there'd be no gas for cooking or electricity for light. Meals in mid-week were often Spartan. Then there was the endless drudgery of housework, all done manually of course.

Mum attempted suicide more than once by putting her head in the gas oven. A cry for help? The answer is a clear 'yes' and 'no'. The 'yes' occasion was when she was found with her head in the gas oven. The kitchen door was never closed and what was going on there could be seen easily from the hallway and through the serving hatch which opened into the dining room. I'm sure Mom knew she would be seen – and saved. At the same time, she could draw attention to her state of mind. There's the thing you see; she couldn't speak openly about how she felt – that would be a sign of weakness, but if someone else, seeing what she was doing, said it for her, well that was the idea. A cry for help? I have no doubt.

But on a second occasion, she was passed the point of no return. She secured the front room door and turned on the gas fire. She could 't be seen – she didn't want to be saved. No one listened, no one understood, no one cared. Death was her only escape and she intended to make it happen. Don't know who but someone worked out that all was not well – the absence of Mom and the barricaded door were indicators. Elder brother kicked the door in and turned off the fire. Mom was saved but I doubt she felt grateful – not for a long time. This was not a cry for help. It alarms me to say that I don't think any of us knew just how many times she attempted suicide. A criminal act? That notion is surely one very sick joke.

That rather clichéd interpretation of acts of self-harm and suicide is a gross over-simplification. It makes no effort to understand the mind-set of anyone so desperate, so devoid of answers and of hope that the only way they feel they can communicate their despair is by trying to take their own lives. For some it may be in the hope, even expectation, that someone will find them and realise the utter desperation that drives people to such acts; for others, there will no such escape, for they do indeed intend to die and of their mind-set we can only conjecture.

I find it incredible that suicide was a criminal offence until the passing of The Suicide Act 1961. Imagine charging someone with murdering themselves - we had Capital Punishment then. It was repealed for a trial period in 1965 and permanently in 1969. Makes one wonder as to the sentence if found guilty. Only people who attempted but failed suicide were charged; the families of those that succeeded were, however, at risk. The idea that suicide was a crime is rooted in religion. Thomas Aquinas (a 13th century theologian and philosopher - Tommaso d'Aquino) held that it was disrespectful to God, the creator, to take away what He had given - it was sin. Offenders were imprisoned.

Mum was, I think, in the first group, she wanted help. I believe that she wanted us all to know how she was suffering and maybe, just maybe one of us might have had some answers, for sure she didn't. She married when she was 19 - she had to, as was the custom of the day when young ladies got pregnant out of wedlock. Shotgun weddings had been around a long time. All that can be said in my parents' case is that Mum's parents were not impressed with her husband-to-be. For the next 23 years, she had and looked after, a growing band of children in the face of poverty and deprivation on all fronts. When each day offers only more of the same and when that same is a constant war of attrition, it's really no surprise that the will to carry on - to live - weakens.

She did her best for all of us. She wasn't worldly, that is to say she had little contact with the world outside 94 Essington Road apart from gossiping with the neighbours and going shopping. You wouldn't find Mum in political debate or such like, she had scant regard for the politicians of the day. She felt that they were in it for themselves' – sound familiar? The truth was plain for all to see, Mum was far too busy for a social life. When television made its appearance in our home in 1954, she did at least have cognisance of events in the wider world and access to some light relief.

Mum liked music and had a broad taste ranging from classical to pop. I imagine her brother, our uncle Jim, may have had some influence there, playing as he did, the organ - he had a perchance for church music. In the early 1950's we acquired a gramophone, they were wind up models then, ones that had to have the stylus (needle) changed regularly if you wanted a decent play-back. It was claimed that the thorns taken from a Hawthorne tree would double as a stylus – never put that one to the test. One of her favourite performers was a tenor named David Whitfield, or Catfield as Dad would have it. Much later when I bought an electric player and started buying the latest pop records, she used to sit and enjoy them with me and it was there that she formed a keen attachment to the playing of pianist Russ Conway.

We're now in the late 1950's and Mum began making efforts to connect with the wider world. She organised coach parties to see some of the big musical films of the day such as South Pacific. She did this through a guy that drove the coach on such occasions. He made the reservations, Mum sold the tickets and off they would go. Unfortunately, on more than one occasion she 'borrowed' the ticket money to pay her way on the understanding that she would be able to replace it by the time the coachman came to collect. There was no dishonest intent, she just couldn't keep up financially speaking. I saw to it that those bills got paid.

Despite her hard life Mum was a very strong woman in terms of survival skills. She had to be in order to keep up with the tremendous daily workload. But in 1974 her resolve was finally broken. That was the year brother David was murdered by the IRA. Mum never really recovered from that trauma. She was prescribed Valium - the anti-depressant drug of the day. It dulled her pain, but she became dependant on it. She also began to complain heavily about various pains she had. We all got used to hearing about them but could make no contribution towards alleviation. On one such occasion sister Carol, tiring of hearing what we all thought to be a constant whinge, virtually frog-marched Mum to her GP. He examined her and sent to New Cross hospital for further tests. Carol and I went to the hospital to learn of the results. The consultant was blunt.

"Your mother has cancer of the pancreas. I'm afraid that it's inoperable, I'd say she has about three months to live"

My sister and I left the hospital and first told Dad who seemed strangely remote - shock perhaps. We then visited every member of the family, most of whom were now married and living away from the family home. We told them of the news. It was a collective opinion that Mum shouldn't be told. The thinking being that she might enjoy her last three months believing that she was going to get well, rather than she was going to die. These are always tough decisions and anyone who suggests that the answer is obvious, you must tell the truth, is an idiot. The answer one should always choose is the one considered best for the dying, not for the conscience of those looking on. We were heavily influenced by the fact that that year Mum and Dad would be celebrating their 50th wedding anniversary and Mum had already started making plans for a big party. Why, we asked, should she not be allowed to carry on making those plans and enjoy what were to be her last days?

We all decided that Mum should come home where we could look after her and allow her to die in her own bed rather than some anonymous hospital ward. Sadly, that arrangement saw the onset of bickering and squabbling amongst the family, doubtless caused by a combination of shock and grief. Dad was still out of it, or did we squeeze him out? Never quite got to the bottom of that one but he didn't ever attempt to assert himself. I took a week off work to help organise affairs, an act that almost cost me my job. Sympathetic my employers were but summarily talking a week off when no one had died - that was going too far.

So, that we could all air our views, I booked a room at a

local school, so we could meet on neutral ground, away from the family home. It was agreed that we would all contribute towards the cost of the funeral and so that no one would feel pressured to committing monies they could ill-afford, I suggested that donations be made anonymously in sealed envelopes. My wife and I agreed that we would make up any shortfall.

There being so many of us it was that much easier to organise 24-hour Mum sitting and as far as individual circumstances would allow we all took our turn. Towards the end, when she slept less, that could mean sleepless nights for the night-watch-men (or should I say nigh-watch-persons?). I certainly suffered from exhaustion at work. Her wakefulness was exacerbated by morphine injections that caused her to hallucinate. There were some touching moments, like when Mum would, in lucid intervals, talk about the plans for the forthcoming wedding anniversary party. Such talk tailed off near the end and I do wonder if she had some inkling of what was happening. There were also the lighter moments like the time Carol and I were on night duty. Mum was restless, and we are on full alert but that didn't help us anticipate what was coming. Mum had a fear of birds, odd because she had kept a budgie in a cage, but she couldn't stand the thought of a bird flying near or much less landing on her. On this night, she swore that there was bird in the room and if we didn't get it out she would get out of bed and leave the room. We tried, in vain, to convince her that there was no bird, but, high on morphine she insisted she could see it. We had to promise to catch it and release it outside. So, there we were, climbing over the furniture at around 2am in the morning making out that we were trying to catch this bird. Eventually we convinced her that I had it in my hands and no. she didn't want to see it (thankfully). Carol opened the front door and we released our imaginary feathered friend. Mum settled down and had some fitful sleep. We didn't dare in case she woke up with another fantasy.

Mum died on the 29th April 1981. As it happened Carol and I were with her at the end. There aren't words to properly describe how it feels to hold the woman that had been there for you all your waking days and whose life was now coming to an end. Mum's death marked what I would call the beginning of the disintegration of the family unit as we had all known it. Some had already married and moved on, but the old ties remained for a while. Her funeral was the last time we were truly united as a family.

On a lighter note, Mom was very superstitious. New shoes were never allowed on a table; umbrellas should never be opened in doors; breaking a mirror consigned the breaker to seven years bad luck and walking under ladders – never happen, she'd take the traffic on first.

Chapter 25

DAD

Dad turned out to be a complex character. In my early teens, I remember him as unsmiling and menacing - even aggressive. I must record though, that Sammy the belt was threatened more often than used. Knowing now what he was going through during the blitz on Coventry, Birmingham and the surrounding areas, it's not hard to understand, at least in part, why he was as he was - the stress levels must have been off the scale. That said, as I've reported elsewhere, he was brought up by very strict parents whose style of parenting would have been typical of the age. I have no doubt but that Dad, quite naturally, simply carried on a tradition that was yet to be challenged.

He spent his working life in the employ of Willenhall Urban District Council - mostly as a driver. Over the years, he drove just about every kind of vehicle they had. In his later years there, he spent most of his time driving the so called 'gulley emptier' - a left hand drive vehicle used to clean and clear drains. They're out there still, we all know them, we've all followed them as they crawl along at 10 miles per hour. Dad had an impeccable driving record, receiving safe driving awards (no accidents) annually. On the few occasions, I sat with him when he was driving I was impressed by his ability to keep the speedometer hovering between 28 and 30 miles per hour - never above. Odd but he wasn't comfortable driving cars. I gave him one once - a Ford Prefect - thought it would be ideal for him to take himself and Mum out for the occasional social drive. He never took it on the road. Maybe he'd driven himself out as it where - couldn't't/didn't want to drive any more.

I wonder too, if his employers weren't alert to a developing reluctance to drive. Towards the end of his working life Dad was offered an 'inside' job - no driving involved. He was to be a part of the team that looked after the swimming baths. I understand that he found the transition difficult. To the best of my knowledge he never drove again after retirement, hence the abandoned Ford Prefect.

*****

Dad was a steady reader; his preferred choice was decidedly low-brow. He took the Daily Mirror during the week and the News of the World on Sundays. Book-wise I recall him reading popular American detective novels of the day - Hank Janson and Mickey Spillane being the stand-out authors. Booker prize winners they'd never be but they offered a cheap escapism I guess. After the war ended the market was flooded with books that covered every theatre of the conflict - from Europe, across North Africa, to the Middle East and the Far East. These books arrived at 94 Essington Road aplenty and I read them all. Learned so much about the war and whilst I've no doubt about the presence of author's license, most of the main facts were borne out by subsequent official enquiries and reports.

Mum and Dad were not what you could call close. They just seemed to jog along with the minimum friction though they did, not surprisingly, have their moments. Again, I think their relationship can be attributed to the social and cultural norms of the time. Men were the breadwinners and women the homemakers or housewives as they called then. The word 'housewife' is a scorned term now. I wonder how longer its replacement will last?

A man's status as head of the house was confirmed in several ways. The one most kids will recall is this: "Wait till your father gets home"

This was supposed to be a scary sanction against any unruly kid. We certainly heard it a lot - there being so many of us.

It was Mum's ultimate deterrent - at least that was the theory. Dad comes home from work; Mum tells of a misdemeanour by one of the others (not me of course) and Dad would punish the offender. The reality was very different. On the rare occasion, Mum did report one of us, Dad's response was likely to be something along these lines.

"Can't you bloody sort it yourself - waiting to bloody moan at me the minute I walk through the bloody door"

Thus, it became an empty threat and when uttered we knew Mum had given up and we had sort of won - whatever that meant.

Dad had only a rudimentary education. The working class was not expected to pass examinations much less to have thoughts of higher education. What he did possess was a miscellany of practical skills such as cobbling (our footwear bore testimony); car mechanics (essential for any driver of the period); building (the pool for Jack Vaughan was the high spot); gardening (our own was very creative, albeit basically executed) and DIY. There are those that would have one believe that the latter half of the 20th century marked the heyday for DIY in the home. They point to B & Q as the inspiration with its bewildering range of fixtures and fittings for bathrooms and kitchens and all points in between. How does one disillusion them? Dad's generation were into DIY out of necessity and were experts at making do – that is, using what was at hand rather than looking for custom made parts. When he retired, Dad showed a surprising talent for wood carving, particularly gypsy caravans. Again, they lacked finesse, but he must be given credit for the ideas. I have little doubt but that a few lessons in basic woodwork would have seen the standard of his work reach a commercial potential.

He didn't communicate with us kids much and when he did

it was usually in some form of admonishment or to be sent on an errand for cigarettes. I don't recall my parents having conversations about things in general – nagging and moaning but no friendly chat. Not that Dad was shy of talking, quite the contrary. He could hold forth on matters politic for hours; he was also an authority on what was wrong with the council and how it could be put right. Mom scornfully called these times his 'soap-box' moments. The army had a name for such speakers – 'barrack-room lawyers' they were called. Always careful to avoid the front-line, they put the world to rights from a very safe distance. They're still with us, the pundits and the hacks, always they know what went wrong and how it should be rectified but you won't find them in the running for the jobs.

With his passing the last threads that had held the family loosely together were severed and, for the most part, we all went our separate ways. The family home, along with parents, was gone. For many years, it had been the meeting place, an easy gathering point for the family. There was no replacement.

Chapter 25

DAVID

It may appear odd to add a chapter concerning an event that was not a part of my early life, coming, as it did very much later. But this was no ordinary event, it was, God willing, a never to be repeated experience. On the 4th July 1974 brother David died from gunshot wounds whilst serving with the army in Northern Ireland.

It began one late June evening. There was a commanding rapping on the front door, two policemen were standing there, they asked for Mr or Mrs Smith. Hard to say what went through Mom's mind at that moment. Did she think one of us had been up to no good? That would have really upset her, it was her proud boast that, despite there being so many of us, not a one of us had been in trouble with the law – no criminal records here. Not every family in the neighbourhood could make that claim. Usually the fear is that someone in the family has been involved in an incident of some sort – a road traffic accident maybe, but we were all accounted for. All that is, save David but he was safe surely, he was with the army – in Belfast. Not the safest of places to be sure and some soldiers had died out there, but it wasn't her automatic default position.

Spare a thought for the police officers sent out to deliver news of a personal tragedy. Whatever they may personally feel they must be very proper and professional, particularly avoiding any errors like mistaken identity or informing the wrong person. So, the two officers went through the drill, confirming Mom and Dad's identity and asking them to confirm that they had a son called David currently on duty with the Cheshire Regiment, serving in Belfast, Northern Ireland. The tension was palpable, the silence ominous.

Mom's face said it all, but she couldn't mouth the words – he's dead isn't he? David's dead.

"David's been shot but he's alive" – the police officer was speaking calmly, reassuringly. The expression on Mom's face went from horror stricken to ecstatic in seconds. Dad remained impassive. David had been leading a small patrol, reconnoitring the streets of Belfast. The patrol was taking cover by hugging the walls of any buildings at hand, David broke cover to take the patrol across the road – zig-zagging from one side of a road to the other was standard procedure. He was mid-way across the road when he was shot from behind, the bullet passed through the side-vent of his flack-jacket (body armour), striking him in the kidney area. David was shot by an IRA sniper. Snipers skulked around the city looking for soft targets. Getting behind a patrol and shooting a soldier in the back, before slinking off, was soft target enough. David had been rushed to the Royal Victoria hospital and was said to be conscious. My parents were given the telephone number of a military contact who would have more information.

Mon and Dad didn't have a telephone at home then so one of the siblings at home repaired to the phone box at the end of the road to summon the family Sue and I were married now and we had a telephone installed. I got the call – get over to Mom's as soon as possible – it's David – that was the cryptic message. It was late at night, close to closing time for the local pubs, letting Mom and/or Dad go to make the call to the military, given their state of mind after the news, would not have been a wise move. The message came back that David was alive and receiving treatment, he was sitting up and talking to the nurses – apparently, he'd asked for some baked beans. That sounded like him, he was fond of baked beans on toast. We were also advised that the military would arrange to fly his parents to Belfast to see David. Hearing that he was alive and seemingly well, Mom was elated but that was short-lived. She said she couldn't fly – she hated flying. It must have been a fear of the thought of flying because she'd never set foot on an airplane before – neither had Dad, who, incidentally, remained rather muted throughout. But the crisis was averted because they said he was sitting up – talking and as soon as he was well enough he'd be sent home on leave, they could wait until then. A bonus was that it was unlikely that he'd return to Northern Ireland.

The next call caused a dramatic 'u' turn. David had relapsed; seems the injury was more serious that had been at first thought – much more serious. The bullet had passed through his kidneys, they were irreparably damaged. David was seriously ill.

Poor parents – plunged into crisis when they thought they would have to fly – elated when that was no longer a 'must' – brought crashing down with terrifying reality. Their heads were all over the place. Mom was adamant – she couldn't fly, thing is, had she done so she would have been a wreck when she got there, not the tonic a wounded soldier needed. Without her, Dad wouldn't have known what to say, he didn't do personal, emotional chat. Whilst we tried to persuade her that flying was safe she came up with her own solution – we should go – 'we' being me, two brothers and a sister. The military had said that they'd arrange transport for David's wife – Olwen, and four family members – we were the ones on hand at the time.

We were rushed to Birmingham airport and put on a plane to Belfast. There were no formalities – tickets, passports – no checks of any kind. This was VIP treatment. The flight was a quiet affair, each of us deep in our own thoughts to what we would find. I'm not given to negative thinking, but I had a strong sense of foreboding. They had said that David was seriously ill, and family should visit without delay. I think that was army speak for 'he's dying'. Regimental personnel, in plain clothes, met us at the airport. We were ushered into two waiting cars, nothing military, just plain family saloons. Two of us and two plain clothes soldiers in one, three plus two in the other. One soldier being the driver, in each car. The non-driver explained that this was for security reasons. They (IRA) know you're coming, out here on the road you're at risk. We sped through the country roads away from the airport at speed, clearly limits didn't apply. At a crossroads, our escort stiffened as two cars, one from each direction, crossed in front of us. Our escort relaxed, they're ours he told us, they had checked that our little convoy was not about to be flanked by terrorists – more security.

The Royal Victoria Hospital was a huge affair, spread over I don't know how many acres. It was an old Victorian building, likely much modernised since we were there in 1974. We were met by a man I assumed to be David's commanding officer. He wasted no time in bringing us up to date on David's condition and on the security situation. Neither gave cause for optimism. David's condition was critical, but he'd leave it to the medics to fill us in with the detail. On security, he was forthcoming and frank. We were dismayed to learn the hospital was far from the sanctuary we had assumed it to be. Medical and nursing staff were as divided as the rest of the province – there were republican sympathisers working alongside unionists. How could one tell? That was easy, just look at their faces as they walked past. During the period, we were there, we got some very hostile looks, I recall one nurse's face – oozing vitriol as she went passed us in a corridor. But, there were enough of the 'good' guys to ensure that we came to no harm. We simply had to be careful as to whom we spoke and when ordering food in the canteen, we made certain that we were served by a sympathiser.

We were assigned an armed escort and told (not advised) not to go anywhere without him. Though a serving soldier, he remained in civvies so as not to draw attention to our party. At last, we were going to see David, on the ward. But first we had to be introduced to the army chaplain, well-meaning but not influential I thought. David was not in a good place. The doctor in charge spoke with us; there was no garnishing of the truth, it was only a matter of time. There was nothing that could be done to save our dear brother. The bullet had irrevocably damaged his kidneys, they were slowly but surely failing, David was dying. The nurses looking after him were wonderfully kind and thoughtful. We were assured that they were doing everything they could to make David's passing as peaceful as possible.

The five of us kept good counsel, we talked amongst ourselves and kept the folks back home up to date whist trying not to raise false hopes. It was a difficult and delicate balance, they had more questions than we had answers. Olwen earned my undying respect and admiration for staying focused and not sinking into a pit of bitter recriminations. Our sleeping quarters were some way from the hospital wards. We always made certain that we went to and from them together. One night, on the way back from sitting with David, our escort picked up on a car engine revving very loudly, he cautioned us to stand still, the roar of the engine suddenly came close – down, down, down he shouted – and we did. I remember the vehicle, an Austin 1800, it came racing through the hospital grounds, no lights, I reckoned there were four men in it – it sped past us at high speed, we got the all-clear. Our escort was convinced they were terrorists, but we weren't their target – this time.

The army chaplain was usually in attendance whenever we visited David, offering support and words of comfort. Well meant, of course, but we were very much a self-supporting group, the five of us looked out for, and after, each other. Asking God to help David get well was a little hard to take. If he has that sort of influence, why wait for someone to get shot? Preventing the miserable wretch who fired the shot from pulling the trigger seemed to me a much more useful act.

David was in intensive care and that's exactly what he got – intensive care. The nursing staff on the unit were wonderful, they did everything possible to make him comfortable; looked after us pretty good too. There was another patient in the unit, in the bed next to David. He was not a pretty sight; his face was burned, as black as coal. There were dark pools where his eyes should have been but, apparently, he could see, after a fashion. Both hands were heavily bandaged and of no practical use to him. I asked a nurse what had happened to him, she told me that he was would-be IRA bomber. He was putting together an explosive device, doubtless to be used against the soldiers and/or the RUC (Royal Ulster Constabulary) later disbanded in an act of appeasement to republicans. Seems the device went off prematurely and the bomber became his own victim. Now that's justice, rough justice I'll grant you but justice nonetheless – hope the chaplain was paying attention.

Up to that point, of finding out who and what he was, we were all sympathetic, that evaporated in an instant when we were enlightened. The nursing staff were cold, even hostile to him. They did their job but expressed no sympathy with him whatsoever. Here was a guy busying himself constructing an explosive device intended to maim and kill indiscriminately; a man who would celebrate the detonation and ensuing pain and suffering, as a success. Fate had decreed otherwise - a premature explosion and he was the only victim – just deserts. Our little party was well out of sympathy.

That changed somewhat on the second night. We were sitting in the waiting area whilst David was readied for visitors. A man in his 60's (I guess) joined us. He was slight in stature with silver grey hair, parted down the middle. He wore a pained expression and seemed uncomfortable in our company, I noticed how he cast quick glances at us but turned his eyes away before there was a chance of engagement. The chaplain whispered that he was the father of the would-be bomber – lying right next to David. Then I saw, not just an uncomfortable stranger, I saw a father, hurting and distressed by his son's suffering – it had nothing to do with condonation or condemnation; nothing to do with the IRA's campaign of violence – it was all about a father, trying to cope with the suffering of his son, he wasn't that much unlike us. I felt for him.

*****

I remember David before he joined the army. He had a dead-end job with Initial Towel company, changing roller towels in shops, offices and factories. He was restless, the job did little more than provide him with an income. He wanted more, two elder brothers had spent time in the army, he and they talked. David wanted some of the travel and excitement that they had apparently enjoyed. One day he came home and told Mum that he was thinking of signing up. Not sure exactly why but Mum was far from pleased. Admittedly one brother had had a near miss in Cyprus causing him to send his wife home for safety, but eldest brother had enjoyed a strife free time serving in Germany. Mum and I talked about it, I argued for David's right to live his life the way he wanted. If he didn't join now he would slowly descend into a pit of boring mediocrity, disillusioned with life. I felt he had to go find out for himself if the army was his future.

It was turning out that way, he blossomed in every regard. He stood tall in his uniform and radiated a new- found assuredness. I know Mum was proud when she first saw him in uniform, she positively burst with pride at his passing out ceremony. He impressed the army too and was progressing through the ranks, at this point he had made corporal and was in line for his sergeant's stipes. On a personal level, he had met and married a lovely girl from Birkenhead, Olwen was her name.

Now, here we were, facing Mum's worst nightmare. We exchanged no words with the would-be bomber's parent, just a few looks – looks that spoke not of hate or hostility, but of understanding and compassion. The man surely loved his son whatever he thought of his activities.

And it was that, on the 4th of July 1974 the doctor in charge of David's case called us to a brief conference. Kindly and clearly, he spelled it out – there was no hope, David was dead. He wasn't breathing – that was the life support machine – switch it off and David would be certifiably dead. The decision to switch off the machine had to be made by us, the next of kin present, it wasn't then, and it isn't now, within the authority of doctors. The five of us repaired to absorb the news and consider the action we had been asked to endorse. I speak here only for what went through my mind. It was this: the doctor had been very clear - David was technically dead. Watching life support cause the rise and fall of his chest, mimicking life, was obscene. He was entitled to dignity in death. So, I said that we should agree to having the machine switched off. It was a unanimous decision. After the machine had been turned off we all retreated to our separate little worlds for a while, absorbing the enormity of what had just come to pass. I will say here that there was none of the melodramatic rhetoric about playing God. Never had much time for such talk.

I was volunteered to formally identify the body. Following a death there are several instances when the harsh reality imposes itself and pushes grief to one side, albeit only temporarily. The formal identification of the body is the first of such instances. David was lying in what looked like a giant tin bath, not very dignified but functional. The identification process is, of necessity, brief and unemotional.

"Is this the body of your brother David Arthur Smith?

Answer: "Yes" and that was it – David was officially dead. In that moment, the dead body became a person.

A harder task awaited – the family back home had to be told. The task befell to me. The Royal Victoria hospital billeted several soldiers for security purposes. David's regiment had a small room where the men could relax after being on duty out on the streets of Belfast. July 1974 was world cup year, on this day, the 4th of July, a match was in progress. Off-duty soldiers were watching it in their billet, we could hear the noise as we approached – shouts of support and derision bounced off the walls. The looks on our faces conveyed all they needed to know – all that they had dreaded; one of their own was down. Now the silence was deafening, the television was switched off, no orders or requests were given or made. Grim faced young soldiers silently filed out of the room. I was invited to sit at a table - a telephone was placed in front of me. The atmosphere was suffocating and charged with emotion, yet still and silent, nothing moved, no one spoke.

My telephone number had been given to the army and it was agreed that all calls should be channelled through my number, rather than having every member of the family making individual calls. It also ensured that everyone got the same news. So, my humble abode became the meeting place for family and friends throughout the crisis. My wife spoke later of the charged atmosphere that hung like a dark cloud, the pressure on them all, particularly my wife, must have been incredibly intense. There is no worse feeling in tragic times than that of impotence – an inability to do anything to ease the stress. To wait is surely, worse than to endure, mentally that is. Now it was coming to a head.

My wife took the call. My exact words are lost in time, I think it was something like. It's all over – he died a few minutes ago. Those few words took more self-control than I could have ever imagined possessing. I felt that I had to keep it together. There was much that had to be done, there would be time for grieving later. Anyhow, I was not given to public outbursts of emotion. Nevertheless, making that call was the hardest thing I have ever done in my life – to this day I shudder at the mental effort it took to keep it together.

As I replaced the receiver I thought of the affects the news would have. For a moment, I felt cut off from the people that mattered most. It was only a moment because all of a very sudden the five of us became the centre of a spate of frantic activity. The order had gone out that every member of David's regiment be pulled off the streets for fear of reprisals by the soldiers.

David's CO wanted to talk about the funeral, he told us that David was entitled to full military honours, as befits a soldier dying on active service. However, he pointed out that the military protocols tended to dominate proceedings at the expense of the grieving family of the deceased. He suggested an alternative, a sort of semi-military funeral, regimental presence would be confined to a senior officer, a couple of junior officers who knew David, a bugler and some of David's colleagues. The regiment would pay for it– all we had to do was to advise him of the arrangements. On reflection, I don't think the army had an appetite for a full-blown military funeral with all the publicity it would attract (so many sought to play down the violence in the Province). But – his point was well made, I didn't think Mum would be up to the stress the pomp and formality would have delivered, so we accepted the alternative.

Olwen wanted it to be in Birkenhead – that was as far as we got. We had to be taken out of the hospital. The IRA would know of David's death – they celebrated those events and they also used them to provoke soldiers on duty. Apparently, we remained targets, IRA supporters in the hospital may well have tried provoking us. They would certainly have let it be known that a British soldier had died. We had to be moved to a safe place, quickly – and here we saw how well the army was prepared. Within minutes we were whisked out of the hospital and into a waiting car – engine running. With minimum regard to the Highway Code, particularly the speed limit, our driver raced off into the suburbs of Belfast. We were delivered to a 'safe house' of which I gather, there were many in and around the city. Our hosts were very pro-British. They had prepared a chicken dinner and all the refreshments we could manage. That had barely been digested before we were on the road again, this time speeding to Belfast airport. We were rushed through the VIP lounge, again no security checks. Seats had been made available on a flight to Birmingham. The flight time was our time for reconciling ourselves to the events of the last few hours. So much to take in – where does one start?

Home was a sombre and sad place. So many questions to answer, understandably, everyone wanted to know everything about David's passing. Mum was devastated – she never got over the tragedy. She wanted David buried at home, but home was now where he had lived with his wife – Birkenhead. I pressed Olwen's superior claim and although Mum accepted it in the end, she never really came to terms with David's body being so far away. One problem solved – another to take its place: David's regiment were willing to pay for the funeral but when it became clear that that meant transporting David's considerable family up the M6 to Birkenhead, his CO admitted that there would not be enough money in regimental funds to cover a fleet of taxis to convey those that didn't have a car – and there were a few. Help came from an unexpected source.

We were approached by a team from Raidio Teilifís Eireann, the national broadcasting service of the Irish Republic. Seems they were making a programme about the trouble in Northern Ireland. Their brief was to put together a trilogy, seeing the conflict from the perspective of those residents of Northern Ireland who wished to remain a part of the UK; from those who fought for the unification of Ireland (the IRA) and from the security forces who were sent in to keep the peace (the British Army). They wanted to use David's story as representative of the latter. In exchange for our co-operation RTE would pay for any transport costs to get the family to the funeral. They were as good as their word, though what other drivers made of the scene I can't say. As the cortege made its way northwards along the M6, at a speed reflecting the occasion, taxis carrying RTE's camera crew sped past filming as they went, then they would wait on the hard shoulder for us to pass by and re-enact the pass all over again.

There was a lighter moment in these proceedings. My wife and I were travelling in our own car, we had a brother and his wife as passengers. We were cruising along as a part of the cortege when suddenly, smoke appeared drifting from the dashboard. Fearing the worst, I pulled over and gingerly inspected the dashboard – nothing. The smoke was coming from a semi-extinguished cigarette courtesy of big brother. At least we had a laugh. But here's the thing, a few months earlier, this same car had burst into flames as we were travelling home from a Christmas fayre. We had our baby daughter with us and only just got out in time before the cat became an inferno. So – I refute any suggestion of over-reaction on the current occasion.

We were right to take the semi-formal route – there was the right amount of formality commensurate with the family's desire for privacy. The most poignant moment came when the young bugler played the last post; he almost choked when the emotion got to him, an officer, standing nearby, whispered quietly "spit – spit". The bugler did just that and went on to play flawlessly and David was laid to rest.

A footnote to these proceedings: Mum was upset at not having anywhere (a grave) to go to visit David. On hearing about this, the vicar of St Matthews church in Walsall gave exceptional permission for a plaque to be laid in church grounds. A very kind gesture.

EPILOGUE

Well, there it is, the first slice of my life. Looking back, it was a sort of aimless meander in the beginning. What I did was done in the moment, there was no great plan at work, in fact, no plan at all. I ask myself what I got out of it, what did I learn? An answer to that question is lurking within these pages. Here and now I'll just say that those early years toughened me up in ways I was yet to fully appreciate.

Writing this book has inevitably required numerous trips down memory lane. Nostalgia can trick us into talking about the 'good old days'. The 'rose tinted' spectacles get an airing. For many of us they weren't so good, they were different. A common mistake is to balance the perceived good things from the past with the perceived negative things from the present. When my generation so indulges, it would do well to reflect on who exactly is responsible for the changes complained of. Kids didn't invent the mobile phone or social media; their elders did and then they made it available to the youngsters. We shouldn't blame them for taking these things up.

Going back to college would be the launch pad for what I would describe as the first of my three careers to date – banking. My time with the bank will be the subject of volume 2. My second career was in education and training and a mixed and varied bag it was. Then came a period that sustains to this day. self-employment, when I set up my own business helping clients cope with mortgage re-possession in particular, and debt problems in general. I think the next 'career' will be the last – this is going to be the time I write to satisfy an ambition to set down as much I have learned in print – so there's another two autobiographical volumes to come. But before that, there are other works in the course of completion and at least one novel to get out of my system.

Tis a long way I have travelled.

That wasn't the only major change I was to experience. College was but a few weeks old when some cheeky young imp of a girl grabbed my scarf. I had to date her to get it back. We're still on that date, there could be something in this – given time.

Her name was Susan Grimes, in the foreseeable future she would be re-christened 'Fred' - don't ask. She was so different to all the other girls I had known (violins please). For a start, she wasn't besotted by the latest pop-singer, her taste in music was much more eclectic. Then there was he interest in matters 'supernatural'; she had a completely open mind and preferred to explore rather than sneer (this being a common reaction at the time). Most important of all, she treated me as she treated everyone else – with respect.

The Grimes family comprised dad – Albert Eric (Grin/Grinner – because he smiled a lot); mum – Winifred (Wyn) and sisters – Christine (Chris) and Margaret (Meg). They all became great friends. Sadly, they are now reduced to two – my wife and her sister Meg.

Sue's maternal grandfather worked in the research department at Rowntree's in York. He was one of the team that invented Smarties – didn't even get an OBE!

Wyn could have been of some renown had she confessed – the great Flying Scotsman was only ever stopped on its travels once – by her. She'd been seeing her sister-in-law off at the station, sister-in-law needed the loo, so she dumped her baby boy in Wyn's arms and went in search of relief. Train started up, chugging out of the station, wherever it was going, Wyn was not going with it and to re-affirm that she pulled the communication chord. She was also a talented artist but never had the chance to exploit her talent – shame.

Sue's father was a very special man. He and I became great friends, I adored him. When I met him, he was transport manager for the Beecham Group – a group of companies long absorbed by Glaxo Smith-Kline. Albert Eric also had a great claim to fame – during the war her served under General Orde Wingate in the famous Chindits. The Chindits were combined British and Indian special forces and operated in Burma and the Far East during 1943/1944. The mission was to infiltrate behind enemy lines and cause as much disruption as they could. The enemy being the Japanese, whose disregard for the lives of their enemies was matched only by their German allies. He never spoke of the atrocities he must have witnessed, as evidenced in sundry historical accounts.

Albert Eric had a remarkable achievement to his name. He was conscripted into the army as a humble private. Because of his great leadership skills, he was commissioned in the field. He rose to the rank of Major. On the cessation of hostilities, he was reduced to the rank of Captain. Apparently, that was the established protocol – a soldier promoted in the field would take one step back so to speak, when peace was restored. Strikes me as being somewhat backward, a man is good enough to get promoted to a senior rank during battle but, when the battle is over, he effectively gets demoted. I would have it that any man who proved himself in battle, to be worthy of the rank say of Major, is surely worthy of being a Major in peacetime. Anyway, regardless of the army, Albert Eric was one special man. He also built a boat, a cabin cruiser, in his garage from plans I presume he bought. Thing is – he had no woodworking or carpentry skills to draw upon – amazing achievement. I must add that the wood came in plain uncut pieces – he had to cut it to shape and steam it, so it would bend. The venture was a remarkable success and the family enjoyed some happy holidays on Maeve – the name given to the boat, or to give it its proper title – cabin cruiser.

Thank you buying and (hopefully) reading and (more hopefully – enjoying) this book. Volume 2 will be different in content, of course, but similar in style I suspect. I have changed, of course. I have an equal right to be here, as does everyone else I'm not deferential to celebrities per se. I don't judge people by what they have but by what they are. Many people in poverty are richer in humanity than some millionaires – wealth should not buy privilege (sadly I know that it does). It happens because we all allow it to.

Anyone wishing to comment to the author about this book may do so at: bjs117@outlook.com

Lightning Source UK Ltd.
Milton Keynes UK
UKHW040822080321
379980UK00003B/1035